The Functional of English

D1549988

Second Edition

WITHDRAWN

The Functional Analysis of English

A Hallidayan Approach

Second Edition

Thomas Bloor and Meriel Bloor

A MEMBER OF THE HODDER HEADLINE GROUP

First published in Great Britain in 1995
Second edition published in Great Britain in 2004 by
Hodder Arnold, a member of the Hodder Headline Group,
338 Euston Road, London NW1 3BH

www.hoddereducation.co.uk

Distributed in the United States of America by
Oxford University Press Inc.,
198 Madison Avenue, New York, NY10016

The advice and information in this book are believed to be true and
accurate at the time of going to press, but neither the author nor the publisher
can accept any legal responsibility or liability for any errors or omissions.

British Library Cataloguing in Publication Data
A catalogue record for this book is available from the British Library

Library of Congress Cataloging-in-Publication Data
A catalogue record for this book is available from the Library of Congress

ISBN 978 0 340 80680 7

3 4 5 6 7 8 9 10

Typeset in 11 on 12pt Times by Phoenix Photosetting, Chatham, Kent
Printed and bound in India by Replika Press Pvt. Ltd

What do you think about this book? Or any other Hodder Arnold title?
Please visit our website at www.hoddereducation.co.uk

Contents

Preface

This edition of *The Functional Analysis of English* was prepared with two main objectives: first, to clarify any confusions and to correct infelicities in the first edition, originally published in 1995; and, second, to incorporate new developments in Systemic Functional Linguistics.

With respect to these aims, we were helped by our students at the universities of Aston, Warwick and Birmingham, who did not hesitate to demand explanations of any passages that seemed to them unclear or to question the accuracy of our analyses. Their input has been invaluable. We were also stimulated by feedback we received from lecturers who had chosen to use the book as course texts. Their comments were sufficiently encouraging for us to believe that revisions would be worthwhile, and we were able to benefit from their experiences in universities and colleges in many countries.

The book retains its original purpose of providing a relatively simple introduction to systemic functional linguistics as it is used in the analysis of English. It sets out the principles and techniques of systemic functional grammar with explanations of basic terminology in what we hope is an accessible way for students who are new to linguistics. Since it also provides the reader with a set of tools for analyzing real samples of English, we believe it will also be of use to specialists in other fields, such as discourse analysis, media studies and gender studies, who have been working with alternative models of analysis and wish to learn new skills. There is still a chapter, somewhat expanded, providing an overview of the applications of functional grammar to social and educational issues and a chapter explaining the place of functional grammar in the history of linguistics.

Since 1995, when the first edition of *The Functional Analysis of English* was published, systemic functional linguistics has grown in substance and expanded in popularity. In the second edition, we have introduced a few of the latest developments and elaborated on the original text to introduce new terms. Inevitably, some aspects of the grammar and its applications are only introduced briefly, but we have tried to make suggestions in the *Further study* sections for readers who wish to consider these in more detail. We still recommend students to turn to *An Introduction to*

Functional Grammar for more depth of treatment of lexicogrammatical matters.

Those readers familiar with our first edition will notice that Halliday's name appears less frequently in this edition. This is not because Halliday is in any way less central to our account, but because, among other things, the new edition of *An Introduction to Functional Grammar* (2004) has a co-author, Christian Matthiessen.

We also acknowledge, in this edition, the increasing number of exciting contributions being made by systemic functional linguists world-wide. Systemic Functional Linguistics is a lively, developing field, which is extending and deepening our understanding of how human language works. Those at the forefront of research in the field are obliged to tackle aspects of language and language use that are poorly understood and have not previously been adequately described.

Inevitably, when people are breaking new ground, we sometimes find disagreement about matters of detail – even sometimes about matters of significant theory. An introductory book is not the place to emphasize differences of opinion. For this reason, with a few exceptions, we tend to focus on areas of agreement within the Hallidayan model, undoubtedly coloured by our own views and our own interpretation of that model. From time to time, however, usually in the *Further study* sections, we have introduced some alternative approaches to certain details without presenting the reasons for or against each position, even though these reasons are clearly very important in establishing the best solutions. Shortage of space would not allow us to present the cases in full. Instead, we provide references so that readers can discover the arguments for themselves.

Much of the book remains unchanged. We were constrained by considerations of length from adding as much as we would have liked. However, there are some important alterations and additions, which are outlined here.

- We have adjusted some sections of the book to clarify difficult points and to reflect small developments in the grammar. We have added an explanation of parts of the grammar that were neglected in the first edition, notably of *grammatical metaphor.*
- We have made some additions to the exercises at the end of Chapters 1 to 10. For the sake of continuity, many exercises remain the same, but a few of the more lengthy sets of sentence analysis have been shortened to make room for the new activities. In response to a number of requests, we have moved the answer keys to the back of the book before the Glossary.
- We have revised *Further study* sections in order to incorporate more recent research and newer references. The Further study sections now additionally contain references to some classic works that have recently been reprinted and are widely available for the first time.

- The Glossary has been improved and lengthened, but readers are reminded that the Glossary alone cannot fully explain complex terminology. It is in the book itself that readers will find full explanations of lexicogrammatical terms with examples of how they can be applied in the analysis of English texts. The Glossary serves as a reminder for those who have already made considerable headway in the field.
- The list of references has been extended to include over 90 new items, most published since 1995. We have retained the bulk of the earlier titles as well, thus providing a rich introductory bibliography.

Thomas and Meriel Bloor
February 2004

Acknowledgements

We would like to thank all the people who helped with the first edition: Michael Halliday, Anne Beale, Mary Bodfish, Malcolm Coulthard, Helen Drury, Gill Francis, Chris Gledhill, Dick Hudson, Susan Hunston, Lorraine Lawrence, Naomi Meredith, Hilary Nesi, Lesley Riddle, Shelagh Rixon, Jane Willis, Dave Willis and Roger Woods.

For help with this edition, we thank: Robin Fawcett for enthusiastic, prompt and precise advice on the Cardiff grammar; Anne Hewings for last-minute provision of the drafts of *Applying English Grammar;* Michael Hoey for affably giving information when we disturbed his Sunday afternoon; Michael Cummings and Martin Davies for advice on stylistics references, and Sheena Gardner and Hilary Nesi for their expertise. We thank, too, our publishers and editors, including Eva Martinez, Rada Radojicic and Susan Dunsmore for their patient co-operation. We are grateful for constructive criticism from a number of anonymous publishers' readers and also from reviewers, including Wendy Bowcher, Chris Butler, Mohsen Ghaddessy, and Anne McCabe. As ever, we owe a great debt to the teachers and students who have used the book and provided us with invaluable feedback. Of course, we alone are responsible for any errors or shortcomings.

List of symbols

S	Subject
F	Finite
P	Predicator
C	Complement
C^{do}	direct object Complement
C^{io}	indirect object Complement
C^{int}	intensive Complement
A	Adjunct
A^{cir}	circumstantial Adjunct
A^{con}	conjunctive Adjunct
A^{mod}	modal Adjunct
|	group boundary
[ ]	embedded group
< >	enclosed elements at clause rank; e.g. Predicator interrupting a discontinuous Subject
||	clause boundary
[[ ]]	embedded clause
<< >>	enclosed clause, i.e. a clause which interrupts another
|||	clause complex boundary
α, β, γ, δ, ε , ζ	alpha, beta, gamma, delta, epsilon, zeta
	Greek alphabetic symbols used to represent dependency. β depends on α, γ on β, δ on γ, and so on.

1

A meaningful approach

1.1 *How to use this book*

This book provides an introduction to the analysis of English. The aim is to provide the reader with the grammatical tools needed to take samples of English apart and find out how the language works. It is by the process of analysis that linguists build up descriptions of the language and gradually discover more about how people use language.

Readers who are new to this subject may find it useful to familiarize themselves with the way in which the book is organized and with the tools that are provided to assist the reader. Of the 12 chapters in this book, the first two are introductory. Chapter 1 introduces some general concepts of the model of grammar and Chapter 2 deals with basic terms used in grammatical analysis. These are followed by eight chapters dealing with different aspects of linguistic analysis. Chapter 11 presents some applications of functional analysis and Chapter 12 provides an overview of some past and present approaches to linguistics in an attempt to see functional linguistics from an historical perspective.

Towards the end of each chapter there is a brief summary of the ground covered and a short *Further study* section, which suggests additional reading and sometimes raises controversial issues. Chapters 1 to 10 end with short exercises. These can be done by individuals or by groups of students. Some are 'open-ended', having more than one possible answer, but most have correct answers, which can be found in the Answer keys at the end of the book.

After the Answer keys, there is a Glossary, which provides brief explanations of technical terminology. Most terms are introduced and explained as they arise in this book. Even so, the large number of technical terms can sometimes present difficulties, and the Glossary is the place where readers can check or remind themselves of the meaning of a term. The Glossary does not offer precise definitions, and the glosses are not intended to be accessible independently of the rest of the book.

The analytical approach taken in this book is, in the main, drawn from the work of the linguist Michael Halliday, in particular, the model of grammar set out in some detail in *An Introduction to Functional Grammar* (1985, 1994, and Halliday and Matthiessen, 2004), henceforth referred to by the initials IFG. This branch of linguistics is known by the name of Systemic Functional Linguistics and is usually referred to in this book as SFL. The grammar that systemic functional linguists have developed is known as Systemic Functional Grammar or SFG.

Other linguists working in a similar tradition also have a significant influence on some sections of this book. References to the work of these linguists can be found in the *Further study* sections and in the bibliography.

Since readers are not expected to be familiar with Systemic Functional Linguistics (SFL), there is some simplification of the more complex and comprehensive work and of the theoretical underpinnings of the grammar.

1.2   *Grammar and meaning*

There are certain theoretical and practical principles that must be introduced because they are crucial to the type of analysis that is presented in this book. In this chapter, therefore, as a first step, we outline the nature of these principles. In Chapter 12, we explain how these principles can be seen as part of a historical tradition in linguistics and indicate something of how they differ from other theoretical approaches.

For SFL, a language is a 'system of meanings'. That is to say that, when people use language, their language acts produce or, or more technically, *construct* meaning. From this point of view, grammar becomes a study of how meanings are built up through the choice of words and other grammatical resources such as singular or plural, negative or positive, and other linguistic forms such as tone and emphasis. This may seem fairly obvious to most people since it accords with a commonsense view of language, but not all linguists have been concerned with meaning in such a direct way as Systemic Functional Grammar (SFG).

Linguists have approached the study of English from different points of view. Some, for example, have tried to account for formal aspects of the grammar of the language largely divorced from meanings. Others have started out by looking at words and sentences (language forms) and then asked how the forms of the language represent meanings. Here, we take the view that the approach that is likely to be most successful will be one that recognizes *meaning* and *use* as central features of language and that tackles grammar from this point of view. It follows from this that the grammar is *semantic* (concerned with meaning) and *functional* (concerned with how the language is used). Moreover, it is also a *lexicogrammar*, a term that embraces the idea that vocabulary (lexis) is inextricably linked to grammatical choices.

1.3   *Linguistic choice*

We have said that the *theory of language* followed in SFL involves the idea that a language consists of a set of systems, which offer the speaker (or writer) an unlimited choice of ways of creating meanings.

Thus, if I want to know the time, I might use one of the following expressions (or any one of many more ways that the language offers us).

(1) What's the time?
(2) Tell me the time, please.
(3) I'd like to know the time.

Although each of these examples includes the word 'time', there is considerable variation in the choice of other words. In addition, the first expression uses the *interrogative form*, the second uses the *imperative form* and the third uses the *declarative form*. (These forms are discussed further in Chapters 2 and 3.)

Linguistic choice is available to speakers not only with regard to interrogatives, imperatives and declaratives; it operates at every point in the production of speech. We may, for example, refer to a shop as 'the supermarket' or 'the store'; we may address our father as 'Dad', 'Daddy', 'Pa' or by the use of his personal name or some invented nickname. Linguistic choice also permits us to use full sentences or indicate meaning by the use of one or two words. Either (4a) or (4b) might be an equally satisfactory answer to the question 'What's the time?'.

(4a) Four-thirty.
(4b) It's half-past four.

Most of the linguistic choices we make are unconscious. We do not usually stop and think about whether to use a past tense or a present tense verb, and the choice between active and passive sentences depends on the circumstances of use, as we can see from the examples (5) and (6) taken from a book for parents[1] on the subject of teaching children to fish.

(5) Last summer, my boys finally *caught* their first fish. [active]
(6) It is said that many more fish *are caught* in May or June than in any other months. [passive]

In (5) the past tense verb ('caught') is used because the language makes this form available for completed actions that took place in the past. In (6) the present tense verb ('are caught') is used. This form is available for events that happen regularly or often. In (6) the passive form is appropriate because the writer has chosen to make the word 'fish' the Subject of the verb 'are caught' rather than a word for the people who catch the fish.

It is not that the author has necessarily made a *conscious* choice among the available language forms. He has created his meaning by drawing on the forms that are available to him as a speaker/writer, partly consciously (as a professional writer) and partly without reflection (as a native speaker). He has made use of what is known as the *meaning potential* of the language by using forms that are appropriate in context.

In everyday speech we are constantly making unconscious context-relevant choices, such as referring to a person as either 'he' or 'she' or to a place as 'here' or 'there'. In part, we select from what linguists term the *paradigms* of the language, a paradigm being a system of choices made potentially available to us by the language we are using. Thus, there is a paradigmatic relationship between *masculine, feminine* and *neuter,* another between *singular* and *plural,* another between *active* and *passive,* and so on. These choices can be represented as *systems,* which inter-relate with each other and can be represented in *network* diagrams (see Section 3.2.2).

1.4   *Language in use*

When people use language to make meanings, they do so in specific situations, and the form of the language that they use in *discourse* is influenced by the complex aspects of those situations.

Thus, to offer some obvious examples, we greet people in different ways depending on the time of day, where we are and who we are talking to. Teachers speak differently when they are addressing a class from when they are talking to a parent or the Minister of Education. Teachers who fail to adapt their speech to different situations and talk to everyone as though they were disruptive children will become, at best, objects of humour, and, at worst, targets of serious resentment. A speaker at an outdoor meeting is likely to use different rhetorical devices and a different tone of voice from a lecturer in a university or an after-dinner speaker at a family wedding.

Situation also affects the form of written English. A business letter requesting payment of a debt is likely to be very different in format and style from a letter on a similar topic written to an old friend who owes the correspondent some money. The situation affects not only the choice of words but also the grammar that is used.

The situation can have such a constraining effect on language that society often develops clear conventions of use (like those associated with business meetings or formal greetings) which have to be learned before newcomers to the circumstances can behave appropriately. The contexts in which language is used frequently (business companies, courts of law, research laboratories, and so on) lead over time to the development of specific socially recognized forms known as *genres* (such as business letters, cross-examination, and laboratory reports) and styles or *registers* (such as business English, legal English, and scientific English). Relevant to the context of situation is the notion of *domain*, a term that is currently used to refer to the range of meaning potential within a particular variety of the language. Loosely, the term *domain* overlaps with the terms *register* and *genre*. Examples of domains given by Halliday and Matthiessen (1999) are recipes and weather reports.

The number of situations to which most very young children are exposed is relatively limited – usually the situations found in the home environment in the company of family and friends – but, as children grow and move into the wider society of the school and community, the range of situations in which they can use language appropriately expands. Most of this language use is acquired without conscious attention, but some situations require such complex language production that training is necessary. Our education system accounts for some of this training; children are helped in school to write narratives, essays or to prepare reports of scientific experiments, for example, and later they may practise debating or public speaking, where they need to communicate orally with a larger audience than is found in one-to-one or small group interaction.

One result of this is that, faced with a fragment of written text, say, from a love letter, a business letter or a newspaper report, adult English-speakers do not usually find it difficult to recognize the situations in which the particular instances of language were used. Often, a recording of a speaker (for example, an announcement by a flight attendant on an airplane, a politician speaking on radio, or a doctor talking to a patient) can be easily recognized and identified. (In Exercise 1.3 at the end of this chapter, you can try your hand at recognizing the situations in which some written texts were constructed.)

1.5   The study of texts

An important feature of a systemic functional approach to linguistic study is its insistence on studying actual instances of language that have been used (or are being used) by speakers or writers. That is not to say that we may never take an interest in sentences that we, as speakers of the language, have simply invented as examples, but that, on the whole, we are more likely to arrive at interesting and useful descriptions of English if we investigate *authentic texts*. Of course, an example may be part of an authentic text when it is presented as an example and is understood as an example by the hearer or reader.

A *text* is any stretch of language, regardless of length, that is spoken or written for the purposes of communication by real people in actual circumstances. Both spoken and written texts are equally valid as objects for analysis. When linguists study or analyze a spoken text, they record the text, or part of the text, either in writing or electronically. Electronic recordings can be *transcribed* (written as accurately as possible, often using some system that can represent pronunciation and intonation). The fact that linguists study fixed written forms of texts could suggest that language itself is somehow fixed or static. This, of course, is not true. A spoken conversation, for example, moves forward in time, and the basis on which speakers and listeners express and interpret meaning is constantly changing. Communication is an interactive process through which meaning is negotiated in real time. Writers attempt to communicate with their readers and expect them to respond emotionally or intellectually to the text. Readers often mentally question what they read and have expectations about how a text will proceed. In a detective story, for example, the facts of the case are introduced gradually by the author so that the readers' perceptions will change as they move though the book until they eventually grasp the secret of the plot. The linguistic context is dynamic and using language is a dynamic process.

In order to explain how human language works, contemporary linguists are often interested in this aspect of language (sometimes called *discourse*) and functional linguists have been in the forefront of this type of work. The text is the data used as the object of study, but we have to remember that it was originally produced as language within a communicative event.

It is via the analysis of texts that we are able to increase our understanding of the linguistic system and of how it enables speakers and writers to produce and process coherent meaning. The choice of words and the word order of one sentence often depends on the sentence that it follows. For example, the language has special words, such as pronouns, that can refer to the same entities as previously used words. For example, in Text 1A, the heading and the first sentence both refer the reader to 'beavers', a large rodent found in North America. Readers of the first paragraph understand that the subsequent uses of *they* and *their* (printed here in bold type) refer to the beavers. Similarly, readers of the second paragraph can see that *another type* and *a third variety* are connected to the expression *one type of beaver house* and understand that all three expressions refer to beavers' dwellings

---

Beavers

Working in colonies, **beavers** perform extraordinary engineering feats. **They** cut large quantities of timber for **their** construction projects and for the green bark **they** eat. **They** build canals on which to transport the wood. **They** build complex houses of various designs and also erect ambitious dams to keep the water level high enough so that marauders cannot find **their** dwellings.

One type of beaver house is burrowed into the bank of a pond, with the entrance underwater and the living quarters above water. **Another type** is constructed in the pond itself and looks like a brush pile. **A third variety** is built as part of a dam.

Text 1A   (Schwartz, *How to Fly a Kite, Catch a Fish, Grow a Flower*[1]).

The linguistic analysis of texts has many practical applications above and beyond knowledge about language for its own sake. It can help us to find out why some texts are more effective than other texts at communication or persuasion. It can help us to understand the nature of propaganda, the success or failure of some types of political speeches, or how breakdowns in communication can occur. It can even sometimes help in the identification of a criminal by revealing the likely author of a text or of a speaker on a recorded telephone conversation. That is to say, text analysis can be used as a tool for the *evaluation* of texts. In addition, text analysis is currently being used to give us a better understanding of the nature of language use in English in specific fields such as business or science, and such work can be applied to the design of teaching syllabuses for language learners. (Some applications are discussed in more detail in Chapter 11.)

1.6   *The notion of rank*

In written English the usual way of grouping ideas or information together is by the use of *sentences*, marked by a capital letter and a full stop. However, in spoken language, there is no such clearly recognizable unit although we intuitively recognize information units by the way spoken English uses intonation. Continuous speech is a series of *tone groups*, indicating which information is 'known' (or familiar to the speakers) and which information is presented as 'new'.

As far as grammar is concerned, the main unit of structure is said to be a *clause*. A clause is made up of identifiable constituents, each of which has its own structure and follows a grammatical pattern. To show the clause *constituents* (or how clauses are structured), SFL employs the notion of *rank*. In brief, this simply states that

> a **clause** consists of one or more groups;
> a **group** consists of one or more words;
> a **word** consists of one or more **morphemes**.

Each of these ranks refers to a unit of meaning at the level of the clause or below (the *rank scale* as it is called) and we explain this in more detail below.

It is, however, possible to link or bind one clause to another clause or even to a number of other clauses. When this happens, the result is known as a *clause complex*. This can be seen in the constructed examples (7a), (7b) and the authentic example (7c).

> (7a) In the lower layers of the sea there are fewer animals. (one clause)
> (7b) In the lower layers of the sea there are fewer animals and they tend to eat each other. (two clauses = a clause complex)
> (7c) In the lower layers of the sea, there are fewer animals and they tend to eat each other because there is no plant life. (three clauses = a clause complex)

Because these are all written examples, we can say that all three are *sentences*. But, grammatically speaking, (7a) is a clause and (7b) and (7c) each consist of more than one clause. We can see then that the term *sentence* in SFL does not carry the same information as the term *clause* or *clause complex*, even though it often used to loosely refer to the same unit/s.

Examples of clauses, groups, words and morphemes can be seen in Figure 1.1. Notice that this figure does not show a full analysis of the constituents of the clauses, but just provides examples at each rank.

Rank	Example
Clause	• in the lower layers of the sea, there are fewer animals • (and) they tend to eat each other • (because) there is no plant life
Group	• the lower layers of the sea • fewer animals • are • each other
Word	• the • lower • layers
Morpheme	• layer • -s • the

Fig. 1.1   Examples of each rank in the clause

1.6.1   The clause and its constituents

In SFG, then, the major unit of grammatical analysis is the *clause*. The clause has a special place in expressing meaning because it is at this rank that we can begin to talk about how things exist, how things happen and how people feel in the world around us. It is also at the rank of clause that we usually use language to interact with others. In other words, instead of simply uttering sounds or single words, we can construct complex ideas and show how one idea relates to another.

As we saw above, a sentence may consist of one or more clauses. As an illustration, the following sentence from Text 1A (Section 1.5) consists of three clauses, shown in Fig. 1.2.

> *They build complex houses of various designs and also erect dams so that marauders cannot find their dwellings.*

The groups in these clauses are separated by slashes (|) and it can be seen that each of the clauses in this sentence has more than one group (although not all clauses do). Some groups consist of only one word, some of two, some of

Clause 1	they | build | complex houses of various designs|
Clause 2	[and] also | (they) erect | dams|
Clause 3	[so that] marauders | cannot find |their dwellings|

Fig. 1.2

three and one of five (*complex houses of various designs*). The words *and also* show the relationship (one of addition) between the ideas constructed by the first two clauses. The words *so that* show the relationship between the second and third clauses (a relationship of purpose and result).

Constituency is concerned with the structural organization of the clause or how it is built up out of its various parts. In a functional grammar, constituency is closely related to the principle of the rank scale. Hence, a *group* is a constituent unit of a clause, and a *word* is a constituent unit of a group. A morpheme, which is the smallest unit of grammatical meaning, is a constituent of a word. A morpheme in English is any word, or part of a word, regardless of length, that cannot be split into constituent parts. Thus, 'water' is a single morpheme whereas 'marauders' consists of three morphemes: *maraud* plus the suffixes '-er' and '-s'. The word 'working' consists of two morphemes: the lexical word 'work' plus the suffix 'ing'.

1.7   *Functions and metafunctions*

In Section 1.2 we said that the grammar described in this book is *functional* and we explained this as being concerned with *language in use*. In fact, the notion of function in grammar is more complex than this. In this section, we discuss two different uses of the word *function* in linguistics and applied linguistics and then we consider how the term *metafunction* is used.

1.7.1   Grammatical functions

The word *function* is often used for the way a word or a group operates in relation to other words or groups in the clause. Each element is said, therefore, to have some *function* within the linguistic system. One type of language analysis depends on assigning grammatical functions to linguistic items. Hence we might say that in the clause || *beavers perform extraordinary engineering feats* || (from Text 1A), *beavers* functions as Subject. Much of this book is about how grammatical function works in English and many examples illustrate the idea.

1.7.2   The communicative function of utterances

In language teaching and applied linguistics nowadays, many people equate the term *function* with situational use. In this sense we can say that each individual utterance in a given context has a particular *use*. For example, a speaker might say the words, 'Good afternoon' as a means of greeting a friend at an appropriate time of day. We can say that the *communicative function* of 'Good afternoon' is *greeting*. In a different context the same words can have a different communicative function. For example, if a student is late for morning school and misses part of the first lesson, the teacher might sarcastically say, 'Good afternoon'. The fact that the words are not spoken in the afternoon indicates to the listeners that in this case the function is not a simple *greeting*, but something that we might term *reprimand*. In this way, the same words can have a different communicative function in a different situation. This way of looking at communication is based on what philosophers know as 'speech act theory'.

In a similar way, different utterances can be used with the same communicative function. So, for example, a woman might tell her child to take off his shoes in a direct way (*Take your shoes off, Robin*) or in a less direct way (*Would you take your shoes off please, Robin?*) or in an extremely indirect way (*You haven't taken your shoes off, Robin*). In each case the function of directing the child to take his shoes off is broadly similar even though the wording and the tone convey different nuances.

SFL takes this issue further by describing more precise ways in which meaning and form are related, either grammatically or intonationally. IFG (Section 4.6) makes the point that the relationship between the forms of utterances and the types of meaning they can express is a complex one which is based on the principle that what speakers say is closely related to the context in which they are saying it. In addition, all adult language is organized around a small number of 'functional components' which correspond to metafunctions (or the purposes which underlie all language use) and that these *metafunctions* have a systematic relationship with the lexicogrammar of the language. We now turn to a discussion of metafunctions.

1.7.3   Metafunctions

The ways in which human beings use language are classified in SFL into three broad categories known as *metafunctions*, (see Fig. 1.3):

● Language is used to organize, understand and express our perceptions of the world and of our own consciousness. This is known as the *ideational metafunction*. The ideational metafunction is classified in IFG into two subfunctions or modes: the *experiential* and the *logical*. The experiential is largely concerned with content or ideas. The logical is concerned with the relationship between ideas.

- Language is used to enable us to participate in communicative acts with other people, to take on roles and to express and understand feelings, attitude and judgements. This metafunction is known as the *interpersonal metafunction*.
- Language is used to relate what is said (or written) to the rest of the text and to other linguistic events. This involves the use of language to organize the text itself. This is known as the *textual metafunction*.

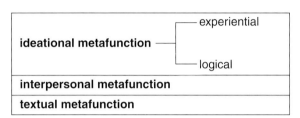

Fig. 1.3 The three metafunctions with subfunctions

Since the grammar of any language has developed through the ages to serve people's communicative needs, Halliday (1978: 22) argues that 'It is the demands posed by the service of these functions which have moulded the shape of language and fixed the course of its evolution'. This very strong claim is the basis of the theory of functional grammar.

Newcomers to functional grammar are sometimes confused by metafunctions because they expect them to operate independently and discretely. This is a mistaken expectation. In almost any instance of language use, all three metafunctions operate simultaneously in the creation of meaning in relation to the context. This is because certain aspects of the grammar support the ideational metafunction, other aspects realize the interpersonal metafunction, and yet others realize the textual metafunction.

We can see examples of the metafunctions in Text 1B, but we will not analyze it in detail at this stage since much of this book is concerned with explaining (and expanding on) the ideas in this section.

There are four things a young child ought to learn about fishing his first time out. *First*, hooks are sharp. Demonstrate this by lightly pressing the point against the fleshy part of his thumb. *Second*, a pole is held in a certain way (usually at the end in two hands, one above the other). *Third*, noise frightens the fish away. *Fourth*, the fisherman must be patient. Perhaps the best way to teach patience is to be patient yourself, since his attitude will depend to a considerable extent on how you behave.

Text 1B (Schwartz, *How to Fly a Kite, Catch a Fish, Grow a Flower*[1]).

This passage is mainly concerned with giving information about the state of the world. Hence, much of the language expresses the ideational metafunction (for example, *hooks are sharp*, *noise frightens the fish away*). Another aspect of the ideational metafunction is realized in *since* in the last sentence. *Since* establishes the logical relationship (in this case of *reason*) between the two main ideas in the sentence.

However, the writer (a man) also reveals his attitude and shows that he is expressing an opinion through the use of modality (for example, *ought to*; *must be*; *perhaps*). This reflects the interpersonal metafunction. The writer is advising parents, the target readers, on how to teach their children to fish. 'Perhaps' indicates that the final point is merely a suggestion, which a reader might reject, in contrast to the earlier advice which indicates more urgent matters by the use of 'ought to' and 'must be'.

Incidentally, he also shows, by the use of *his* and *fisherman*, that he expects the child who is learning to fish to be a boy rather than a girl, a view that we might wish to question. This use of language also reveals certain attitudes of the writer (his *ideology*), but in this case he is presenting the ideas as being representative of the world as he sees it and so his attitude could be said to be 'hidden' within the ideational framework.

The textual metafunction is realized through the word order of the sentences, through which the writer sequences the message for the reader, and also through the numerals, *first*, *second*, *third* and *fourth*, which the writer uses to signal the salient points of his message.

It is the meshing of these metafunctions in the lexicogrammar of the clause that realizes the meaning of the text as an act of communication between the writer and his readers.

Summary

In this chapter we have looked at various points of grammatical theory. We began in Section 1.2 by explaining the importance of *meaning* in a functional grammar. Then, in Section 1.3, we discussed the question of *linguistic choice* as an inherent part of the potential of language and introduced the terms *paradigm* and *system networks*. Section 1.4 considered the importance of *situation* in the creation of *language in use* and of functional varieties (*registers*) and text types (*genres*). This was followed, in Section 1.5, by an explanation of how the term *text* is used in SFL and a discussion of how grammar is utilized in stretches of language with an example of cohesive reference. Section 1.6 briefly introduced the notion of *rank*, and finally, in Section 1.7, we looked at two different uses of the term *function*, grammatical function and communicative function, ending the chapter with an explanation of the three metafunctions: ideational, interpersonal and textual.

Further study

Note that all references to 'IFG' are to the 2004 edition unless otherwise specified. Since our book focuses on the practical application of SFL to the analysis of written English, articulatory features (phonetics and phonology) and prosodic features (intonation, rhythm and stress) are barely discussed. IFG provides a brief introduction to prosody in Section 1.2. A detailed account of English intonation is available in Tench (1996). For details on the analysis of casual conversation, see Eggins and Slade (1997). On spoken discourse in general, a broad range of topics is covered in the collection of papers edited by Coulthard (1992).

The concern about issues of context places SFL firmly in the tradition of Firth, a British linguist of the first part of the twentieth century. Context is of theoretical importance to the study of grammar, phonology, prosody and discourse. It has been classified into *context of culture, context of situation* and *co-text* (or the linguistic environment of an utterance), and for discussion of this and related issues; see, for example, Firth (1957: Ch. 3, 10), Halliday (1978, especially Chapters 1, 5 and 13) and Hasan (1996: 37–50). See also Chapter 12 in this volume for more on historical influences.

The clearest short account of the three metafunctions is in Halliday (1971) although the reader should be aware that, in that early work, they are simply referred to as *functions*.

A fuller account of constituency and rank in SFG is found in Butler (2003a: 5.2.2). A simple, but slightly more detailed explanation of morpheme is given in Butt *et al.* (2000: 32–3). The rank scale, while widely used and well established in SFL, has been subjected to some criticism since the mid-1960s, for example, in Matthews (1966). The hypothesis was well defended at the time by Halliday (re-printed in Halliday 2002a: 118–26). There was, however, to be an on-going debate on the issue, which is neatly summarized in Fawcett (2000a: Appendix C). Fawcett himself replaces the rank scale with a different approach to linguistic units. For advanced study, this is well worth reading, but we continue to use the concept of the rank scale, and associated concepts such as rankshift, in this book.

Examples of system networks can be found in IFG, Sections 4.5.2, 6.3; 9.2 and Halliday (2002a: 127–51). There has been some debate about the best way to develop systemic networks in SFL. For a clear introduction on how system networks are constructed, see Fawcett (2000a: Appendix A.2 and elsewhere). For another approach, see Hasan (1996: 104–33).

Exercises

Many of these exercises can be done very effectively in discussion with a partner or in a small group.

Exercise 1.1

Imagine you are in a room with someone you know well. You would like the other person to turn the radio on. Think of three ways of asking them to turn the radio on, using an interrogative form, a declarative form and an imperative form.

Exercise 1.2

(a) How many ways can you think of asking someone to stop smoking?
(b) Would the way you speak differ depending on whether you are talking to: (a) your boss (or professor); (b) a 12-year-old child; (c) a new friend that you don't know very well; (d) your sister?

Exercise 1.3

Each of the following short texts is taken from a different published source. They were all, originally, written to be read. Read them carefully and decide on the possible origin of each text.

1. Are you disqualified by a court from holding or obtaining a driving licence?
2. Mix all the ingredients together and drop spoonfuls of the mixture onto a greased baking sheet. Cook them in a hot oven for about twelve minutes. While they are still hot, curl them round the handle of a wooden spoon and leave them to dry.
3. Granulated flourspar being fed into a steel making furnace.
4. Feet should be clean and dry. Moisten adhesive surface of pad with water and apply to foot with aperture directly over painful or sensitive area. Press pad down firmly to ensure complete adhesion.
5. There are A kg of apples in one bag, and B kg of apples in another bag. What is the total weight of apples in the two bags?

Exercise 1.4

Read the following short text from a travel brochure and discuss the textual and interpersonal metafunctions as they are realized in (a) the order in which the information is presented and the way in which this order is signalled by the writer; (b) which sentences or phrases (if any) reveal the attitude of the writer to the places described; and (c) which words or phrases (if any) refer to the writer and which to possible readers of the brochure.

Welcome to Singapore, a city of many colours and contrasts, cultures and cuisines. . . .

Even if your visit is a short stopover between flights, it is possible to take in some of Singapore's sights before departure. An evening out with a tour group can lead to all sorts of fun and adventure.

One tour unveils the cultural diversity of Singapore and features its Indian, Chinese and Peranakan heritages. It takes in Little India and samples local food, including the flakey, pancake style bread, *roti prata.*

Next stop is the *Kong Meng San Phor Kark See Temple,* Singapore's largest Buddhist temple, with its magnificent statues, including one carved from a 10-ton block of marble.

The tour then continues to the Straits National Gallery where you can discover the unique Chinese/Malay Peranakan culture.

The final stop is Arab Street to explore the vibrant Malay culture and the old charm that the area has retained.

Text 1C   From *Singapore: An Official Guide* (edited).

Notes

1. Schwartz, Alvin 1967: *How to Fly a Kite, Catch a Fish, Grow a Flower.* New York: Macmillan Pocket Books.
2. This example is from Martin, E., Larkin, S. and Barnbaum, L. (eds) 1976: *The Penguin Book of the Natural World.* Harmondsworth: Penguin Books Ltd.

2

Labels

2.1 Music, mathematics, medicine and motor-vehicle maintenance

All disciplines use technical terms. The field of music uses the labels *chord, note, semitone, octave, tonic, dominant, subdominant* and many, many more. In mathematics books, we find terms such as *angle, decimal, fraction, factor, hypotenuse* and *ratio*. Doctors talk about *hypothermia, gastritis, lesions* and *oedema*. Motor-vehicle mechanics make use of terms such as *spark plug, gear, cambelt,* and *solenoid*. The study of language also has its specialized vocabulary of technical terms.

2.2 A political parable

Suppose some mad dictator, believing that people who worked in garages were using specialist language in order to bewilder and cheat their customers, decided to ban the use of technical terms for motor-vehicle maintenance. Under this lunatic regime, mechanics would be permitted to talk about the parts of an engine in 'ordinary' language but would not be allowed to use the specialist terms which they use today. For example, mechanics might refer to the *brake* as the *thing that puts pressure on the wheels to stop them turning* but they could not refer to it as a *brake*. (This assumes that *wheel* is not a technical term, which is a questionable assumption.) It does not require a great leap of the imagination to see that insuperable difficulties would arise, particularly when they came to talking about items which are known in the repair shops of more tolerant societies as the *power train control module* or the *reverse gear selector pivot pin*. Almost certainly, this mad enterprise is entirely impossible. But, even if it were possible, mechanics would fairly soon be using shorthand terms for these descriptions: the *thing that puts pressure on the wheels to stop them turning* might be called the *wheelstopper* or the *squeezer*. Would the dictator's thought police feel that this was a breach of the law? How long would it be before names like *brake, power train control module* and *reverse gear selector pivot pin* re-emerged?

Clearly, the whole scenario is ridiculous. Yet our hypothetical dictator's position is not a million miles from the attitude taken by some people to the use of technical terms in the study of language. These people seem to perceive grammatical terminology as part of a conspiracy to baffle the general public. Some think that we can make the discussion of language easier by using descriptive statements rather than labels, or, if labels are used, they prefer labels which sound less technical: for example, the label *naming word* instead of *noun*; *doing word* instead of *verb*. There are a number of problems here which parallel those in our hypothetical dictatorship. Such terms have very limited potential for application, and we would soon run out of them. If an *adjective* (such as *quick*) is called a 'describing word', what are we to call an *adverb* (such as *quickly*)? And how accurate is it to call a verb a 'doing word'? *Are* is a verb in the sentence *Whales are mammals*, but it cannot with any precision of meaning be called a 'doing word'.

Some people argue that it is not necessary to use technical terms for language because we can use language efficiently enough without describing it in this way. It is true that people may have an excellent command of their mother tongue and know little about the analysis and labelling of the language that they speak; it is even possible to learn a foreign language without conscious recourse to such considerations. The fact remains, however, that if you wish to talk about language, you must have a vocabulary for doing so. After all, it is not inconceivable (though it does not often happen) that people might manage to repair car engines, play musical instruments or even perform an appendectomy without acquiring related technical terminology, but, in order to systematically discuss these matters, they would have to acquire or invent the appropriate language for such discussion. No one questions this obvious truth in mathematics, medicine, music or motor-vehicle maintenance; it is only in the field of language and, with rare exceptions, only in the Anglophone world, that this happens.

Language for talking about language is *metalanguage*, and it has come into existence because there is a need for it. Linguists are not unique in using metalanguage. All people talk about language with varying degrees of metalinguistic detail. When a child says that a book has a lot of long words in it, that is a metalinguistic comment. The term *word* itself is a technical term used in discussing language; it just happens to be one that most people are very familiar with. The word *greeting* is a metalinguistic term of a different kind, identifying a speech act, as are *question, answer, denial*. Such terms are accepted by the anti-terminology lobby because they are familiar and clearly useful. However, linguists need a very large technical vocabulary for language just as mechanics need a large technical vocabulary for car engines. How familiar we need to be with linguistic descriptions will vary in accordance with our professional concerns and our personal interests and motivation.

One difference between labelling parts of an internal combustion engine and labelling language items is that the former are concrete physical phenomena and the latter are not – or at least only partially so. Language form is essentially an abstraction although it is realized concretely as sounds or written symbols. Moreover, by and large, motor-car parts have one function each so that we need only one label for any individual unit. A language is vastly more complex than an automobile engine, and linguistic items, being multifunctional, can be looked at from more than one point of view, and hence given more than one label on different occasions even within the same analytical framework.

2.3   *Word classes*

One of the great contributions that the grammarians of ancient Greece and Rome made to our understanding of language was the development of a set of categories for classifying words. These categories came to be known in English as *parts of speech*, and traditionally eight (or sometimes nine) of these are presented as if they were a full and true account of the possible classes into which words fall. They are usually given as *noun, verb, adjective, adverb, pronoun, preposition, conjunction, article* and/or *interjection*.

Nowadays, among linguists the term *parts of speech* is not often used, and categories of this kind are called *word classes*. Modern linguists have raised a number of objections to the traditional classification and particularly to the criteria for assigning these labels to items, yet most of them still use all or most of these labels to indicate the word classes of lexical items. Although they serve a purpose, there is nothing sacrosanct about these labels; nor are they self-evident. Indeed, it took the ancient Greeks several centuries to work their way from two identified word classes to the eight that they ended up with, and the categories were not always the same as the ones listed above. Some of the eight are also subdivided into various subcategories.

Like traditional grammar, SFG also features eight word classes, but they are not quite the same as the traditional ones. They are *noun, adjective, numeral, determiner, verb, preposition, adverb* and *conjunction*. One way of analysing a sentence is to label each word in it according to word class. The analysis of (1) given in Fig. 2.1 reveals samples of all eight of Halliday's word classes.

(1)   Soon a massive system was developed, consisting largely of numerous flood barriers, two dams and several branch canals.

Unfortunately, questions of classification rarely have an obvious or conclusive answer, and so analysts may disagree on how to classify items without anyone necessarily being wrong or, for that matter, entirely right. Hence you

noun	system, flood, barriers, dams, branch, canals
adjective	massive
numeral	numerous, two, several
determiner	a
verb	was, developed, consisting
preposition	of
adverb	soon, largely
conjunction	and

Fig. 2.1

will find considerable variation in different publications on this as on many of the issues discussed here.

2.3.1   Nouns

Some of these items can be subclassified, for example, *noun* subdivides into *common noun*, *proper noun* and *pronoun*. These have qualities in common, hence their overall classification as *noun*, but they are also grammatically distinct from each other in some respects, and so there are distinguishing labels available, too. All the nouns in (1) are common nouns, but we can find other subclasses in further examples.

(2) Wedgwood experimented ceaselessly.

In (2), *Wedgwood* belongs to a subclass of nouns known as *proper nouns*, which are traditionally described as the individual names of persons (such as *Abdullah, Picasso, Shakespeare, Kurosawa*), places (*Japan, Sydney, Alberta, South Island*), ships, trains and aeroplanes (*the Titanic, the Orient Express, Concorde*), institutions and organizations (such as *Toyota, the United Nations*), book and film titles (*The Godfather*), and similar categories. In English a proper noun is normally written with a capital letter. Nouns (other than pronouns) which do not fall into this class are labelled *common nouns* (for example, *ant, cheese, concept, donkey, evidence, faith, grass*). These words too have often been called 'naming words'.

Some linguists prefer to identify word classes not in such conceptual terms but rather in terms of (i) their potential for interaction with other parts of the linguistic system; and (ii) their morphology, that is, the 'shapes' they can take, their 'endings', etc. Thus a noun might be described as: (i) a linguistic item which can function as (among other things) Head of a nominal group (see Section 2.5), the nominal group being a unit which can (among other things) realize the function of Subject or Complement in a clause (see Section 2.4 and Chapter 3); or (ii) an item which can take a possessive inflection (as in *Shakespeare's*, *donkey's*). A *common noun* might be described as an item that may be preceded by *the*. A *countable noun* might be described as a noun which may be modified by *a/an* or a numeral, and which may have plural inflection (usually an added -*s*), and so on.

It is not entirely frivolous to suggest that one defining characteristic of a noun is that it is not one of the other categories in the set: not a verb, adjective, adverb, preposition, and so on, for it is only by contrast with (and by interaction with) the other items that a word class has significance.

Some readers may query the analysis of *flood* and *branch* as nouns in Fig. 2.1 since they function as modifiers of other nouns: *barriers* and *canals* respectively. We do not classify all modifiers of nouns as adjectives, however. See Chapter 7 for more details on this.

2.3.2   Pronouns

Why are pronouns included within the broad category of nouns in SFG? Consider the following example, written by the medieval Italian traveller, Marco Polo, and translated into English:

> (3) Let me add only that the Great Khan has no authority over them and they render no tribute or other acknowledgement.

Pronouns in this example are *me*, *them* and *they*. They are classed as a type of noun because they realize the same grammatical functions as common and proper nouns. In the example given, the pronoun *me* refers to the writer. If someone else told the story, *me* might be replaced by *he* or by *Marco*. *Them* and *they* refer to some third party, an already identified group of people. Grammatically, it makes little difference whether we write 'the Great Khan has no authority over *them*' or 'the Great Khan has no authority over *these people*'; '*they* render no tribute' or '*these people* render no tribute'. Contrariwise, instead of using the expression *the Great Khan*, the author could have written *he*. These choices differ in the amount of information that is made explicit, and there may be good textual reasons for preferring one or the other, but they perform similar grammatical functions. To some extent, then, pronouns are like other items that are classed as nouns, and there is a case for treating them as members of the same class.

There are also, however, characteristics which set them apart from the other two types of noun, which is why we want to subclassify them, giving them the distinguishing label of *pronoun*. Common and proper nouns are *open sets*; that is to say that the community that uses the language can go on adding new members to the set with little difficulty. If, for instance, a new gadget is invented, it may be given a new name, thereby extending the set of nouns in English (as occurred with the computer). In the seventeenth, eighteenth and nineteenth centuries, English vocabulary expanded enormously to accommodate new scientific concepts, adding words like *biology*, *botany*, *hydrogen*, and *scientist*. Later we acquired *cybernetics*, *hyperspace*, *microchip* and *software*. English readily takes in nouns from other languages; a large portion of English vocabulary was acquired by such borrowing. Obvious modern examples are sports terms such as *judo* and *karate* from Japanese, *kung fu* and *tai chi* from Chinese and *ski* from Norwegian; or food terms such as *biryani*, *pasta* and *sushi*, from various sources.

Pronouns, in contrast, are a closed set of items which cannot easily be added to or diminished, as witness the seeming impossibility of introducing a gender-neutral pronoun for human beings (*he/she*), for which there has been some demand. Also, unlike common nouns, but like most (not all) proper nouns, pronouns are not normally preceded by words like *this* or *a/an* (determiners).

There are various kinds of pronouns, including the personal pronouns in Fig. 2.2. The personal pronouns in the right-hand column can be distinguished from those to their left by the fact that they occur as modifiers of other nouns (for example, *my book*, *her prize*) whereas the ones on the left can 'stand alone' (*mine* referring to *my book*, *hers* to *her prize*, and so on, but without the common noun *book* or *prize* being mentioned). Some traditional grammars call the ones on the right possessive adjectives, but we call them possessive pronouns.

Another class of pronouns is the so-called wh-pronouns (*who*, *whom*, *whose*, *which*, *what*) and *that* when it means *who/whom* or *which* (for example, *the book that you gave me*). This account does not exhaust the class of pronouns, but it covers most of them.

Singular		
First person	I, me, mine	my
Second person	you, yours	your
Third person	he, him, his	his
	she, her, hers	her
	it, its	its
Plural		
First person	we, us, ours	our
Second person	you, yours	your
Third person	they, them, theirs	their

Fig. 2.2 Personal pronouns

2.3.3   Verbs (and verbal groups)

Traditionally defined as 'words which express an action or state' (a rather feeble definition), verbs show the greatest degree of variation in form (morphology) of any of the word classes. Verbs can be subdivided in many different ways. IFG lists three basic subclasses – lexical, auxiliary and finite – but there are many possible approaches.

Somewhat confusingly, the term *verb* has long been used to refer to such items as *write, writes, wrote, writing, written*, and to *is, was, were, has*, and also to *was writing, were writing, has written*, and so on. That is to say that conventionally *verb* may refer to *verbal groups* as well as to the components of those groups.

The structures *writes, wrote, am writing, are writing, is writing, was writing, were writing, has written, have written, has been writing, have been writing, had been writing, will write, may write* (one could continue) can be described as different forms of the verb *write*. Thus, *write* is the form by which we may refer collectively to all or any of the forms in the list just given; it is the *citation form*. If we look for the word in a dictionary, we do not look under the heading *wrote*, or *was writing* or any of the other forms but under this citation form *write*. (Some people tend to give the *to*-form for citation purposes: *to write*.)

The various forms of *write* in the incomplete list above are in some instances supported by other verbal elements (*am, are, is, was, were, has, had*, and so on). We can refer to *write* as the *stem* and to *is, are, was, were, has*, and so on, as *finites, finite operators* or simply as *operators*. Since *write* is a dictionary item in a way that none of the finite operators is, we can also refer to it as a *lexical verb*. Most grammars do not make the division between finites and auxiliaries as such, but speak of *finite auxiliary* and *non-finite auxiliary*. In *might have been reading, might* is the *finite* (modal operator) and *have* and *been* are (non-finite) *auxiliaries*.

The finites and auxiliaries are closed sets; lexical verbs are an open set: *write, chase, conceal, dig, diversify, sweat, overcompensate*; there is virtually no limit. As with nouns, though perhaps not quite so freely, new concepts can inspire new verbs; computer activity has given us such verbs as *hack, download* and *interface*, just as physics once gave us verbs like *electrify* and *electrocute*. It is hard to imagine how we could add to the set of auxiliary verbs. This is not to say that auxiliaries are inevitably and eternally impervious to change, but they are strikingly different from lexical verbs in their resistance to innovation.

A significant subset of finites is the set of *modal operators* (or *modals*): *can, could, may, might, must, shall, should, will, would*. One distinctive characteristic of these verbs is that they do not add *-s* for third person singular: *she can* but not **she cans*. (An asterisk before an item indicates an abnormal form.)

Another way of looking at verbs, setting aside the issue of auxiliaries, is to consider the forms which each lexical root can take. Thus, if we count the *to*-form as a separate entity, we can say that *dig* is a five-form verb showing up as *dig, to dig, digs, dug, digging*, whereas *write* is a six-form verb: *write, to write, writes, wrote, writing, written*. More limited are verbs like *cut*, which is a four-form verb: *cut, to cut, cuts, cutting*. Excluding third person singular present which adds *-s*, *cut* serves for present simple tense, past simple tense, and *past participle*, whereas *dig* has *dug* as simple past and past participle; and *write* distinguishes between simple past and past participle in the forms *wrote* and *written*. The reason for the variation in the number of forms is largely historical. All present participles have the ending *-ing*.

In all lexical verbs, the base form (*dig, write, cut*) doubles as (i) all persons of the simple present tense except third person singular (*I write, you write, we write* and *they write*); and (ii) what is sometimes called the *bare infinitive* (the form we referred to earlier as the citation form), which combines with modal auxiliaries to give *may write, must write, can write*, for example. The form with *to* is known as the *to-infinitive*. Either of these can simply be called the *infinitive*.

The richest variety in English verb forms is found in the verb *be*, which has eight forms: *be, am, is, are, was, were, been, being*. Most English verbs distinguish third person singular from the other persons in the present tense, but *be* is the only verb in English that does so for the past simple tense: *was/were*. Compared with most European languages and many others, the variation in morphology of English verbs is extremely limited, but it is still greater than for any other word class in English.

In addition to *person* (first, second, third), *number* (singular/plural) and *tense* (present/past), an important system affecting verbs is that of *voice*: *active* or *passive*. When passive voice is selected, some form of the auxiliary *be* (or less frequently *get*) is present, and the lexical verb is in the form of a past participle, as in (4) (italics added):

(4) Current from one input *is channelled* to two or more different gates.

We return to these and other characteristics of verbs in Section 2.4 and Chapter 3.

2.3.4 Adjectives

Adjectives have two main functions: (i) as modifiers of nouns (for example, a *large* deficit); (ii) as Head of a group that is Complement of a copular verb such as *be, seem, become*; for example, the deficit is *large*. (Groups are discussed later in this chapter and also in Chapter 7. Complement and related functions are discussed in Chapter 3.) The typical morphological potential of an adjective is inflection for comparative and superlative forms:

-(e)r and *-(e)st;* for example: *larger, largest.* Comparative and superlative may also be indicated by *more* or *most* placed before the adjective. Also most adjectives can be modified by items like *very, fairly, rather, quite, somewhat;* hence *very large, quite large*, and so on.

However, not all adjectives have this potential for comparative, superlative or other grading; exceptions are known as *nongradable adjectives*, and include such items as *male, female, left, right, single, married, total* and *unique*. Only when playing with words, as a sort of joke, do we speak of someone being *very female* or *slightly married*, since one either is or is not female, married, and so on, or so the language suggests. The fact that many people describe things as *rather unique* or *very unique* probably says something about their perception of the meaning of the word as a near-synonym of *rare* rather than as meaning, in the words of the *Shorter Oxford Dictionary*, 'of which there is only one; single, sole, solitary'.

2.3.5   Determiners

The term *determiner* is a more comprehensive category than *article*. The articles in English are *the (definite article)* and *a/an (indefinite article)*; but these two make up only a subclass of words that have a similar grammatical role, or, to put it differently, that show up in the same positions. Others include the words *this, that, these, those*; for example, the italicized words in (5) and (6). Like pronouns, determiners are a closed set.

> (5) *This* microprocessor directs *the* car's engine-control system.
> (6) *These* two groups of figures are binary and decimal equivalents.

The words *some* and *any* are also determiners when in the modifying function, as in (7).

> (7) He melted down *some* silver coins.

In some traditional grammars, determiners other than articles (and sometimes articles, too) were classed as *adjectives* on the grounds that they modify nouns, but there are very good reasons for treating them as separate from adjectives. Although it is true that they modify nouns, they do not do so in the same way as adjectives, and they differ on the question of grammatical obligatoriness. Where both occur together, determiners precede adjectives as in (8) but not vice versa as in (8a).

> (8)   The greater danger is that of flooding.
> (8a) *Greater the danger is that of flooding.

Sometimes a determiner before a noun is a grammatically obligatory requirement whereas an adjective never is: we say (9) or (9a) but not (9b) (except possibly in 'telegraphic' style).

(9)   *A* microprocessor works by responding to electrical impulses.
(9a)   *This* microprocessor works by responding to electrical impulses.
(9b)   *Microprocessor works by responding to electrical impulses.

Putting an adjective before the noun does not solve the problem, as we see from (9c).

(9c)   *New* microprocessor works by responding to electrical impulses.

2.3.6   Numerals

Numerals were also frequently classed as adjectives in traditional grammars, but again their grammatical role is sufficiently dissimilar to justify classing them separately. In some instances – certainly not all – numerals are more like determiners than like adjectives. On other occasions (for example, in abstract mathematical calculations such as *five times ten equals fifty*), they seem rather to resemble nouns. In fact, numerals are a rather anomalous set and are perhaps best treated as a class of their own.

2.3.7   Adverbs

The most unsatisfactory word class is that of *adverb*, which is often described by commentators as a ragbag or dustbin category; in other words, it is the category into which an amorphous collection of linguistic items goes when they have not been fitted in anywhere else. Traditionally, the adverb category was even more comprehensive than it is now, but it has to be admitted that in modern linguistics it still embraces a range of markedly dissimilar items. Since adverbs vary so greatly, it is difficult – perhaps even impossible – to come up with any feature which they all share.

One of the primary functions of adverbs is as the Head word of a group functioning as Adjunct at the rank of clause (see Chapter 3 for a fuller explanation of this statement). One type of adverb is characterized by the morphological feature *-ly*: *quickly*, *cleverly*, *silently*, *bravely*, and so on. Obviously these items have a regular correspondence to certain adjectives and are said to *derive from* the corresponding adjectival forms: *quick*, *clever*, *silent*, *brave*. Sometimes, the *-ly* suffix is missing and we have what appears to be the same word for both adjective and adverb; for example, *fast* in (10) is adjective in the first instance and adverb in the second.

(10)   He is a fast runner but he can't swim very fast.

Another set of adverbs (depending on what criteria we use to group them, traditionally usually semantic criteria) includes *now*, *then*, *later*, *earlier*, and yet another set: *here*, *there*, *everywhere*, *nowhere*, *anywhere*. Thus, we can speak of adverbs of manner (*quickly*), time (*now*) and place (*here*). Items like *seldom, never, often, frequently, always, invariably* are sometimes described as adverbs of frequency. *Upwards, downwards, sideways, left, right, forwards, backwards* and so on are often called directional adverbs. Another set includes such items as *however, moreover, nevertheless, thus, consequently, finally,* and, closely related to this group, *frankly, honestly, clearly, apparently*; both these types often occur at the beginning of a clause and they are sometimes called sentence adverbs. (See the discussion of Adjuncts in Section 3.4.)

All these subgroups have a strong family resemblance at least, and one can see why they end up with the same label. More questionable are items like *very, fairly, rather, quite, somewhat*, whose function, as mentioned above, includes the modification of gradable adjectives. It also includes the modification of gradable adverbs (*very quickly, very quietly*). There is something very messy about putting these items in the same large class as adverbs of time, manner and place, and some grammarians set them apart as *intensifiers*; there is a lot to be said for this approach, but it is common to treat intensifiers as a subclass of adverbs.

The rules regarding the sequential position of adverbs in relation to other items in the clause are very complicated and vary according to the subclasses of adverb. We will not pursue this further here, but the invented example (11) gives some indication of a range of adverb types and their distribution in the clause.

(11) Honestly, they are usually still working very energetically now, but tonight they are probably waiting outside or going home exceptionally early.

2.3.8 Prepositions

Confusion may arise with words like *up, on, in, over, under, near, by, inside, outside*. These often occur in a role which indicates that they are adverbs. Perhaps even more frequently they seem to be prepositions. Consider (12) from an introductory book on computers.

(12) For example, they can process sounds coming in through a microphone and reproduce them through speakers or onto special disks. They can monitor temperatures in laboratories or manipulate images on television.

The first occurrence of *in* (*sounds coming in*) is an adverb; the second occurrence of *in* (*in laboratories*) is a preposition. Other prepositions in this example are *through* (*through a microphone*), *onto* (*onto special disks*) and *on* (*on television*). *Through* can also be an adverb as in (13):

(13) I can't get through.

Perhaps the easiest way to deal with this problem is to say that they are homonymous pairs (looking and sounding alike but different in meaning): that just as there is an adjective *hard* (e.g. *a hard surface*) and an adverb *hard* (e.g. *Work hard*), there is also an adverb *in* and a preposition *in*, two different words belonging to different word classes but which happen to be pronounced and written in the same way. The same applies to *through*, or any of the others. Not all linguists would accept this position, however.

By definition, prepositions occur in prepositional phrases with a nominal group as Complement (see Section 2.5). A preposition does not vary in its form.

2.3.9 Conjunctions

Conjunctions are of two types: *linking conjunctions* or *linkers* (also known as co-ordinating conjunctions or co-ordinators) and *binding conjunctions* or *binders* (also known as subordinating conjunctions or subordinators). The linkers are a small set: *and, but, or, for, so,* and possibly *then.* Of course, in some cases, what appear to be the same 'words' may be items of a different word class that happen to look and sound alike. For example, in (14) the item *for* is a conjunction; in (15) *for* is a preposition.

> (14) Such a picture neatly explains A.V. Hill's observations, for clearly the number of molecules of APT consumed will depend on the length of rope hauled in.
> (15) The Air Force surrounded him with medical orderlies specially cleared for security.

The binding conjunctions are a larger group and they include: *because, since, when, whenever, until, before, after, while, if, unless, whether, although, even though, in case, given that, so that,* and many more. A clause which begins with a linking conjunction must follow the clause to which it is linked, but a clause which begins with a binding conjunction may generally follow or precede the clause to which it is bound. Note that once again duplication occurs: there are items here which are identical in pronunciation and spelling to items classed as prepositions or adverbs.

It is undeniable that the proliferation of terminology presents problems for the student of grammar. In part, the profusion of terms is arbitrary; simply because of the fact that there is no systematic attempt by the profession to agree on one set of labels. A more significant reason is that different linguists have different perceptions and different aims and so break language down differently. This is exacerbated by the fact that most categories in language are not discrete, neatly separable classes but *clines*, or gradations with clear central examples and more peripheral ones shading into other classes. For example, *and* and *or* are the most central – or most typical – examples of conjunction.

However, one point that we want to make is that there are good reasons why one linguistic realization (word, group of words, and so on) may carry more than one label even within the same model of grammar. Therefore, we will suspend discussion of word classes and look further at some functions of nouns and the groups in which nouns and other word classes play a key role.

2.4   *Subjects*

A traditional term (not a word class) still widely used is *Subject*. In (2), repeated here, *Wedgwood* is the Subject. It is also a noun.

  (2) Wedgwood experimented ceaselessly.

To say out of context that *Wedgwood* is a noun is quite viable. The quality of being a noun is a feature of the word *Wedgwood* in virtually all circumstances. We cannot say out of context that *Wedgwood* is a Subject, however, since being a Subject is not an intrinsic feature of the word *Wedgwood* but only a function which it sometimes realizes. Now consider (16).

  (16) Money is the root of all evil.

What we just said about *Wedgwood* is equally true of *money*. It is always a noun and in this example it is a Subject. It is not always a Subject, however. For instance, in (17) and (18), *money* is a noun but it is not a Subject.

  (17) They offered money.
  (18) He is obsessed with money.

It is only in some specific instance of a clause that an item can be labelled Subject. In SFG, *money* in (17) is said to be the *Complement* (see Chapter 3), and the pronoun *they* is the Subject. In (18) *he* is the Subject and *money* is part of a prepositional phrase (*with money*).

Not all the personal pronouns in Fig. 2.2 can function alone as Subject in Standard English clauses. *I, you, he, she, it, we, they*, from the left-hand column, and *mine, yours, his, hers, its, ours, theirs* may do so. For example, in Standard English, we say *They offered money* but not **Them offered money*. In fact, *I, she, he, we, they* nearly always realize the function of Subject (one exception is intensive structures like *It is I*, which most native speakers avoid as pedantic). *Me, her, us* and *them* never realize Subject in Standard English (though they do in some dialects).

How do we decide then whether some word or group of words is the Subject? With pronouns, as we have just seen, the form of the word itself (its morphology) often reflects its function. *I, he, she, we* and *they* are all forms which realize the Subject function, and *me, him, her, us* and *them* realize Complements. However, pronouns are untypical in this respect. In some languages, most words consistently vary according to their function, but in English most words do not. So what formal clues are there to help in identifying the Subject? One is that it often determines the form of the verb. Thus we say *He is obsessed with money* but *They are obsessed with money* or *I am obsessed with money*. As we have already seen, the verb *be* has more forms than other English verbs and so this *agreement* (or *concord*) with the Subject is noticeable more frequently than with other verbs, where evidence tends to be more restricted. Most verbs require an *-s* in the third person singular form, so that a third person singular Subject such as *The computer chip* co-occurs with the verb form *uses* as in (19), but with a plural Subject as in (19a) there is no *-s* inflection on the verb. (It is a strange quirk of English morphology that *-s* is the suffix denoting singularity in verbs and plurality in nouns. No one, presumably, would wish to suggest that the *-s* on verbs is grammatically the same morpheme as the *-s* on nouns even though they look and sound the same.)

(19)   The computer chip uses this battery of information [...]
(19a) Computer chips use this battery of information [...]

However, once again, English does not always display even these limited distinctions, and, as already mentioned, verbs like *can*, *may* and *should* (the modal operators) and most past tense main verbs do not vary according to Subject – or for any other reason.

IFG (Section 4.2) proposes one diagnostic test (or *probe*) for Subject which works fairly well. The Subject is the item in the clause which is picked up in the pronoun in a *mood tag* (also known as a *question tag*). A tag question is a question which is made up of a clause with a short form interrogative tagged on at the end; for example, (19b) or (19c). The mood tag is the bit at the end, after the comma.

(19b) The computer chip uses this battery of information, doesn't it?
(19c) Computer chips use this battery of information, don't they?

It in the first example is the pronoun equivalent of *the computer chip* and *they* in the second example picks up from *computer chips*. Hearing a sentence like (20), we can deduce not only the Subject but also the gender of the person the Subject refers to:

(20) The doctor prescribed these pills, didn't she?

The choice of *she* is not intrinsically identified with the word *doctor*, but determined by an aspect of the situation, in this case the sex of the doctor in question. If the doctor were a man, the pronoun would reflect the fact. This is further evidence that grammar is intimately bound up with context of situation and not just relationships within the clause.

Even given a declarative clause without a tag, the analyst can easily imagine a tag and thereby identify the Subject. We look at this issue again in Chapter 3.

2.5   *Groups*

2.5.1   Nominal groups

Not all nouns can stand alone in the way that proper nouns and many personal pronouns usually do or as some common nouns may, for example, *money* in (16). The nouns *computer* and *microchip*, for example, when they occur in the singular form, are always modified in some way by a word such as *the* or *a* (a determiner) or the numeral *one*. (Such nouns are labelled *count* or *countable nouns*. Nouns like *money* are *non-count* or *uncountable*.)

Nouns can also, of course, occur with more extensive modification. We can speak of *a sophisticated computer* or *a computer with an external drive*, or, if we are being more expansive, *a sophisticated computer with an external drive that meets all the requirements*. In a modern analysis we would say that, in (21), the Subject is *a computer with an external drive*, and not just the noun *computer*.

(21) A computer with an external drive works in the same way.

It is not quite right therefore to say that a *noun* can realize the Subject. It is rather a *nominal group* that has this potential. Thus, in (21), *a computer with an external drive* is a nominal group functioning as Subject of the clause. In fact, in all the examples the Subject is realized by a nominal group, regardless of the number of words involved. *The Great Khan, current from one input, this microprocessor, these two groups of figures, the greater danger, a microprocessor, such a picture, the number of molecules consumed, the Air Force, the doctor, a computer with an external drive* are all nominal groups, but so are *Wedgwood, money*, and *he*.

It may seem surprising that we should label a simple unmodified noun (*Wedgwood, money* or *he*) as a nominal group, but this is in keeping with the hierarchical, paradigmatic structure of the grammar. According to the rank scale (introduced in Chapter 1), a group is made up of *one or more* words and a clause is made up of *one or more* groups.

The key grammatical item in the group is called the Head. The remaining elements are Modifiers. Some of the nominal groups functioning as Subject that we have already considered are (with the Head in italics): current from one input, this *microprocessor*, these two *groups* of figures, the greater *danger*, a *microprocessor*, such a *picture*, the *number* of molecules consumed, the *Air Force*, the *doctor*, a *computer* with an external drive; *Wedgwood, money*, and *he*.

To sum up, a nominal group is typically a group with a noun (or pronoun) as its Head, and that noun may be modified, but it does not have to be modified in order to constitute a group in this technical sense. To make an analogy with a non-linguistic situation: a boat has a crew, and one person is the captain of that boat, but a boat may have a crew of one, and that one is by definition the captain. We have also seen that one of the functions which a nominal group can realize is that of Subject. We can now deal very briefly with other groups.

2.5.2   Verbal groups

Just as a nominal group may consist of a simple noun, a *verbal group* may consist of a simple verb; for example *directs* in (5), *is* in (8), *works* in (9). A verbal group may also be more complex, as with *was developed* in (1); *is obsessed* in (18); *must be based* in (22) or *had been developing* in (23).

(22) Price movements must be based on the beliefs of the investing public.
(23) They had been developing a similar process before this.

Finiteness is a quality which is not exclusive to the subclass of *finite opera-tors*. Where the verbal group is a single word (e.g., *directs, uses, prescribed, works* in the previous examples), it may be referred to as a *simple finite verb*. That word is the Head of its group. Where the verb is more complex, the Head is the finite: *must* in *must be based* in (22), *had* in *had been developing* (23).

The verbal group *may have been being written* has five elements. The breakdown here is as follows:

may: (modal operator)
have: auxiliary (bare infinitive)
been: auxiliary (past participle)
being: auxiliary (present participle)
written: lexical verb (past participle)

In fact, a more abstract analysis would cut across most of the words to give:

have plus the past participle morpheme (*-en*), which together indicate per-fect aspect (completion)
be plus present participle morpheme (*-ing*), which together indicate con-tinuous (i.e., progressive) aspect
be plus past participle morpheme (*-en*), which together indicate passive voice.

So, on this analysis, this verbal group is modal perfect progressive passive. In (22) *must be based* is modal passive, and in (23) *had been developing* is past perfect continuous. There is further discussion of the verbal group in Chapter 3.

2.5.3   Other groups

Adverbial groups tend to have less complex structure than nominal or verbal groups. The adverbial group normally has an adverb as its Head. In (24), *somewhat earlier* is the adverbial group; *earlier* is the Head, and *somewhat* the Modifier.

(24) Somewhat earlier the first application of glaze to pottery was made.

A *conjunction group* usually consists of just the conjunction as Head, and is rarely analyzed as such. Conjunctions can have Modifiers, however: in the clause *just until you go*, the conjunction *until* is modified by *just*; in *even if he answers*, *if* is the Head and *even* is the Modifier. Linking conjunctions are not modified.

A *prepositional group* has a preposition as Head and this is not often modified. Some prepositional groups do contain Modifiers, however; for instance: *just inside* has *inside* as Head and *just* as Modifier. Other examples are *right on* (as in *right on target*), *slightly over* (as in *slightly over the edge*), *far beyond* in *far beyond our expectations*.

Except in elliptical structures, a prepositional group (with or without modification) always occurs with a nominal group to make up a *prepositional phrase*. For example *in the office* is a prepositional phrase made up of a preposition *in* (strictly speaking a prepositional group without a Modifier) and a nominal group *the office*. *Slightly off the point* is a prepositional phrase made up of a prepositional group *slightly off* (*off* Head; *slightly* Modifier) and a nominal group *the point*.

Groups of the same type can be linked together to make up a group complex. *Jack and Jill* is a nominal group complex, and so is *the truth, the whole truth and nothing but the truth* in *Do you swear to tell the truth, the whole truth and nothing but the truth?* A verbal group complex can be formed similarly: She *speaks and thinks* like a lawyer. Also classed as verbal group complexes are the italicized items in: She *wants to understand*; Things are *beginning to develop*; They *seem to thrive* here.

2.6   *Three ways of looking at a clause*

We have said that any item of language may have more than one function. Any sample of language would serve to illustrate this. Take the following sentence, for instance:

(25) Boole had already written an important paper on this subject.

We can examine this from various points of view. We can analyze the structural relations of the clause, commenting on its *mood*, which concerns the fact that it is a statement (in grammatical terms, a *declarative*) and not a question (an *interrogative*), and therefore the Subject *Boole* comes before *had*. If the sentence were a question, the interrogative form would require *had* to be placed before *Boole* to give (25a).

(25a)   Had Boole already written an important paper on this subject?

This has something to do with the nature of the exchange between the speaker (or writer) and the listener (or reader). The fact that the writer is asking rather than telling leads to the choice of a particular ordering in the wording, a choice made from a number of possible options in the structure of clauses in English. In order to examine this aspect more fully, we would need to consider such matters as which items take on the functions of Subject, Complement, and so on. In this case, *Boole* is the Subject. The remaining functions will be discussed in Chapter 3.

On the other hand, we might be more interested in considering what some people might think of as the 'meaning' of the clause, but what for Systemic Functional linguists is just one of several kinds of meaning. What kind of event or state of affairs is being represented here? Or, in the words of the limerick: Who does what, which way up, and to whom? Here, the analyst's attention is directed to the question of whether the process is one involving action, or thought/feeling, or speech, or whether it specifies some relationship such as identity or similarity. In this case, we might label *Boole* as *Actor* on the grounds that this is an action and that Boole is the one who performs it. So we see that we have now labelled *Boole* twice: once as Subject and once as Actor. Each label says something different about the function of the item *Boole* in this clause.

There is yet another way in which we can look at it. We can concentrate attention on the choice the writer has made about which item to place first in the clause. Once a declarative has been opted for, *Boole* is the obvious choice for starting point, because in most declarative clauses in English the Subject comes first. The grammar of English would also permit other choices, for example, one of the following:

(25b)   Already, Boole had written an important paper on this subject.
(25c)   On this subject, Boole had already written an important paper.
(25d)   An important paper Boole had already written on this subject.

It is true that some of the choices seem less likely than others, but all are possible. In all these alternatives, the function of Subject is realized by the nominal group *Boole*, and in all of them *Boole* has the role of Actor; but in (25b), (25c) and (25d) the author has chosen to start off with something other than the Subject/Actor. The item with which we start a clause can usually be labelled the *Theme*. In the original, authentic example, (25), *Boole* is Subject, Actor and Theme. In the others, *Boole* is Subject and Actor, but not Theme. The Themes in the other examples are as follows: *Already*, *On this subject*, and *An important paper*. Chapters 4 and 5 return to the question of Theme and related issues. If (25d) seems a little odd out of context, compare (26) from the same page of the same text.

(26) He also began to have some ideas of his own. These he wrote up [. . .]

In the second clause here, we have the same sort of structure as (25d). The author might have chosen to place the Subject/Actor *he* first in the clause, as in (26a), but for textual reasons opted for *These*, thereby pushing the Subject into second place.

(26a) He also began to have ideas of his own. He wrote these up [. . .]

So, we have suggested three different ways of looking at the clause. The first, involving such functions as Subject, is described in Halliday's grammar as the 'clause as exchange' and relates primarily to the interpersonal metafunction. The second, involving such functions as Actor, is the 'clause as representation' and relates primarily to the ideational metafunction. The third, which concerns the choice of starting point and the optional ordering of elements and which involves the function Theme, is the 'clause as message' and relates primarily to the textual metafunction. Each of these will be discussed further in subsequent chapters.

Summary

In this chapter we have argued that grammatical terminology, rather than being a device intended to exclude the public from the deliberations of specialists, is valuable, even necessary, for talking about the way in which a language works. Starting with the familiar notion of word classes (or parts of speech), we see that the criteria for classification may produce different groupings of items, and we list Halliday's eight word classes, paying particular attention to nouns and their subclass, pronouns. Verbs can be described in a number of different ways and various subclassifications emerge. The functions Subject, Actor and Theme serve as an illustration of the fact that the same samples of language can be usefully labelled in more than one way, reflecting co-existing dimensions. Functions such as Subject are realized not so much by nouns as by nominal groups. Nominal groups consist of a Head (usually a noun) and possibly Modifiers.

Further study

Many linguists working within a Systemic Functional framework posit the existence of *adjectival group* with an adjective as Head (for example, Downing and Locke, 2002; Fawcett, 1974; in later Cardiff analysis it is labelled *quality group* but is essentially an adjectival group: Fawcett, 2000a;

Tucker, 1998). This appears to be consistent and predictable in terms of the analysis of other groups. (Note that in IFG adjectives which occur as Modifier in a nominal group are not themselves groups.) Halliday himself, however, dispenses with adjectival groups, classifying these structures as nominal groups with adjective as Head on the grounds that, like nominal groups with noun as Head, they frequently function as Complement (see Chapter 3) and in other roles typical of groups with noun as Head. In comparing Fawcett and Halliday on this point, Butler (1985, p. 101) seems to favour Fawcett, and much later (Butler 2003a) his remarks on Halliday's position on this issue are slightly negative.

Different Systemic Functional linguists vary in the use of the term *prepositional group*. In much Systemic literature, the prepositional group applies to combinations of a preposition and a nominal group: for example: *on your bike, over the rainbow*. Halliday, at least in later writings, calls this structure a prepositional phrase, and treats it, somewhat ambivalently, as outside the rank scale of clause, group, word, morpheme. As explained in Section 2.5, he applies the term prepositional group to the preposition itself (as Head) plus Modifiers, if any (IFG Section 6.5).

IFG Section 6.3 discusses the verbal group in somewhat different terms from those used here. The SFL treatment of tense and aspect in particular is strikingly different from that of most other linguists. More conventional treatments of verbs can be found in Palmer (1974; 1979; 1986).

Exercises

Exercise 2.1

Read Text 2A and carry out the tasks below.

---

[1] Water makes up over three-quarters of most living things and is constantly used up in cell processes. [2] Small plants are kept upright by being distended with water [3] just as a motor car tyre is firm when filled with air. [4] A tyre, [5] when it is flat, [4 *continued*] cannot support the car, and [6] a plant short of water on a hot day wilts. [7] Most of the water taken up by a plant is lost by evaporation from the leaves, a process called transpiration. [8] A maize plant loses about two litres a day because, [9] when the stomata are open to exchange gases during photosynthesis, [10] water vapour is lost very rapidly. [11] Transpiration actually helps to draw water up the plant in a way similar to sucking liquid up a straw.

Text 2A　(Martin *et al.* (eds), *The Penguin Book of the Natural World*, (1976 p. 42), numbers added).

   (a) 1. Identify the nominal groups which function as the Subjects of the numbered clauses in the text. (Clauses without an explicit subject are not numbered.)
       2. Identify the Head noun in each group.
   (b) Identify each word in the last sentence according to its word class. (Treat *to draw* as a single unit.)
   (c) Label the following groups as nominal, verbal, adverbial or conjunction. Clause numbers are given in parentheses.

constantly (1)	evaporation from the leaves (7)
cell processes (1)	about two litres (8)
just as (3)	is lost (10)
wilts (6)	very rapidly (10)

Exercise 2.2

   (a) Identify the verbal groups in the following examples and label them as active or passive.
   (b) Label the elements of the verbal groups as lexical, non-finite auxiliary, finite operator, modal operator.
   (c) Identify the nouns and label them as: common noun, proper noun or pronoun.
   (d) Identify prepositional phrases and label the preposition and the nominal group.

1. Robins had quoted a passage from Stevenson.
2. The government was willing to use that strategy.
3. Johnson must have smiled.
4. Eventually seventeen people were wiretapped by the FBI.
5. One more ingredient must be mentioned [. . .]
6. He worked with Bronstein, who had been brought into the firm by Kaplan.
7. [. . .] we did not know it at that time [. . .]
8. Her future in corporate public relations must have looked rather dim at that moment.

Exercise 2.3

One of the eight parts of speech in the most widespread version of traditional grammar is *interjection*. This is exemplified by such expressions as *Ouch! Oh! Ah! Help!* Try to think of reasons why many grammars exclude this category.

Exercise 2.4

From texts of your own choice, find examples of *numerals* functioning as (a) Modifier of a Head noun (b) as Head.

Exercise 2.5

Think about the alternating pronouns in the following examples or discuss them with a friend or colleague. You might consider questions of 'correctness', common usage versus grammatical regularity, and so on.

1. (a) I don't mind giving money to they who need it.
   (b) I don't mind giving money to them who need it.
2. (a) He first met my wife and I during our honeymoon.
   (b) He first met my wife and me during our honeymoon.
3. (a) Me and Bill go back a long way.
   (b) Bill and I go back a long way.
4. (a) Unlike She Who Must Be Obeyed, he was kind enough to laugh.
   (b) Unlike Her Who Must Be Obeyed, he was kind enough to laugh.
5. (a) Speaker 1: Who did this? Speaker 2: It was I.
   (b) Speaker 1: Who did this? Speaker 2: It was me.

Exercise 2.6

Go to example (11) in Section 2.3.7 and pick out all the adverbs.

Note

1. Martin, E., Larkin, S. and Bernbaum, L. (eds.) 1976: *The Penguin Book of the Natural World*. Harmondsworth: Penguin.

3

Structure of the clause

The night before Easter Sunday, 1920, Otto Loewi, an Austrian physiologist, awoke in the night with an idea which he jotted down on a tiny slip of paper and then went back to sleep. When he awoke again about six, he remembered that he had written down something of the greatest importance, but he could not decipher his own scrawl. The next night, at three a.m., the idea returned. It was a way of determining whether there is any chemical substance involved in nerve transmission.

The nerve impulse was known to be electrical in nature, but it was a mystery why some nerves stimulate an organ and others depress it. For instance, the vagus nerves slow down the rate of heartbeat, while the accelerator nerves increase it. Seventeen years before, it had struck Loewi that there might be a connection between this fact and the way in which some drugs stimulate while others depress.

Text 3A   (Taylor, *The Science of Life*,[1] p. 298).

3.1 *Subject revisited*

In Chapter 2, we pointed out that the Subject (S) is a function which is realized by a nominal group. At its simplest, this can be a personal pronoun such as *he* in a clause like (1).

   (1) [...] he could not decipher his own scrawl [...]

Or it may be an 'empty' pronoun such as *there*, as in the clause in (2).

   (2) [...] (whether) there is any chemical substance involved in nerve transmission.

It can also consist of a straightforward nominal group with a common noun as Head such as *the idea* in (3).

   (3) The next night, at three a.m., the idea returned.

3.1.1 Apposition

The Subject of the first clause in Text 3A, example (4), is *Otto Loewi, an Austrian physiologist*, which is complicated slightly by the nominal group *an Austrian physiologist*, placed alongside the personal name. Such a group is said to be *in apposition*; in this instance, *an Austrian physiologist* is in apposition to the nominal group *Otto Loewi*.

> (4) The night before Easter Sunday, 1920, Otto Loewi, an Austrian physiologist, awoke in the night with an idea which he jotted down on a tiny slip of paper.

With some sacrifice of informational detail, the author could have chosen to place either *Otto Loewi* or *an Austrian physiologist* alone as Subject to give (4a) or (4b):

> (4a) Otto Loewi awoke in the night [. . .]
> (4b) an Austrian physiologist awoke in the night [. . .]

Both expressions refer to the same individual. In (4a), the Subject function is realized by a proper name, and in (4b) it is realized by a more complicated nominal group with a common noun *physiologist* as its Head. In the event, the author combined the two by using the device of apposition. We shall regard *Otto Loewi, an Austrian physiologist* as a *group complex* realizing the function Subject.

3.1.2 Subject-Finite agreement probe

We mentioned in Chapter 2 that, although agreement with the finite element of the verb is one way to find the Subject, this is often – perhaps usually – not a reliable guide, because English verbs rarely vary in form to reflect person and number except in the third person singular present tense, where they often add *-s*. In such instances, it is easy to see that a change of number or person in the Subject may coincide with a change of number in the verb. (By 'number' we mean the choice of singular or plural and by 'person' we mean: first person – *I* and *we*; second person – *you*; and third person – anyone else).

In Text 3A, the prevailing tense is past simple and so the feature of agreement is not manifest. The verb *awake*, for example, is invariably *awoke* in the past, regardless of how many people are involved or whether the person doing the awaking is the speaker or the addressee or some third person.

Texts written predominantly in the present tense, therefore, obviously offer more examples of explicit subject–verb agreement. A geography textbook, describing existing conditions or general truths, is a case in point, offering such examples as (5), (6), (7) and (8), all with verbs in the present.

> (5) Erosion depletes the grasslands.

(6) The failure of the rain brings disaster.
(7) All savanna lands experience a period of drought [. . .]
(8) Rich pastures support more animals [. . .]

In (5) the verb ends in *-s,* the third person singular morpheme. There are two nominal groups: *erosion* and *grasslands. Erosion* is singular and *the grass-lands* is plural. Therefore the Subject is *erosion.* In (7) we also have two nominal groups: *all savanna lands* and *a period of drought.* The verb is plural; *all savanna lands* is plural whereas *a period of drought* is singular. Therefore the Subject is *all savanna lands.* In these two cases the relation between the Subject and the verb is very clear.

In (6) and (8) the probe (i.e. test or check) does not work quite so well. In (6) the verb is singular but both nominal groups are singular and in (8) the verb is plural and the nominal groups are both plural. But the probe can still work if we ask ourselves what effect it would have to change the nominal groups from singular to plural or vice versa. In (6) if we change *disaster* to *disasters,* it has no effect on the verb. But if we change *the failure of the rain* to *the failures* (or some other plural group) we have to change the verb from *brings* to *bring.* Therefore, *the failure of the rain* is Subject, and not *disaster.* The same sort of thing happens in reverse for (8).

This probe works for the past tense with the verb *be* only. Text 3A gives us (9), where *It* is a third person singular pronoun referring to *the idea,* mentioned in the previous sentence.

(9) It was a way of determining whether there is any chemical substance [. . .]

If Loewi had had more than one idea the pronoun would have been *they* and the verb would have been *were* as in (9a).

(9a) They were ways/a way of determining whether there is any chemical substance.

3.1.3 Other probes

We mentioned in Chapter 2 another probe for Subject. This is based on the fact that in a tag question, the Subject of the main clause is reflected in the tag. Thus, we can probe for the subject of a declarative clause by adding to it a question tag (also known as a mood tag). Adapting our original example (4) from the source text, this gives (4c).

(4c) Otto Loewi awoke in the night with an idea, didn't he?

The pronoun in the tag reflects *Otto Loewi* and so takes the form *he* rather than *it,* which it would have to do if it reflected *the night* or *an idea.* In (3), where the subject actually is *the idea,* the tag would have *it,* as in (3a).

(3a) The next night, at three a.m., the idea returned, didn't it?

The application of the tag probe on (5), (6), (7) and (8) works as a diagnostic for Subject in a similar way to the Subject-agreement probe, that is, more straightforwardly for (5) and (7) than for (6) and (8) (see (5a) to (8a) below).

(5a) Erosion depletes the grasslands, doesn't it?
(6a) The failure of the rain brings disaster, doesn't it?
(7a) All savanna lands experience a period of drought, don't they?
(8a) Rich pastures support more animals, don't they?

An equally reliable probe (advocated by Fawcett, 1999) might be crudely paraphrased as follows: reduce the clause to its simplest declarative form (if it is not in such a form already); then re-express it as a yes–no question. The Subject is the nominal group which immediately follows the finite operator in the interrogative. Thus, (5) can be re-expressed as (5b) and (6) as (6b) and so on:

(5b) Does erosion deplete the grasslands?
(6b) Does the failure of the rain bring disaster?

To signal the change of mood (from declarative to interrogative), *erosion* and *the failure of the rain* 'change places' with the finite operators and are thus identifiable as Subject.

3.1.4 Passive clauses

In the first sentence of the second paragraph of the text about Loewi, we have the clause given below as (10).

(10) The nerve impulse was known to be electrical in nature [. . .]

This is a passive clause, a clause in which the verbal group includes some form of the auxiliary verb *be* and a past participle, in this instance, *known*. The probes suggest that *the nerve impulse* is Subject.

Passive clauses are, in a sense, the inverted form of corresponding active clauses. To take an example from the source text but not included in the above extract.

(11) Loewi was obsessed by the idea.

This has a hypothetical corresponding active clause (11a).

(11a) The idea obsessed Loewi.

In the first one, the passive clause, the hypothetical tag is *wasn't he?* and in the second, the active, the tag is *didn't it?* Thus, we can ascertain that the Subject of (11) is *Loewi* but that of (11a) is *the idea*.

In passive clauses, there is sometimes a phrase made up of *by* plus a nominal group, as in (11). The by-phrase in the passive matches the Subject of the corresponding active clause; that is, the nominal group following *by* in the passive clause has the same referent as the nominal group realizing the Subject in the corresponding active clause (see Fig. 3.1).

Much more frequently, however, we find passives without a by-phrase. This brings us back to the first clause in the second paragraph of the source text, our example (10) above (*The nerve impulse was known to be electrical in nature*), which is an instance of exactly this phenomenon. Presumably, there is some hypothetical 'knower' assumed, but there is no mention of this person and we cannot safely deduce who it might be; in fact, there is an implication that the precise identity of the knower is not significant.

Voice	Subject	
Active	The idea	obsessed Loewi
Passive	Loewi	was obsessed by the idea

Fig. 3.1

3.1.5   'Dummy' Subjects

We mentioned above the 'empty' Subject *there* which occurs in the first paragraph of the source text. Such Subjects are also known as 'dummy' Subjects. In the second paragraph, we find another of these. This time the pronoun is the first *it* in (12).

> (12) [. . .] it was a mystery why some nerves stimulate an organ and others depress it.

What is the function of the first *it* in this clause? Superficially, it resembles the *it* in the previous sentence of the text, our example (9), but there is a big difference. In (9) (*It was a way of determining* [. . .]), the pronoun *it* refers to the same concept as the nominal group *the idea* in the sentence before that, but in (12) the Subject *it* is simply a sort of stand-in, holding the Subject position until the meat of the Subject comes along, namely: *why some nerves stimulate an organ and others depress it*. In contrast, the second *it* in the same sentence, (12), is a fully referring pronoun (not a 'dummy') and is co-referential with *an organ*.

Where empty *it* temporarily stands in for more substantial matter (that is, as a dummy), we treat the *postposed* structure (placed afterwards) as an embedded clause (see Chapter 8). We analyze the dummy *it* and the embedded clause together as making up the Subject. Thus, the subject of (12) is: *it* [. . .] *why some nerves stimulate an organ and others depress it*. (We return to this kind of structure in detail in Chapter 8.)

3.2   *Finites and Predicators*

Verbal groups realize the functions of *Finite* (F) and *Predicator* (P), and the two are often combined in a single word. If we take all the simple verbal groups from the source text, we have: *awoke, jotted (down), went, remembered, returned, stimulate, depress, slow (down),* and *increase*, some occurring more than once. Each of these is analyzed as a simple verbal group realizing the functions of Finite and Predicator at the same time. In each instance, the Finite and Predicator are said to be *fused*. Where the verbal group consists of one word, the fused Finite/Predicator function is represented as F/P.

It can perhaps be more easily understood what this means if we look at the instances of unfused Finites and Predicators. These can be found among the remaining verbal groups: *had written, could not decipher, was known* and *had struck*. Each of these falls into two parts, the first part (the finite operator) being Finite and the second part (the lexical verb stem) Predicator. The Finite is that part of the verbal group which carries the agreement (person and number) in so far as agreement shows up at all in English; the Predicator is the remainder of the verbal group.

In this text, as it happens, we have no examples with more than two verbal elements, but non-complex verbal groups can contain up to five words, not counting the negative polarity element *not* or the particles (for example, *down* in *had written down* or *slow down*). An example of a five-part verbal group is *might have been being written* as in *It might have been being written during that period*. Admittedly, such instances are not very common, but four-word verbal groups (*might have been written*) are, and so are groups of three words or two. In all such instances the first element (in our example, *might*) realizes the Finite function whilst the rest of the verbal group (in our examples, *have been being written* or *have been writing*) realizes the Predicator function (see Fig. 3.2).

In other words, the Predicator is realized by the lexical verb, that part of the verb which you might look up in a dictionary (*awake, jot, go, remember*, and so on), but it also incorporates all auxiliary elements other than

Finite	Predicator
was	writing
had	written
was	written
has	been writing
might	have been writing
might	have been being written

Fig. 3.2

the operator, which carries the agreement function (though agreement is not always made manifest in the substance of the language). So, in *might have been writing*, only *might* realizes the Finite function, whereas *have been writing* realizes the Predicator. In *has been writing*, *has* is Finite and *been writing* is Predicator. Fig. 3.2 offers a random selection of various verbal groups with *write* as the lexical verb, analyzed into the functions Finite and Predicator.

In any verbal group made up of more than one word in English, only the Finite carries the agreement, and there is only one Finite to a group. When they stand alone, finite forms of *be* (*am, is, are, was, were*) and finite forms of *have* (*has, have, had*) are usually analyzed as Finite and not as fused forms. Clauses featuring Finites of this kind have no Predicator, for example, the first clause partially analyzed in Fig. 3.3 (i). Compare this with the other two clauses in Fig. 3.3: (ii) a fused Finite and Predicator and (iii) a separate Finite and Predicator.

(i)	it	was	a way of determining	
	S	F		
(ii)	he	awoke	again about six	
	S	F/P		
(iii)	he	has	written	the letter
	S	F	P	

Fig. 3.3

3.2.1   Negatives and interrogatives

In English, the grammar of interrogatives and negatives (and certain related structures) is much more complicated than in many other languages, such as most other European languages. Where the positive declarative contains a separate Finite and Predicator, as in *had written* in our source text, the negative counterpart is identical except that *not* (or *n't*) is present immediately after the Finite. Let us consider modified data to avoid some confusing problems irrelevant to our present concerns. Thus, illustrating the positive–negative options, we have the pairing (13) and (13a).

(13)   He has written the letter.
(13a) He has not written the letter.

Interrogatives   likewise   have   a   fairly   straightforward   systematic correspondence with declaratives in that the Finite and the Subject are inverted; thus we have (13b).

(13b) Has he written the letter?

So far, so good. Look at it from the point of view of the non-English speaker (say, a German teenager) trying to master English usage. This corresponds very nicely with what happens in her own language. In German, for example, she might say (14) when forming a positive declarative, (14a) when forming a negative and (14b) when forming an interrogative.

(14)   Er hat den Brief geschrieben.
       (lit. *He has the letter written.*)
(14a) Er hat den Brief nicht geschrieben.
       (lit. *He has the letter not written.*)
(14b) Hat er den Brief geschrieben?
       (lit. *Has he the letter written?*)

The order of the words is not quite the same, but the relationship between the two is otherwise consistent with the English pattern.

So long as we stick to samples where the verbal group in the positive declarative realizes distinct Finite and Predicator, all is well, but the unsuspecting young German will get into linguistic trouble if she tries to do the same thing with all verbs because, working on the same principles, she could come up with the paradigm (15).

(15)   He awoke in the night.
       *He awoke not in the night.
       *Awoke he in the night?

That sort of thing might have been all very well for Shakespeare, but it will not do for English today. In modern English, we have the paradigm (15a), analyzed for S, F and P in Fig. 3.4.

(15a) He awoke in the night.
       He did not awake in the night.
       Did he awake in the night?

He	awoke	in the night	
S	F/P		
He	did not	awake	in the night
S	F	P	
Did	he	awake	in the night?
F	S	P	

Fig. 3.4

This particular complication in English grammar, which has no parallel in German (or French, Spanish, Italian or most other) grammar, requires that the negative or interrogative counterparts of positive declaratives with a simple verb must feature a form of the verb *do* as Finite. Put another way, the rules in English are as follows:

- To convert a positive declarative into a negative, add *not* after the Finite. If there is no separate Finite, make *do* the Finite and add *not*.
- To convert a declarative into an interrogative, invert the order of Finite and Subject. If there is no separate Finite, make *do* the Finite and place it before the Subject.

The native English student learning German needs only the first part of each rule (suitably translated), since the second part is unique to English.

Incidentally, *do* and other finite auxiliary verbs often occur in isolation in elliptical structures such as short form answers to yes/no questions (*Yes, I did*; *No, they can't*); short form emphatic agreement (*So they did! So they should!*); and many other structures, including question tags. These are clear instances of Finite without a Predicator.

Of course, we are not obliged to explain the relationship between regularly corresponding clause types as involving some kind of conversion process from one to another. This is just one of the many metaphorical devices we may employ in talking about language. Another might present the whole of the vocabulary and grammar of the language as a vast network of inter-related systems, through which the users thread their way each time they use the language, committing themselves to a series of options, some of which determine later choices to varying extents. This last metaphor is closer to the SFL perception.

3.2.2   Mood

In Section 3.2.1, we looked at some of the grammatical characteristics of declaratives and interrogatives. This leads us to a brief consideration of the treatment of Mood in SFG.

SFG divides the clause into two parts: the Mood and the Residue. The Mood is made up of the Subject and Finite; the Residue is the rest of the functions in the clause (Predicator, Complements and Adjuncts).

Recall that we have mentioned the representation of the grammar as an intricate set of sets of choices. Each of these sets is called a system and the systems link up with each other as networks. The realization of the MOOD function in any clause involves making choices from the MOOD system network (see Fig. 3.5).

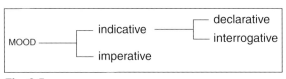

Fig. 3.5

Not all clauses have MOOD. Examples of moodless clauses are (16), (17), or the italicized section of (18) (see Chapter 8).

(16) Closed for lunch.
(17) Happy New Year!
(18) *Subsequently released*, he escaped to England.

In clauses which do have mood, an obligatory choice is made between indicative and imperative. (We could call indicative 'non-imperative'.) If indicative is chosen, an obligatory choice is made between declarative and interrogative. Each choice precludes the others; that is to say, you cannot have a clause which is simultaneously declarative and interrogative, or imperative and declarative, and so on. In the network, this MOOD system links up with the system of POLARITY shown in Fig. 3.6. In addition to selecting one of the three options from the MOOD system, we are required to choose between positive and negative. (Names of systems and networks – not functions – are conventionally presented in small capitals.)

In the second sentence in Text 3A, presented here as (19), there are four clauses, listed separately below. Each of them realizes the choice *declarative* from the MOOD system; the first three realize the choice of positive and the last one realizes the choice of negative from the POLARITY system.

(19) When he awoke about six, he remembered that he had written down something of the greatest importance, but he could not decipher his own scrawl.
  • When he awoke again about six: *positive declarative*
  • he remembered: *positive declarative*
  • that he had written down something of the greatest importance: *positive declarative*
  • but he could not decipher his own scrawl: *negative declarative*

Subject and Finite are the key exponents of the mood choices in that (i) the sequencing of Subject and Finite is affected by the choice between declarative and interrogative (already discussed above) and (ii) the choice of imperative permits us to leave out the Subject. Polarity has a bearing on mood because,

Fig. 3.6

as we have pointed out, with verbs in the simple present tense and simple past tense, Finite and Predicator are fused in a single word in the positive option, but in the negative option the separate auxiliary finite operator *do* must realize the function of Finite.

To label the rest of the clause 'Residue' is not to suggest that it is of little importance. It is simply the Residue (what remains) after the Mood is taken out. It is possible to analyze a clause in terms of the functions SFPCA without discussing Mood and Residue, but they are part of the same package.

3.3   *Complements*

If you are familiar with traditional grammar, you may have already learned to interpret the term *complement* in a more narrow sense than it has in SFG. (In other grammars the term is used with various meanings.) The use of the term in SFG is more comprehensive than in traditional grammar. In her seminal *Introduction to Systemic Linguistics*, Margaret Berry identifies it as follows: 'A complement is the part of a sentence which answers the question "Who or what?" (or, if one wishes to be pedantic, "Whom or what?") *after* the verb' (Berry, 1975, p. 64)

Berry refers to definitions of this type as 'helpful but unscientific' (Berry, 1975, p. 84), and that is a fair comment. If we were to apply it to Text 3A, we would find it helpful in some cases, less helpful in others. Since our aim here is to elucidate rather than confuse, we will take the liberty of being selective in our application.

If on reading the first sentence, shortened here as (20), we ask 'Loewi awoke who or what?', there is no obvious candidate to fill the *Who or what?* slot.

(20) Loewi awoke in the night.

Loewi awoke *in the night*, but *in the night* does not answer the question *Who or what?* The sentence goes on to say that he awoke in the night *with an idea*, but this too fails to meet the *Who or what?* criterion. Therefore, there is no Complement.

This is a correct deduction. In fact, many clauses have no Complements. It happens that, even though it does not have a Complement in this instance, the verb *awoke* could have one, though this is not true for all verbs. For example, Loewi might have decided to tell his bright idea to his wife, assuming that he had one and that she was present. In this case, we might wish to say (21).

(21) He awoke his wife.

Now, if we were to ask Berry's 'who or what?' question, we get the answer *his wife*. Thus the Complement is *his wife*. In (22), however, there is no possibility of a Complement.

(22) Night fell.

Dipping into Text 3A at a later point, we get (23):

(23) [. . .] he had written down something of the greatest importance [. . .]

This time when we apply Berry's question as *He had written down who or what?*, we get the answer: *something of the greatest importance*. We have identified a Complement. This time, the presence of the Complement is obligatory since *had written down* must take a Complement (see Fig. 3.7).

he	had	written down	something of the greatest importance
S	F	P	C

Fig. 3.7

A further dip into the text brings out example (3) again, repeated here:

(3) The next night, at three a.m., the idea returned.

The idea returned who or what? we ask. No answer. So again, no Complement.

Try again with (9), also repeated:

(9) It was a way of determining whether there is any chemical substance in nerve transmission.

Apply Berry's question: *It was who or what?* Answer: *a way of determining whether there is any chemical substance in nerve transmission.* We have identified another Complement, a long and complicated one this time, but there is nothing in the grammar that says that Complements cannot be long and complicated.

One last dip. This time we take a dependent clause, (24) (see Chapter 8 for dependent clauses).

(24) [. . .] while the accelerator nerves decrease it [. . .]

Ask: *While the accelerator nerves decrease who or what?* Answer: *it.* Therefore, the Complement is *it*. A complement does not have to be long and complicated, then, or even very explicit out of context.

Alas, this probe is no more rigorous or reliable than the probes for Subject. The best that can be said for it is that it often works. If you try the rest of the clauses in the extract, you may well get into difficulties at times. This is the price of using authentic data rather than invented 'The cat chased the mouse' type of sentences that are designed to suit the needs of the moment. Some of the problems will be resolved in later chapters. Part of the source text is analyzed and labelled for SFPCA in Section 3.5.

3.3.1   The name of the rose and Complement subcategorization

Like flowers, Complements come in various kinds. On one occasion, it may be enough to describe an object as a *flower*; on another occasion, we may wish to be more specific and refer to it as a *rose* or *jasmine* or *magnolia*. Some people might want to specify what kind of rose they are talking about and so they classify it as a *tea rose* or a *rambling rose*. Rose growers may go into even greater refinements of categorization. In the same way, with many grammatical categories, we can classify items with varying degrees of delicacy. Though they are less variegated than flowers, Complements are no exception to this tendency. For some purposes, we may be happy with the label Complement; sometimes we may wish to go further and say what kind of Complement we are dealing with.

The Complements (italicized) in the clauses 'he awoke *his wife*'; 'he had written down *something of the greatest importance*'; 'he could not decipher *his own scrawl*'; 'others depress *it*' are all classed, with greater delicacy, as *object Complements*. Or, at somewhere around the 'rambling rose' stage of delicacy, they can be classed as *direct object Complements* (C^{do}).

Direct object Complements (C^{do}) normally follow those verbs listed in dictionaries as transitive: *decipher, depress, stimulate*, from our extract. Verbs marked in the dictionary as intransitive tend to occur without an object Complement. One problem for someone trying to give a neat account of all this is that most verbs in English (not all) seem to be able to function both 'transitively' and 'intransitively'; that is, with or without a Complement. For example, in the extract we find both (25) and, a little later, (26) (with C^{do} in italics):

(25) [. . .] some nerves stimulate *an organ* and others depress *it*.
(26) [. . .] some drugs stimulate while others depress.

A Complement which follows a copular verb (such as *be, seem, appear, become*) is called an intensive Complement (C^{int}). Examples: *Brasilia is the capital city*; *she seems a brilliant woman*; *he appears stupid*; *the terrain eventually became a desert*. The text provides a more complicated example of this in (9), repeated here with added italics.

(9) It was *a way of determining whether there is any chemical substance involved in nerve transmission.*

To sum up, all the following items are intensive Complements: *the capital city, a brilliant woman, stupid, a desert* and *a way of determining whether there is any chemical substance involved in nerve transmission.*

Some verbs allow two object Complements: a direct object Complement and an *indirect object Complement* (C^{io}) (see Fig. 3.8). (27) is taken from another chapter of the source text.[1]

(27) Mendel promptly sent him 140 packets.

Mendel	promptly	sent	him	140 packets
S		F/P	C^{io}	C^{do}

Fig. 3.8

Here the C^{do} is *140 packets* and the C^{io} is the pronoun *him*. The verbs that permit C^{io}, called *ditransitive* verbs, are a limited set; typical ones are *give*, *send*, *offer*. In a simple independent declarative clause the C^{io} normally comes immediately after the verb and the C^{do} follows it, as in (27). Such clauses systematically correspond to clauses where the C^{do} immediately follows the Predicator and the other Complement is expressed as a prepositional phrase with *to*. Thus, the author might have written (27a):

(27a) Mendel promptly sent 140 packets to him.

Many linguists reserve the term indirect object for the structure without the preposition. One label that has been applied to the *to*-phrase in such structures is *oblique Complement* (C^{ob}). Some class it as an Adjunct. However, some analysts prefer to apply the term indirect object Complement to both structures, regardless of the form and sequence, which is what we shall do, as in Fig. 3.9.

Mendel	promptly	sent	140 packets	to him
S		F/P	C^{do}	C^{io}

Fig. 3.9

Sometimes a C^{io} corresponds not to a *to*-phrase but to a *for*-phrase, but it is analyzed similarly. For example, in the case of the invented clause (27b), the corresponding clause is (27c).

(27b) Mendel bought him 140 packets.
(27c) Mendel bought 140 packets for him.

A different kind of structure with two Complements is to be found in (28):

(28) Loewi called the substance released by the vagus nerve 'vagus-stuff'.

There are two Complements here: (i) *the substance released by the vagus nerve*, and (ii) *vagus-stuff*. The first is the C^{do}, but the second is another kind of intensive Complement (C^{int}), sharing identity with the C^{do} (see Fig. 3.10). (Two is the maximum number of Complements that a simple clause can contain.)

A standard textbook instance of this type of structure is (29).

(29) They elected him President.

Loewi	called	the substance	'vagus-stuff'
S	F/P	C^{do}	C^{int}

Fig. 3.10

Here *him* is C^{do} and *President* is C^{int}. Comparable structures in common use are the so-called performative expressions, such as (30), (31) and (32).

(30) I now pronounce you man and wife.
(31) I find you not guilty.
(32) I declare this supermarket open.

A literary example of this structure is the well-known first sentence of the great American novel *Moby Dick:* 'Call me Ishmael' (which because it is imperative lacks a Subject). An old joke plays on the potential ambiguity of such structures:

Hotel guest: Call me a taxi!
Hotel porter: All right, you're a taxi.

Normally in our analysis we label Complement as C without indicating the more delicate subcategory. Only when the distinction is important for the purposes of the discussion do we go into the more delicate analysis.

3.4   *Adjuncts*

Adjuncts, as their name suggests (etymologically: something 'joined to'), are slightly peripheral in the clause. The information they give may be just as important as that of S, F, P or C items, but Adjuncts are for the most part grammatically optional in a way that the others are not.

The first sentence in Text 3A begins with an Adjunct: *The night before Easter Sunday, 1920*. Other Adjuncts in the same sentence are: *in the night, with an idea, on a tiny slip of paper* and *then*. (Some analysts might want to add *down*, but we have decided to place it with the verb as part of the Predicator.) In the following sentences in the same paragraph, we find: *again, about six, the next night, at three a.m.*, and *in nerve transmission*.

Adjuncts fall into three subtypes: *circumstantial, conjunctive* and *modal*, corresponding more or less to the three macrofunctions: experiential, textual and interpersonal. As in the case of Complement, whether or not we need to go into such details depends on the immediate purpose of our analysis. It may be enough to classify an item as Adjunct or we may wish to subclassify it.

3.4.1 Circumstantial Adjuncts

Most of the Adjuncts in the first paragraph concern information about time or place; in other words, they deal with the *circumstances* of the events or states described in the text. For this reason, such Adjuncts are called *circumstantial Adjuncts* (A^{cir}).

The realizations of A^{cir} cited here are as follows:

the night before Easter Sunday, 1920: nominal groups
in the night: prepositional phrase
with an idea which he jotted down on a tiny slip of paper: prepositional phrase
on a tiny slip of paper: prepositional phrase
about six: prepositional phrase
the next night: nominal group
at three a.m.: prepositional phrase
in nerve transmission: prepositional phrase.

As you can see, Adjuncts have considerable flexibility with regard to the items which realize them. Most typically, though, they are realized by prepositional phrases or adverbs. Nominal groups which express points of time and to that extent resemble adverbs are not rare either, but in this extract prepositional phrases dominate.

Circumstantial Adjuncts express information about the circumstances of a process: they convey information about such matters as place, time, manner, the associated participants (with whom? with what?); they are, therefore, part of the ideational (experiential) meaning of the clause. Grammatically, they are part of the Residue though they may sometimes be placed separately.

The by-phrase in passive clauses is also A^{cir} because it expresses the meaning: by what? Example (11) is analyzed as in Fig. 3.11.

Loewi	was	obsessed	by the idea
S	F	P	A^{cir}

Fig. 3.11

3.4.2 Conjunctive Adjuncts

You may have noticed that in the previous section we omitted from the list of realizations the adverbs *then* and *again*, although we originally identified them as Adjuncts. This is because *then* and *again* have subtly different functions from the items in the list, and are therefore discussed in this section. But before we continue with the adverb *then*, let us consider the second paragraph of the extract, where we find an Adjunct that is clearly of a different kind from the circumstantial Adjuncts listed.

(33) For instance, the vagus nerves slow down the rate of heartbeat, while the accelerator nerves increase it.

In (33) the prepositional phrase *for instance* functions to show the link between the clause it introduces and the previous text. In the sentence that precedes (33) in the text, we have a general statement: *some nerves stimulate an organ and others depress it.* The information that (33) offers is a specific example of the type of thing initially described in these general terms. It is an instance of the discourse pattern Generalization: Example (Hoey, 1983). What the expression *For instance* does is to signal the nature of that relationship. It does not actually add to the propositional content of the second sentence, but it does make clear for the reader how it fits into the text. It helps to show the link between this clause and what precedes it. For this reason, Adjuncts of this type are called *conjunctive Adjuncts* (A^{con}).

To return to *then* (in the clause *and then went back to sleep*), although it resembles most of our examples of circumstantial Adjuncts in that it is concerned with time, its primary function seems to be to relate this event to the events previously recounted in the text. This seems to suggest that it is A^{con}. The adverb *again* in *When he awoke again* is similar. By the same reasoning, *Seventeen years before* might also be classed as A^{con} instead of A^{cir} (though this is perhaps more debatable). Here we have evidence of the way that labelling needs to take account of the possibility of a *cline*, a gradation between two clear ends of a line (in this case, indisputable instances of A^{cir} and indisputable instances of A^{con}); *then* seems to have some qualities of both, but to be closer to the Conjunctive end of the cline.

The book from which we took our extract continues with the passage in Text 3B. In the first sentence here we find another A^{con}: the time adverb *now*. In the subsequent sentence, we have the adverb *then*, and in the last sentence the adverbs *equally* and *afterwards. Now, then* and *afterwards* signal conjunction relating to time, and *equally* signals a kind of comparison. All are A^{con}, and they can be contrasted with the other Adjuncts in the same text fragment.

The experiment which now occurred to Loewi was to take a frog's heart, put it in Ringer's solution (a solution containing the salts which normally bathe cells, and which keep them alive for a while), and stimulate its vagus nerve repeatedly, in the expectation that some chemical substance would be liberated into the solution. Then to put a second frog's heart in the solution and see if it slowed down. Loewi got out of bed, went to his lab, and did the experiment. It worked. Equally, if he stimulated the accelerator nerve, the solution would afterwards accelerate another heart.

Text 3B   (Taylor, *The Science of Life*[1]).

3.4.3 Modal Adjuncts

The remaining Adjuncts in Text 3B can be split up into two sets. On the one hand, we have the circumstantial Adjuncts: *in Ringer's solution, into the solution, in the solution, out of bed,* and *to his lab.* On the other hand, we have: *normally, for a while,* and *repeatedly.* These three fall into a subclass of Adjuncts not yet mentioned, to which we give the label *modal Adjuncts* (A^{mod}). The function of A^{mod} is to indicate some aspect of the speaker/writer's attitude to the message or her comment on its relevance, reliability, interest, and so on. Sometimes, it may be difficult to distinguish between a modal Adjunct and a circumstantial Adjunct, or, indeed, even between a modal and a conjunctive.

Clearer examples of modal Adjuncts are (34) to (37) from an earlier page of the same book.

(34) [. . .] the sodium ions which enter are *somehow* pumped out again.
(35) [. . .] it was *probably* the same substance [. . .]
(36) [. . .] one nerve cell does not *quite* touch another.
(37) These proved big enough for the voltage *actually* observed.

The adverb *probably* can be taken as the prototypical item realizing the function of A^{mod}. It represents the degree to which the speaker/writer is committed to the proposition being made. For this chapter, we are using as our main source a popular textbook, a history of biology. In texts of this type, there is a tendency to present propositions in a relatively unmodified way as scientific truths. We say 'relatively' because, as the samples just given demonstrate, such 'hedging' is certainly not absent. However, in articles written by scientists reporting their own research, there tends to be a greater amount of hedging, that is, signals of a degree of caution in the making of claims. This can show up in the use of various modifiers such as *approximately, about, around,* usually as part of a nominal group, and also in the use of modal operators like *may, might* and *could,* realizing the Finite in the verbal group. In addition, more significantly for our present discussion, the hedging can take the form of modal Adjuncts realized by modal adverbs like *probably.*

Modal Adjuncts have something in common then with modal operators, hence their shared part of the label. On a scale of commitment to a proposition, we might have *certainly* at the positive end and *certainly not* at the negative end, with such items as *probably, possibly, conceivably* at various points along the line, along with expressions like *perhaps, maybe, indisputably, without doubt, imaginably, surely.*

Less obvious examples, perhaps, are the items which we identified in Text 3B: *normally, for a while,* and *repeatedly.* These tell us about the frequency, duration or regularity of the process. At the positive end of this scale we might have *always* or *invariably* and at the negative end *never, not once* or *at no time*. Incidentally, *not*, analyzed in Fig. 3.4 as part of Finite is perhaps better treated as a modal Adjunct along with items like *never* and *seldom*.

Discourse analysts and scholars who are interested in how scientists write about their work have paid considerable attention to modality in text, and one thing that has emerged is that reports of scientific research in newspapers and popular magazines feature less hedging than do the reports in specialist scientific journals. In contrast, school textbooks, histories and biographies tend to resemble newspapers rather than specialist texts, in this respect if not in others. One good reason, perhaps, why there are fewer hedging expressions in our source text than in original research reports is that what is recounted here is seen with hindsight to be reliable information. Moreover, politeness factors (modesty and lack of encroachment on other people's space) that are significantly present when scientists report their own work do not apply when a historian reports it retrospectively. This is discussed further in Chapter 11.

Examples of other modal Adjuncts that serve a similar purpose are *in our view*, *in my opinion*, *according to our calculations*, *on present evidence*. A similar expression found later in the same book is (38) (italics added).

(38) Diluted by a lot of Ringer's solution, it would, *one would expect*, be much too weak to exert any effect.

This expresses the author's caution with regard to the likelihood of the proposition even though it exploits the impersonal pronoun *one* to do so. If we remove the italicized words, we have a more strongly committed claim. Although this hedging device is a clause, it is something like a fixed expression functioning as a simple Adjunct. (See Chapters 9 and 10 for a discussion of clause complexes.)

All these modal Adjuncts have a similar function, namely that of hedging or modulating the proposition. As we have said, they have much in common in this respect with modal verbs (*may*, *might*, and so on), which function as Finites within the Mood of the clause. Thus, they can with greater delicacy be labelled *mood Adjuncts* to distinguish them from the other subclass of modal Adjuncts which we call *comment Adjuncts*. For most purposes, however, it is not necessary to make such subtle distinctions.

Comment Adjuncts are typically realized by such adverbs as *frankly*, *fortunately*, *obviously*, and *regrettably*. These offer the speaker/writer's comment on the proposition, but that comment does not say anything about probability, frequency or generality. An example from later in our source text is (39) (italics added):

(39) *Oddly enough*, a case where the transmission actually was electrical was discovered soon after.

The modal (comment) Adjunct that begins it (*Oddly enough*) serves to indicate to the reader something of the author's surprise at the fact which he is reporting. Incidentally, (39) also includes another modal Adjunct, this time the mood Adjunct: *actually*, and a conjunctive Adjunct: *soon after*.

3.4.4   Adjuncts and conjunctions

As we have said, Adjuncts are normally realized by prepositional phrases, adverbial groups, and sometimes even nominal groups, but they are not realized by conjunctions. This is deducible from the statement made in Chapter 2 that conjunctions are not part of the structure of the clause. Although the word *then* can be a conjunction, in this text it is not a conjunction but an adverb, as are *now* and *afterwards*. All function here as Adjunct.

As their name suggests, conjunctive Adjuncts have a function similar to that carried out by conjunctions; they signal the rhetorical organization of the text, which places them as part of the textual metafunction. The distinction between *conjunctions* and *conjunctive Adjuncts* can be a source of some confusion.

Conjunctions are a word class within the same system as *noun, verb, adjective, adverb, determiner, preposition*, and *numeral* (see Chapter 2) whereas Adjunct is a function in the clause and is realized by such word classes as adverbs and nominals as well as by prepositional phrases. In our analysis, conjunctions fall outside the clause structure SFPCA. Although conjunctive Adjuncts often seem to convey a similar meaning to that conveyed by conjunctions, they differ from them grammatically. For instance, the conjunction always occurs at the beginning of the clause which it links or binds, whereas conjunctive Adjuncts can occur at various points within the clause that they affect. Consider (40).

> (40) He remembered that he had written down something of the greatest importance, but he could not decipher his own scrawl.

There are three clauses here: *He remembered ‖ that he had written down something of the greatest importance ‖ but he could not decipher his own scrawl.* The first two go together and we will ignore that relationship here and focus on the link signalled by *but*. The conjunction *but* indicates to the reader that there is an adversative relation between the two parts of the sentence, or rather, that the second is in an adverse relation to the first. Now, suppose we reword this as (40a).

> (40a) He remembered that he had written down something of the greatest importance. However, he could not decipher his own scrawl.

The adverb *however* here carries something akin to the force of *but* in the actual sentence, but, in addition to the change of lexical item, there is a grammatical change. Instead of a two-part sentence linked by a linking conjunction, we have two separate sentences with an adverb as A^{con} in the second. That this is not just an arbitrary labelling distinction is clear if we try to move the words in question. We can say in the same linguistic context (40b) or (40c).

> (40b) He remembered that he had written down something of the greatest importance. He could not, however, decipher his own scrawl.
> (40c) He remembered that he had written down something of the greatest importance. He could not decipher his own scrawl, however.

But there is no other position for the conjunction *but* without a change of meaning. We do not, in modern Standard English, say or write (40d) or (40e) (though archaically (40d) could occur with a different meaning and (40e) might still be heard in parts of Scotland).

> (40d) *He remembered that he had written down something of the greatest importance, he could not but decipher his own scrawl.
> (40e) *He remembered that he had written down something of the greatest importance, he could not decipher his own scrawl but.

Plainly, *however* and *but* behave grammatically in very different ways. That is why we classify them differently, assigning them different labels as word classes (*adverb* versus *conjunction*) and functionally (since *however* is an Adjunct and no comparable function can be assigned to *but*). Also, that is why orthographic conventions prescribe a full stop (or a semi-colon) between the two clauses with *however* and permit a comma with *but*. The same can be said, with appropriate changes, of the other items in Fig. 3.12.

Conjunctive Adjunct (adverb)	conjunction
moreover, furthermore, also however, nevertheless, alternatively meanwhile, simultaneously thus, therefore, consequently	and but, yet or, whereas when, while so that

Fig. 3.12

Note that *yet* can be a conjunction, similar in meaning to *but*, or it can be a temporal adverb and hence function as Adjunct (*He has not spoken yet*).

When analyzing clauses into SFPCA, conjunctions are omitted from the analysis, but conjunctive Adjuncts are included though they are technically outside the Mood and Residue.

3.5   *Sample analysis*

The first three sentences of Text 3A are analyzed in terms of SFPCA in Fig. 3.13. The first two sentences are clause complexes, that is, they consist of more than one clause (see Chapter 9), but this does not present any problems for analysis here. The first sentence also contains another clause (*which he jotted down on a piece of paper*), but this is left unanalyzed. The fourth sentence in the paragraph contains multiple embedding of clauses, which does make for some difficulty in analysis, and so the sentence is omitted here, but similar structures are dealt with in Chapters 8 and 9. In future chapters, the subclassification will normally be left out of such analyses because the labels C or A are usually sufficient without further detail.

The night before Easter Sunday, 1920,		Otto Loewi, an Austrian physiologist,		
A^{cir}		S		

awoke	in the night	with an idea which he jotted down on a tiny slip of paper,		
F/P	A^{cir}	A^{cir}		

and	then	went	back to sleep.	When	he	awoke	again
	A^{con}	F/P	A^{cir}		S	F/P	A^{con}

about six	he	remembered	that	he	had	written down
A^{cir}	S	F/P		S	F	P

something of the greatest importance	but	he	could not	decipher
C^{do}		S	F	P

his own scrawl.	The next night	at three a.m.	the idea	returned.
C^{do}	A^{cir}	A^{cir}	S	F/P

Fig. 3.13

Summary

In this chapter, we deal with the five clause functions: Subject (S), Finite (F), Predicator (P), Complement (C) and Adjunct (A). A nominal group with a nominal group in apposition is treated as a group complex. Three probes for Subject (Subject-Finite agreement; question tag formation; mood change) are followed through in detail. The pronoun *it* can be a personal pronoun referring to some entity or it can be a dummy, empty of content and filling only a grammatical role. When dummy-*it* occurs with a post-posed clause, we analyze the whole as a discontinuous Subject. Subject interacts with Finite in Mood, and MOOD system choices are realized in the sequence of S and F. Complements subclassify as direct object Complement (C^{do}), indirect object Complement (C^{io}), intensive Complement (C^{int}). Adjuncts subclassify as circumstantial (A^{cir}), conjunctive (A^{con}) and modal (A^{mod}). Finally, we stress the difference between conjunctive Adjuncts and conjunctions.

Further study

Subject

The last probe for Subject mentioned is adapted from a more technically pre-cise formulation by Fawcett (1999). His article is a close examination of the notion of Subject: how to test for it and what its meaning is.

Finite and fused Finite/Predicator

The lexical items *be* and *have* have given lot of trouble to linguists over the years, and there is still widespread disagreement about how to treat them. Part of the difficulty resides in the fact that each has very varied functions; some-times they resemble operators like *can* and *may*, and sometimes they have characteristics of lexical verbs.

Consider *was* in the sentences from our source text discussed above as (9) and (12), repeated here:

(9)   It was a way of determining whether there is any chemical substance involved in nerve transmission.
(12) [...] it was a mystery why some nerves stimulate an organ and others depress it.

In (9) and (12), *was* is analyzed as Finite alone, just as it is in its obviously auxiliary role in (10), repeated here.

(10) The nerve impulse was known to be electrical in nature [...]

Thus, finite forms of the verb *be* are exceptions to the general principle that we implied earlier, though we did not explicitly state it, that a finite verbal group made up of a single word consists of a fused Finite and Predicator (F/P). Thus, in intensive clauses (e.g. *Time is money*) some form of *be* realizes the function of Finite and there is no Predicator at all.

An exception can be made, however, for the very rare use of *be* meaning *exist* as in (41).

(41) I think; therefore I am.

The analysis of this as a simple Finite rather than fused F/P is not entirely plausible, since it functionally parallels so closely comparable clauses with *exist*; see (41a).

(41a) I think; therefore I exist.

In (41a), the second verbal group (*exist*) is clearly to be analyzed as F/P; so it seems to follow that the same analysis could apply to *am* in (41). But this is a rare use of *be*.

The lexical item *have* is in some ways even more slippery than *be*. Its most frequent occurrence is as an auxiliary in present perfect or past perfect constructions, such as (42).

(42) [...] he had written down something of the greatest importance [...]

However, there are other instances (not, unfortunately, in our source text fragment) where finite forms of *have* (*has, have, had*) might be construed as more like fused F/P. For example, where *have* means *take,* as in *Fred had coffee,* the question tag would be *didn't he?* This provides evidence for the analysis of *had* in this instance as F/P. If *had* were a simple Finite, the tag would be *hadn't he,* which would not work here.

A possible logical case might go something like this:

- Where *have* is the unfused Finite in the declarative clause, it is repeated in the tag (for example: *You have read it, haven't you?*).
- Where *have* is a fused Finite/Predicator (lexical verb), the finite operator in the tag must be some form of *do,* as with all other fused F/Ps (for example: *You had breakfast, didn't you?*)
- If the tag has *have* rather than *do,* then the first *have* must be unfused Finite.

A more complicated issue arises with structures like (43).

(43) Mary has a cold.

English speakers who would tag this as (43a) are clearly treating *has* here as a simple Finite and not a fused F/P.

(43a) Mary has a cold, hasn't she?

Unfortunately for the tidiness of our grammar, not all English speakers do say (43a). Some say (43b).

(43b) Mary has a cold, doesn't she?

Are we to assume that for such speakers *have* is a fused F/P and for others it is a simple Finite? It seems very likely. It is probably the case that this use of *have* is a point of change in the language, moving towards a more fully lexical quality. There are variations in usage not only among individuals, but also on a large regional basis across the English-speaking world. Anyone who uses *got* as in (43c) is likely to use the tag *hasn't she?*

(43c) Mary has got a cold.

Of course, if *have* appears in a non-finite form, it is all or part of the Predicator. For example, in (44) *has* is Finite and *had* is Predicator and in (45) *had* is Finite and *been having* is Predicator.

(44) Mary has had a cold.
(45) He had been having difficulty with the proofs.

Exercises

Exercise 3.1

Analyze the following examples, labelling them for SFPCA. If you wish, you may try subclassifying Adjuncts and Complements, but identification as A or C will suffice.

1. They cannot choose.
2. The nature of the city around us changed.
3. This required positive effort.
4. All over the city the divisions increased.
5. The locations filled beyond capacity.
6. The Ninomaru Palace itself is a national treasure.
7. Industrialization brought a flood of people to the city.
8. Telephones are reserved for trivialities.
9. Now we too were singing songs in the bath.
10. In Japan, the word 'duty' has special meaning.
11. Every appointment must be kept.
12. He handed me the document.
13. The papers declared the strike a failure.
14. The castle was built in 1603.
15. In its day it served as a symbol of the power and authority of the Tokugawa military government.
16. No word may be carelessly spoken in front of the children.
17. The transoms are carved from massive cypress blocks.
18. We had been protected from criticism for years.
19. These have been designated Important Cultural Properties by the Japanese Government.
20. The disciplines are never obliterated.

Exercise 3.2

Identify two conjunctive Adjuncts and two modal Adjuncts in the following text fragment.

> Since then, it has become clear that these 'recognition' systems are widespread in the body. [. . .] No doubt they explain why sperm of one species will not normally fertilize eggs of another species. Furthermore, certain diseases, including possibly arthritis, are due to the body making the mistake of treating part of its own tissue as if it were foreign.[1]

Exercise 3.3

Explain in terms of SFPCA functions the joke mentioned earlier:

Hotel guest: Call me a taxi!
Hotel porter: All right. You're a taxi.

Exercise 3.4

Open-ended activity. See Further study section above.

(a) Think about your own use of English and decide whether you treat non-auxiliary *have* as a simple F or a fused F/P.
(b) Listen for examples of this usage in other speakers and find out which seems more prevalent. If you have the necessary skills and access to a corpus of spoken English, you might try a computational investigation.

Note

1. G.R. Taylor, 1967: *The Science of Life*. London: Thames & Hudson (Panther Books).

4

Information structure and thematic structure

4.1 *Organizing ideas*

An extremely important aspect of a functional grammar is the way information is structured in communication. If we are explaining something to another person, whether in speech or writing, we instinctively try to organize what we say in a way that will make it easier for the hearer or reader to understand (unless, of course, we are deliberately trying to confuse).

Most of us are aware of the way in which we structure large chunks of information in writing because this is something that is usually taught in school, especially for particular genres like *essays* or *business letters*, where we are encouraged to plan what we are going to write about, paragraph by paragraph.

Genres with which we are very familiar from childhood, like stories, come more naturally to us, and most children can tell a joke or even write a reasonably well-organized story without too much thought by the time they are eleven or twelve years old. That is not to say that conscious knowledge does not help us to construct stories better. Successful writers are often well aware of the ways in which they construct their texts even though they produce sentences intuitively.

Spoken language too is sometimes carefully planned and sometimes totally spontaneous. The context makes a big difference to how we talk and how far we think in advance about what we are going to say. We can make a distinction between *prepared speech* and *unprepared speech*. Prepared speech, as, for example, in an after-dinner speech or a formal lecture, is similar to the letter or the essay in that a lot of planning can go into the organization of ideas and the structure of the text. A speaker may write down the ideas in note form before the spoken event takes place, and politicians and other official speechmakers may have their whole speech typed out in full, sometimes even prepared by a professional speech-writer. With an ordinary conversation, however, we rarely even think about what we are going to say, let alone how we are going to structure it; it just 'comes naturally'. Yet, when we study language, we can see that we do subconsciously impose a structure on our speech as part of the act of communication.

This structure is something which is built into the grammar of the language and happens at the level of the clause (although it affects longer stretches of text as well). All clauses have information structure and we make use of this in spoken as well as written language.

In SFG, we recognize two parallel and interrelated systems of analysis that concern the structure of the clause with regard to organizing the message. The first of these is called *information structure* and involves constituents that are labelled *Given* and *New*. The second is called *thematic structure* and involves constituents that are labelled *Theme* and *Rheme*.

We do not use the term 'information structure' to refer only to clauses that state facts or give 'information' in the strict sense of this word. Any type of clause can be analyzed for its information structure, including clauses which give opinions or instructions, for example. Similarly, any type of clause can be analyzed for its thematic structure.

Information structure and thematic structure are introduced in Sections 4.2 and 4.3 respectively.

4.2 *Information structure: Given and New information*

An independent clause is a clause that can stand alone. Given and New information is found in both dependent and independent clauses and in combinations of the two, but for the sake of simplicity we will consider only independent clauses at this stage.

In order for a person to understand what someone says, he or she must be able to understand what the speaker is talking about. Another way of saying this is that an interlocutor must be able to 'use the sounds uttered by another to locate some appropriate area within his own store of accumulated and generalized experience' (Moore and Carling, 1982, p. 168). This means that in order to communicate effectively, the speaker must bring to the hearer's attention some element of shared or 'mutual' knowledge. This shared information is usually found at the beginning of a clause and is labelled Given information. Most clauses also include information that is the focus of the speaker's message, information that is considered New. The two elements together make up an *information unit*.

Thus, if a woman expects her friend to make tea and calls to him, 'The kettle's boiling', she is making the assumption that her friend knows what a kettle is and more particularly can identify the particular kettle referred to. That is to say that they share the knowledge about the kettle, and this knowledge is taken for granted in the statement. The main focus of the information (the New element) is *is boiling*, which is found at the end of the clause. The information unit is analyzed in Fig. 4.1.

The kettle	's boiling
Given	**New**

Fig. 4.1

With this meaning, the woman would speak the clause with a falling tone on the final element in the clause (the tonic foot), in this case 'BOILing'. The syllable in small block capitals is known as the *tonic* syllable and is the one on which the main pitch movement of the voice takes place.

Of course, this is not the only way in which the words can be spoken. A different context might require a different intonation, but the most common form is the one where the Given information precedes the New information. It is said to be the *unmarked form.*

4.2.1   Given and New in written English

Text 4A is an extract from a computer manual. The text begins with the heading in the form of a question ('What is an Operating System?'). The function of a question is often to *ask for information* and here the writer of the manual uses a question that he imagines (quite reasonably) is in the mind of the reader who has opened this book. This is a common device in textbook writing and is used to establish the area of mutual knowledge. Having posed the question, the writer can then begin the first paragraph with the words 'operating system' presented as Given and the rest of the sentence, the explanation of what an operating system does, is New. In fact, every sentence in this text begins with a reference to this shared concept of operating systems (although the third sentence also includes the shared reference to *a computer*), so the text is a clear example of the principle that the New information is regularly presented in the second part of the clause.

What is an Operating System?
An operating system runs a computer. It controls how the parts of a computer interact and organizes information in and out of the computer. Without an operating system, a computer cannot be used effectively. Some operating systems are DOS, CP/M, OS/2 and UNIX.

Text 4A   (Chua Chooi See, *DOS 5: A Step by Step Guide*[1]).

GIVEN elements in Text 4A:
Sentence 1. An operating system
Sentence 2. It
Sentence 3. Without an operating system, a computer
Sentence 4. Some operating systems

There are, however, two main exceptions to this general statement. One is at the beginning of a fresh topic of conversation or of a new section of a written text, where the whole of the information is new (although even there the speaker or writer is likely to identify or assume some 'shared' element). A classic example of a clause without a Given element is the opening of the Jane Austen novel *Pride and Prejudice* seen in Text 4B.

> It is a truth universally acknowledged, that a single man in possession of a good fortune must be in want of a wife.

Text 4B   (Austen, *Pride and Prejudice*[2]).

In this case *It* carries no information at all (see discussion of the *empty it* in Chapters 3 and 8). The rest of the clause, of course, carries what is technically called the New information. Remember that the message may be something other than 'information' in the general meaning of the word; in the case of the quotation from Jane Austen, of course, it is an ironical comment on the social pressures on families in the early nineteenth century to find rich husbands for their daughters.

The second exception comes when, by using ellipsis, we leave out the Given information and express only the New. Examples of this can be seen in the computer manual text above. The second sentence contains two clauses (a) and (b):

(a) It controls how the parts of a computer interact
(b) organizes information in and out of the computer

In clause (b), the information is all New. The subject of the verb *organizes*, which would normally carry the Given part of the clause, is omitted. However, the reader understands that the subject is also 'it' (referring to 'operating system'). The grammar of English allows ellipsis of this type in certain contexts where the meaning is clear.

Thus we can say that an information unit consists of Given, which is optional, and New, which is obligatory (brackets indicate the optional element):

(GIVEN) ———— NEW

4.2.2   Given and New in spoken English

In real life (and in fiction and drama that imitate real life) language is always set in a social context. It is this context that usually provides the source of the Given information. The words that feature most commonly as Given in conversation are pronouns referring to the interlocutors: *I*, *we* and *you*. Proper nouns, the names of the people or places one is talking about, are also very common.

Look at the example (Text 4Ca) from a famous English play *The Importance of Being Earnest* by Oscar Wilde. Immediately before the section quoted, which takes place at tea time, Jack and Algernon have been discussing divorce, but then Jack does something which causes Algernon to change the topic of conversation. Notice that he does this by using an imperative clause.

Algernon: Divorces are made in heaven. [Jack puts out his hand to take a sandwich. Algernon at once interferes.] Please don't touch the cucumber sandwiches. They are ordered especially for Aunt Augusta.

Jack: Well, you have been eating them all the time.

Algernon: That is quite a different matter. She is my aunt. Have some bread and butter. The bread and butter is for Gwendolen. Gwendolen is devoted to bread and butter.

Text 4Ca   (Wilde, *The Importance of Being Earnest*[3]).

In an imperative clause like *Please don't touch the cucumber sandwiches* all the information is effectively New. Part of the shared element is the unspoken *you*. This can be unspoken, because, as in most imperatives, the context makes clear who the request is directed at, in this case, Jack. The word *please* is a conventional reduction of *If it please you* but here the meaning is more like *It would please me if you don't touch the cucumber sandwiches.*

In Text 4Cb, a version of the same text as 4Ca but with only the conversation reproduced, the information units have been separated by slashes (//) and the New elements in the information units have been presented in italics.

Please don't touch the cucumber sandwiches.// They are *ordered especially for Aunt Augusta.//*

Well, you *have been eating them all the time.//*

That *is quite a different matter.//* She *is my aunt.//* *Have some bread and butter.//* The bread and butter *is for Gwendolen. //* Gwendolen *is devoted to bread and butter.//*

Text 4Cb

We can see that, with the exception of the imperative, all the clauses have Given elements that are referentially linked either to the interlocutors or to previously mentioned elements in the conversation. However, in this case, each clause begins with a different Given element, each taking up information from some idea that was presented as New in an earlier clause. In this way a speaker or writer can structure the clause so that the Given element is already understood by the listener. Thus *They* refers to the same cucumber sandwiches mentioned in the previous sentence. *That* refers to the whole of the information in the previous sentence (*You have been eating them all the time*), and *She* refers to the same person as *Aunt Augusta*. *Bread and butter* and *Gwendolen* both also have previous identical mentions. This type of organization is extremely common in everyday conversation, but it is also found in written texts in many contexts.

As we said in Section 4.1, where a speaker or writer constructs a clause in the way outlined above (with the Given information first and the New information second), the clause is said to be *unmarked*. This is a matter primarily of *intonation*, the way in which the different levels of pitch (or *tone*) are used in the language to express meaning.

In an unmarked declarative clause, the New information is said to have the most *communicative dynamism* (to use a term from the Prague School linguists) and is signalled intonationally by a falling tone.

4.2.3   Difficult cases of Given and New

Not all clauses are as clearly structured as the ones in our examples above. The letter in Text 4D, written by the English novelist D.H. Lawrence after his return to England from New Mexico, contains an interesting example of a difficult case in the first paragraph.

110, Heath St,
Hampstead,
7 December, 1923

Dear Bynner,
Here I am – London – gloom – yellow air – bad cold – bed – old house – Morris wallpaper – visitors – English voices – tea in old cups – poor D.H.L. perfectly miserable, as if he were in his tomb.

You don't need his advice, so take it: Never come to England any more.

In a fortnight I intend to go back to Paris, then to Spain – and in the early spring I hope to be back on the western continent.

> I wish I was in Santa Fe at this moment. As it is, for my sins, and Frieda's, I am in London. I only hope Mexico will stop revolting.
>
> De profundis,
>
> D.H.L.

Text 4D   (Lawrence, *Selected Letters*[4]).

The meaning of this letter is not difficult to decipher even though it was written a long time ago and was written to someone we do not know. Moreover, the rhetorical structure of it is quite clear:

Paragraph 1: The writer complains about life in London.
Paragraph 2: The writer advises the reader to stay away from England.
Paragraph 3: The writer explains his plans for future travel.
Paragraph 4: The writer repeats that he is in London and wishes he was back on the American continent.

What is happening, however, in this letter at the level of information structure? How is the Given and New information organized? The first paragraph is particularly interesting because, after the first clause *Here I am*, the information is not presented in complete sentences or even complete clauses. Every word and phrase represents new information: that is to say, the reasons why 'poor D.H.L.' is 'perfectly miserable'. He seems to have found it superfluous to his communicative requirements to present the Given information in each clause and so he has just left it out. It is certainly not difficult for us to guess what the Given elements would have been had he chosen to express them.

There are a number of different types of text which present mainly New information. One common genre is the shopping list, a list of words or phrases, sometimes written for others to follow but more often written for oneself as a simple reminder of what to buy.

toothpaste
soap
12 eggs
fish
1 kilo rice
2 kilos flour

Text 4E   A shopping list

We could claim that each item in a shopping list has a sort of implied clause, like (*We need*) *toothpaste*, or (*I want*) *some rice*, but we do not need to go as far as imagining some missing words to realize that the information in the list is the information that matters, that which holds the information focus.

A more formal text of this type, usually carefully prepared, is the encyclopedia or gazetteer entry, which conventionally can omit all but the new information. In Text 4F the headword 'Cheetah' with its alternative name 'or hunting leopard' represents the Given information and the rest of the entry is New.

Cheetah or 'hunting leopard', the large spotted cat of Africa and Southern Asia, the swiftest four-footed animal alive.

Text 4F   (Cook and Barker, *Pears' Cyclopaedia*[5]).

4.3   *Thematic structure: Theme and Rheme*

We now turn to the second system of analysis involved in text organization, thematic structure. Thematic structure, like information structure, operates at the level of the clause. All full clauses have thematic structure, but we do not find it in expressions like 'Good morning' or 'Hi' or nominal groups such as we might find in book titles (*Great Expectations*; *David Copperfield*; *A Tale of Two Cities*), captions (*desert locust*; *red kangaroo*) or newspaper headlines (*Faulty brakes on death crash wagon*; *Hepatitis link to pigs*).

In some ways, thematic structure is similar to information structure and in many clauses there is a parallel equivalence between Theme and Given on the one hand and between Rheme and New on the other. Some linguists conflate these concepts (see Further study). However, in this chapter (following Halliday), we treat them as separate structures, and by the end of the chapter the difference between them as tools of analysis should be made clear.

A simple explanation of Theme in English is to think of it as *the idea represented by the constituent at the starting point of the clause*. This has been expressed by Halliday as 'the point of departure of the message', where he is thinking of the 'message' carried by one clause. In simple terms, then, a clause begins with a realization of the Theme. This is followed by the realization of the Rheme, which can be explained as being *the rest of the message*:

THEME ——— RHEME

Another way of explaining this idea informally is to say that the Theme tells the listener or reader what the clause is *about*, but this explanation can sometimes be misleading. In this book, we distinguish between the idea of *topic* (or what the language user is speaking or writing about, a non-linguistic issue) and Theme, the starting point of the message, realized in the clause, which is a linguistic category.

All clauses in English incorporate what is known as a *topical* Theme (and sometimes other types of Theme as well, as we see in Section 4.3.4). The term *topical Theme* does not imply that this Theme always represents the topic of the discourse in the popular sense of the term 'topic'. An after-dinner speaker may, for example, take as the topic (or 'theme' in the non-technical sense) of a speech 'The Social Value of the Family' but this does not mean that any clause in the speech will *necessarily* have any part of that title as Theme of specific clauses. The Themes chosen by the speaker may, for example, refer to place (*in this country*) or time (*in the last century*); they may indicate when the speaker is about to express attitude (*in my opinion*) or introduce an example (*for example*); a Theme may even begin a rhetorical question (*What are we going to do about the lack of values?*). The last mentioned example is particularly interesting: the topic of discussion is 'lack of values' but the Theme is *what*, because the speaker's starting point here is the question he or she is asking about the Complement of the clause.

The so-called *topical Theme* in any clause is the first constituent that is part of the meaningful structure of the clause. To put it another way, we can say that the topical Theme always represents a *Participant*, *Circumstance* or *Process* (these terms are introduced in Chapter 6).

The topical Theme is always realized by one of the following elements: Subject (S), Predicator (P), Complement (C), or circumstantial Adjunct (A). As we see later, in some interrogative clauses, the Finite (F) precedes the Subject and hence can be Theme, but in this case it is not a *topical* Theme.

In Text 4G, each of the topical Themes is Subject of the clause it introduces. Themes are presented in bold type to assist recognition.

Europe, after 1500, entered a time of far-reaching mechanical and scientific discovery and development. **Inland Africa**, by contrast, did not. **Inland peoples** continued with the steady but slow development of their own civilization.

Text 4G

4.3.1   Nominal groups as Theme

As we saw in Chapter 3 on SFPCA, declarative clauses frequently begin with the Subject and so it is usually the case (as in the examples in Text 4G) that the Subject of a clause is in Theme position. In the first clause of Text 4A, for example, the Subject is also the Theme, as shown in Fig. 4.2.

An operating system	runs	a computer
S	F/P	C
Theme	Rheme	

Fig. 4.2

When a Subject is in Theme position in a declarative clause, it is said to be *unmarked*. Some further examples of clauses with unmarked Themes appear in (1), (2) and (3), analyzed in Fig. 4.3. The starting points of the clauses are listed in the first column of Fig. 4.3. In this case, all the Themes are nominal groups.

(1) The capital of Malaysia is Kuala Lumpur.
(2) Kuala Lumpur is the capital of Malaysia.
(3) It's the capital of Malaysia.

The capital of Malaysia	is	Kuala Lumpur
Kuala Lumpur	is	the capital of Malaysia
It	's	the capital of Malaysia
S	F	C
Theme	Rheme	

Fig. 4.3

In example (1), we can assume that the speaker is engaged in discourse about, say, Malaysia or capital cities and so chooses to begin the clause with a reference to what has been previously discussed. In (2), on the other hand, the chosen Theme is *Kuala Lumpur*. This would be the appropriate wording for, say, the first clause in a paragraph about the city. Example (3), which might be the response to the question 'Where is Kuala Lumpur?' shows how a pronoun might be chosen as Theme in certain contexts.

In the following examples, we see a contrast between a clause with a verb in the active voice and one with a verb in the passive voice (see Fig. 4.4).

(4) Ziggy played guitar.
(5) Guitar was played by Ziggy.

Example (4), the opening line from the David Bowie song *Ziggy Stardust*, begins with the Theme as topic (*Ziggy*), which is followed by the Rheme (*played guitar*) which provides the first essential information about the char-

Ziggy	played guitar
Guitar	was played by Ziggy
Theme	Rheme

Fig. 4.4

acter described in the song. Consider the change of focus in (5). Whereas (4), the original line, describes Ziggy's professional talent or general ability, the clause *Guitar was played by Ziggy*, with *guitar* in Theme position could appear in a situation where a speaker or writer was describing the line-up in a band, as in *Piano was played by John, drums by Ali, and guitar by Ziggy*. Thus, we can see that although there may be a semantic relationship between a clause with an active voice verb and its passive inversion, the selection of a different thematic structure changes the focus of the clause in significant functional ways.

In (2), (3), (4) and (5) above, words acting as Subject and Theme consist of only one Nominal Group. In (1), however, there are two nominals (*the capital* and *Malaysia*) making up the Theme. Similarly, in (6) and (7) below, two nominals together make the Theme of the clause (in italics).

> (6) *Incorrect eating habits and insufficient exercise* disturb or alter the fat metab-
>   olism of the organism.
> (7) *Assessment and evaluation* are increasingly based on the performance of
>   communicative acts.

In fact, the Theme may be quite long or have a complicated structure, but we will not consider too many complexities at this stage.

4.3.2   Interrogatives, imperatives and exclamations

In Chapter 3, we discussed the structure of declarative and interrogative clauses in English, in terms of SFPCA. To recapitulate, we showed that while the declarative mood followed the S,F order of constituents, the interrogative mood reversed the order of the Finite and the Subject as in examples (8) and (9) where *had* is the Finite and *he* is the Subject (see Section 3.2.2).

> (8) **What** did he write down?
> (9) **Did he** write down anything of importance?

In interrogatives, the Subject is not necessarily the first element in the clause, and so it follows that the unmarked Theme is not the same as in declarative clauses. In (8), the first element in the clause is *What*. This is the realization of Complement in this example since the speaker is taking for granted that 'he' wrote *something* and is asking what he wrote. So in interrogatives that begin with a question word, such as *what, who, which, where, when, why,* and so on, the question word itself realizes Theme.

If we look in more detail at Theme in wh- interrogatives, we can see that question words represent different elements from the SFPCA structure. In the question *Who wrote down the idea?*, the word *who* represents the Subject of the verb *wrote* (because the question is asking the name of the person who did the writing). In the alternative question *What did Loewi write down?*, *what* represents the Complement of the clause. In *When did he write it down?* and *Why did he write it down?*, *when* and *why* represent an Adjunct of time and reason respectively.

In (9), where the question begins with a Finite, we have two Themes *did* and *he*. This is because the Finite alone cannot realize Theme even though it is the first element in the clause. We also need the second element 'he', which, in this case, realizes the Subject. This is explained further in Section 4.3.4.

The imperative mood also realizes Theme in a typical way. In this case the Theme is normally realized by Predicator as in (10) or by two Themes – a negative Finite and the Predicator – as in (11).

(10) **Write** it down, please.
(11) **Don't write** it down now.

The exclamative mood is slightly more complicated as the Theme is the exclamative word (*what* or *how*) followed by the Complement or Adjunct of the clause, so in (12) the Theme is *how sweetly* and in (13) the Theme is *what neat writing* and (14) is *how dirty.*

(12) **How sweetly** she sings! (*how* + adverbial/Adjunct)
(13) **What neat writing** he has! (*what* + nominal/Complement)
(14) **How dirty** your shoes are! (*how* + adjectival/Complement)

We can say that each Mood has a typical unmarked thematic pattern, which is summarized in Fig. 4.5.

MOOD	THEME
declarative	Subject
interrogative (yes/no)	Finite + Subject
interrogative (wh-)	Question word (wh-word)
imperative	Predicator
exclamative	Wh- word + Complement Wh- word + Adjunct

Fig. 4.5

4.3.3   Marked Theme in declarative clauses

We said above that, in a declarative clause, the Theme is said to be unmarked where the Subject is the starting point of the clause. However, other elements are frequently found in Theme position in English clauses, and in these cases the Theme is marked. The most common element to appear as marked Theme is the circumstantial Adjunct, as in the following examples from Russell's

History of Western Philosophy[6] (p. 116). Each example is the beginning of a consecutive paragraph.

(15) After the war, the Spartans erected a memorial on the battlefield of Thermopylae [. . .]
(16) For a long time, the Spartans proved themselves invincible on land [. . .]
(17) Apart from war, the reality of Sparta was never quite the same as the theory [. . .]

In these clauses the Theme is realized by the prepositional phrases which are acting as circumstantial Adjuncts (see Section 3.4.1): *After the war*; *For a long time*; *Apart from war*. Russell could have, had he wished, put each of these Adjuncts at a later position in the clause (as in, *The Spartans erected a memorial on the battlefield at Thermopylae after the war*), but the language allowed him to select the initial position. This flexibility of position makes it easier for a writer to present a Given element in Theme position, which can assist in making a text coherent.

A more unusual, but interesting, case of marked Theme, occurs where the first constituent in the clause is the Complement. Complements more usually follow the verb in declarative sentences (see Section 3.3), but occasionally, for special effect, we find them as Themes. This phenomenon occurs in conversation, often in response to questions concerning Complements, and also in English poetry, as in the following well-known example, where the Thematic Complement is in italics.

(18) I strove with none; for none was worth my strife.
Nature I loved, and, next to nature, Art;
I warmed both hands before the fire of life;
It sinks, and I am ready to depart.
(Walter Savage Landor, 1775–1864)

In (18), the more usual prose order would have been *I loved Nature*. In (19) a lecturer is talking to a student about an assignment that he has just marked.

(19) Oh yes, I dropped one of your pages, so some of the comments I've scrubbed out. They're all rubbish. Ignore them.

It can be seen that in the second clause (*some of the comments I've scrubbed out*) the Complement is in Theme position. The unmarked form of this clause would have been *I've scrubbed out some of the comments*.

A prose example of Complement as Theme can be seen in Text 4H. Notice that the clause in question consists of only three words (*Hard it is*), but a longer section of the text, with the complex series of clauses that follow, is reproduced since it makes it easier to understand the writer's stylistic intent in fronting the word *hard*.

> *Hard* it is, no doubt, to read in Stanley's pages of the slave-traders coldly arranging for the surprise of a village, the capture of the inhabitants, the massacre of those who resist, and the violation of the women; but the stony streets of London, if they could but speak, would tell of tragedies as awful, of ruins as complete, of ravishments as horrible, as if it were in Central Africa.

Text 4H   (Booth 'In darkest England and the way out'[7]).

The Themes in all the marked examples we have looked at so far are still part of the *ideational* (*experiential*) element of the clause, which is to say that they tell us something about the world that the writer is describing or discussing.

4.3.4   Multiple Themes

All clauses which have one thematic constituent, like most of those we looked at in Section 4.3.2, are said to have *simple* Themes (even though the thematic constituent may have more than one part to it, as in (6) and (7) in this chapter). However, some clauses have more than one theme or what is known as a *multiple* thematic structure. We consider these in this section.

The explanation of multiple Theme relates to the three metafunctions discussed in Chapter 1: *ideational* (*experiential*), *interpersonal*, and *textual*. Basically, a clause has a Theme which relates to the ideational metafunction. This is the Theme which usually represents *what the clause is about*, or the *topic* of the clause. For this reason it is known as the topical Theme. In all the examples of Simple Theme given above, where only one Theme was identified for each clause, the Theme is the topical Theme.

However, in addition to the topical Theme, some clauses also have a textual and/or an interpersonal Theme. When speakers in a conversation, for example, use expressions like *well*, or *anyway* in order to indicate that they are about to continue an idea or refute an argument, they are commenting, in a sense, on the previous speaker's text. This indicates that they are using a textual Theme. Words such as *then, however, nevertheless, therefore,* introduced as conjunctive Adjuncts (see Section 3.4.2) are often, but not always, selected as textual Theme.

A speaker or writer frequently begins a clause with an adjunct that comments on the substance of the following clause. By using a word like *honestly, really, probably, possibly* or *presumably* we can commit ourselves to the truth or correctness, certainty or strength of the proposition that follows, and with words like *happily, unfortunately, tragically,* or *clearly* we can display our attitude to something or evaluate a situation. Words and phrases of this type are known as modal Adjuncts or comment Adjuncts (see Section 3.4.3) and when they are used before the topical Theme in a clause, they are analyzed as interpersonal Theme.

There are two other types of interpersonal Theme. The first is when a speaker or writer addresses someone or some people directly, by using a name or familiar address term (*John, Mother*) or a term of affection or insult (*my dear, darling, idiot*) but only when the vocative term comes before the topical Theme.

In the example in Fig. 4.6, the speaker uses each type of Theme in turn, ending with the topical Theme, which, in this case, is an unmarked Theme, Subject of the clause.

Well,	children,	the story	is about to continue.
textual Theme	interpersonal Theme	topical Theme	Rheme

Fig. 4.6

The storyteller directly addresses the children who are listening to the story. In a similar way, in the example in Fig. 4.7, the speaker (a lecturer in biochemistry) uses an interpersonal Theme to address the students, but here the topical Theme is a marked circumstantial Adjunct: *last time*. The speaker uses the phrase *last time* in order to get the students to recall the previous lecture. The Rheme is the New information that the lecturer wants the students to focus on.

Ladies and gentlemen,	last time	I was talking about the concept of theory.
interpersonal Theme	topical Theme (marked)	Rheme

Fig. 4.7

Another type of interpersonal Theme functions simultaneously as topical Theme. This can be seen in interrogative clauses, such as those in Fig. 4.8. These are sometimes known as mood-marking Themes because the mood of the clause is indicated by the use of the Finite or wh- word in Theme position.

Did	he	write down anything of importance?
Could	I	have your name?
interpersonal Theme	topical Theme	Rheme

Fig. 4.8

In (19), discussed in the last section, we see two examples of multiple Theme, analyzed in Fig 4.9. The first clause begins with a textual Theme (*Oh yes*, meaning something like 'There's something I must tell you') followed by topical Theme (*I*). The second clause is particularly interesting. Here, we have a textual Theme (*so*), followed, as we explained above, by a marked topical Theme. This special ordering of the constituents, which is unusual but perfectly possible in English, allows the speaker to save the unexpected (New) information (in this case the fact that he has crossed out some comments he made on the student's work) until the end of the clause in Rheme position. The marked SFPCA structure is indicated in brackets.

Oh yes,	I (**S**)	dropped (**F/P**) one of your pages (**C**).
So	some of the comments (**C**)	I've (**S**) scrubbed (**F/P**) out.
textual Theme	**topical Theme**	**Rheme**

Fig. 4.9

4.4 *The interaction of information structure and thematic structure*

As we have seen in this chapter, it is possible to analyze clauses for both their Given–New structure and for their Theme–Rheme structure. We have seen that it is usually the case that the Given element is the same as the Theme, but this is not always so. In imperative clauses, for example, we draw a distinction between Theme and Given (see Fig. 4.10). Slightly more complex examples can be seen in Figs 4.10 and 4.11.

(*You*)	Have	some bread and butter.
	Theme	**Rheme**
Given (implied)	**New**	

Fig. 4.10

(*You*)	Please don't	touch	the cucumber sandwiches.
	interpersonal Theme	**topical Theme**	**Rheme**
Given	**New**		

Fig. 4.11

The fact that we have both Thematic structure and Information structure in the language makes it possible for a writer or speaker to choose to put New information in Theme position and Given information in Rheme position.

In spoken English, we can use special emphasis and intonation to indicate that we are presenting New information in Theme position instead of the more normal Rheme position. We can make a contrast, for example, between *The kettle's **boiling***, which has New at the end, and *The **kettle's** boiling* (not the milk) which has New in initial position.

In written English prose, however, it is more difficult to vary the relationship of Theme and Rheme to Given and New respectively. In the vast majority of English written sentences, Theme is realized by the same constituent as Given, and the Rheme and the New information are realized by the rest of the clause. However, there are certain expressions in English which signal special cases. Where the substance of a clause is all New information, we often find *it* or *there* in Theme position as in (20) and (21).

>   (20) There are twenty-four tables in the classroom.
>   (21) It's very wet today.

Since *there* and *it* are relatively empty from the point of view of meaning, they can hardly be said to represent Given information.

Not only x but also y is an expression that enables a writer to signal a double Theme (or a double Rheme) where the first nominal group represents Given and the second represents New. So in an essay on curriculum planning we find (22), where *Ministry of Education* is Given, having been mentioned previously, and *specialist linguists* is New, even though the nominal group appears as part of the Rheme.

>   (22) It was not only the Ministry of Education but also specialist linguists who were involved in producing the first national syllabus for English.

As well as has the opposite function allowing a speaker or writer to put New information in Theme position as in the (constructed) example (23).

>   (23) Specialist linguists as well as the Ministry of Education were involved in producing the first national syllabus for English.

In Section 4.2 we discussed the role of Given and New in a letter written by D.H. Lawrence (Text 4D), and we observed that, after the initial clause, the first paragraph was largely New information. Since Lawrence is not using full clauses, it is difficult to assign a Theme–Rheme structure to the fragments of information that we find here. As we said above, Thematic structure does not apply to minor clauses. However, it is arguable that *Here* realizes the function of (marked) Theme in relation to all the minor clauses up to *tea in old cups*, and that we then have the new Theme *poor D.H.L.* In looking at the interaction of Theme and Rheme, it is important to take into account not only the particular clause that we are analyzing but also the context in which that clause is set.

The context may involve issues like prior knowledge of speaker and hearer or the prior knowledge that a writer expects his or her readers to have on a particular topic. It may also involve the co-text (the rest of the text) since, if a writer or speaker has previously introduced a topic of discussion, that topic may later appear as Given information in Theme position in the clause.

Summary

This chapter begins with a discussion of the way we organize information in discourse, but most of the chapter is concerned with the way information is ordered in the clause. In Section 4.2 we explained the principles of Information structure, first in written and then in spoken English, and looked at the ways in which speakers and writers usually present Given (or shared) information first in the clause and save New information until later in the clause, where it has the most communicative dynamism. In Section 4.3 we discussed how Theme and Rheme combine to make up the Thematic structure of the clause and examined different ways in which the Theme of a clause is realized, including the difference between marked and unmarked Themes. We then examined the difference between textual, interpersonal and topical Themes and looked at clauses with multiple Theme. Finally, Section 4.4 dealt with the interaction of information structure and thematic structure.

Further study

Prague School linguists (for example, Daneš, 1970, and Firbas, 1972) identify utterances as being ordered on the basis of Theme and Rheme, but do not distinguish Theme from Given. They describe sentences as 'theme followed by rheme' (without upper case 'r' or 't') where the starting point of the utterance is shared information and as 'rheme followed by theme' where the starting point of the utterance is new information. The Prague School account is, therefore, substantially different from the account described in this chapter even though it is an attempt to capture the same features of the language. One interesting contribution of the Prague School was the concept of thematic progression (usually attributed to Daneš, 1970; 1974). We discuss this further in Chapter 5.

Other approaches to Theme (and some possible problems of analysis) are discussed in Fries and Francis (1992) and Francis (1990) and some articles in Noel (1992) and Ghadessy (1995). More recently, a number of researchers have compared Thematic organization in different languages, sometimes in specific domains, such as McCabe's (1999) study of thematic patterns in Spanish and English history texts. See also chapters in Ghadessy *et al.* (2001).

Markedness is a concept which is useful in language study as a whole, not only with respect to issues that are discussed in this chapter. Markedness, in the sense in which we use the term here, concerns the probability of a grammatical occurrence in the language as a whole rather than in any particular use of the language in context. Clauses can be said to be marked (the unusual form) or unmarked (the usual form). In spoken English, when a clause is marked for information structure, special intonation or emphasis will indicate to the listener that shared (Given) information appears in the second part of the clause and New information in the first. The use of corpus data has great potential in establishing the statistical likelihood of specific forms.

Exercises

Exercise 4.1

(a) Identify the Given and New information in the short biography of Kazuo Ishiguro (Text 4I).

> **Kazuo Ishiguro**
> Kazuo Ishiguro was born in Nagasaki, Japan, in 1954 and came to Britain in 1960. He attended the University of Kent at Canterbury and the University of East Anglia. He now lives in London. His first novel, *A Pale View of Hills*, was awarded the Winifred Holtby Prize by the Royal Society of Literature and has been translated into thirteen languages. His second novel, *An Artist of the Floating World*, won the Whitbread Book of the Year award for 1986; it has been translated into fourteen languages.

Text 4I   (From cover of Ishiguro, *The Remains of the Day*[8]).

(b) Write a brief encyclopaedia entry for Kazuo Ishiguro, following the example for **Cheetah** (Text 4F above), and then underline the Given information.

Exercise 4.2

Text 4J is boxed information from the middle of a magazine article on the subject of protecting your body from the sun. Identify the Given and New information in Text 4J.

> Sun safety tips
> The best way to avoid developing skin cancer is to protect yourself from the sun. Follow these guidelines:
>
> ● Avoid the midday sun.
> ● Wear loose-fitting, tightly woven clothes and a wide brimmed hat.
> ● Protect your eyes with proper sunglasses.
> ● Use a sunscreen with a high protection factor (at least 15 SPF).

Text 4J

Exercise 4.3

(a) Read Text 3A about Otto Loewi again and look at the Theme of the first clause in each sentence. Make a note of any marked Themes.
(b) Suggest reasons why the author uses marked Themes in these clauses.

Notes

1. Chua Chooi See, 1992: *DOS 5: A Step by Step Guide.* Kuala Lumpur: Federal Publications.
2. Austen, Jane 1813: *Pride and Prejudice.*
3. Wilde, Oscar 1895: *The Importance of Being Earnest.*
4. Lawrence, D.H. 1950: *Selected Letters*. Harmondsworth: Penguin Books.
5. Cook, C. and Barker, I.M. (eds) 1980: *Pears' Cyclopaedia* (89th edition). London: Pelham Books Ltd.
6. Russell, B. 1961: *History of Western philosophy* (2nd edition). London: George Allen & Unwin.
7. Booth, W. 1890: 'In darkest England and the way out'. In Hampton, C. 1984: *A Radical Reader*. London: Penguin.
8. Ishiguro, Kazuo 1989: *The Remains of the Day.* London: Faber and Faber.

5

Grammar and text

5.1 *Text and texture*

In the last chapter we looked at the ways in which the grammar of English allows speakers and writers to structure information within the clause by making use of the two independent patterns: (a) Theme + Rheme structure and (b) Given + New structure. In this chapter, we consider how this type of patterning works in longer stretches of discourse and how the thematic choices made by a language user can help to make a text coherent. In addition, this chapter seeks to explain how other elements of the language – cohesive devices – are combined with structural elements to give a sense of continuity to discourse.

In Section 1.7.3, we explained that one of the three metafunctions of language is the *textual*, which organizes the text itself. When we use language to talk about the language we are using and when we use language to link other pieces of language or help our ideas 'hang together', we are exercising the textual function.

A stretch of language which is coherent and 'makes sense' is said to have *texture* (originally discussed in Halliday and Hasan, 1976, pp. 2–3). *Texture* is simply the quality of being a text, rather than a set of unconnected bits of language such as one might find in a collection of independent sentences used as exercises in a language textbook.

This is illustrated in the two samples of language in Texts 5A and 5B. Of these, only Text 5B has texture, even though the individual sentences in Text 5A 'make sense' as separate items. In Text 5A, the sentences are not linked together in a textual way. Although we have called it a 'text' for ease of reference, in fact Text 5A, which is an extract from a translation exercise in an Italian language course book, consists of four unrelated sentences. It is not really 'text' in the true sense at all, since, by definition, a text has texture. We could say that this sample of language consists of four separate short texts, numbered 1 to 4.

1. Give it to me, not to him.
2. Those two men with the oxen will arrive tomorrow.
3. I met them in town, this morning, but I did not see her.
4. That book was written by him.

Text 5A   (Speight, *Teach Yourself Italian*[1]).

In Text 5A the pronouns (*me, him, them, her*) do not have any common referents with any other nouns or pronouns in the extract. The reader does not know who the pronouns refer to in any sense. What is more, we do not have any basis on which to decide whether or not *him* in sentence (1) refers to the same person as the *him* in sentence (4) or not. This kind of link between the sentences is not necessary since each one is a separate entity within the context of the larger actual text, a language teaching book. We can contrast this with the pronoun reference in Text 5B.

Wole Soyinka, dramatist and scholar, is a Nigerian. He was born in 1934, and has devoted his life to drama for the theatre, both as a dramatist and as a university teacher of drama and English in his own country. He is also an accomplished writer of stories, novels and poetry. His background and his professional life have made him uniquely able to write plays with an African setting which can absorb the conflict between past and present, tradition and novelty, tribal beliefs and the ideologies of the Western world today.

Text 5B   (Lott, *A Course in English Language and Literature*[2]).

Text 5B, which is the first half of a summary of the life of Soyinka from a book on language and literature, is coherent and textured. How cohesion is realized in language is discussed in detail in the next section.

5.2   *The textual component of the grammar*

Halliday (1994: Chapter 9, Section 6) identifies the *textual component* of the grammar of English (and hence *texture*) as consisting of the features associated with two groups of resources: the *structural* and the *cohesive*. The first (the structural) is subdivided into the two areas we discussed in Chapter 4. The second (the cohesive) is subdivided into four further areas, as can be seen in the following summary:

Structural component
  1. Given and New: information structure and focus
  2. Theme and Rheme: the thematic structure
Cohesive component
  1. reference
  2. ellipsis and substitution
  3. conjunction
  4. lexical cohesion

Text 5B provides a straightforward example of the textual component in operation. This text comes at the end of a book, which includes some extracts from a play by Soyinka, so the readers of the text already have some familiarity with the dramatist's name. The author is able to assume that the reader has already heard of Soyinka and takes *Wole Soyinka, dramatist and scholar* (two nominal groups *in apposition*, referring to the same person) as Theme of the first clause, presented as Given information. The subsequent clauses, with the exception of Clause 3 (discussed below) take up the same Given information either by referring to the dramatist as the Theme of each clause or as a crucial part of the Theme. We will look at this example in some detail because a similar use of Theme often occurs in encyclopedias and dictionaries, where it is assumed that the readers will have 'looked up' a person, place or thing that they have previously heard of.

The analysis of Text 5B is shown clause by clause below with the Theme given in italics:

Clause 1. *Wole Soyinka, dramatist and scholar*, is a Nigerian.
Clause 2. *He* was born in 1934.
Clause 3. *[he]* has devoted his life to drama for the theatre, both as a dramatist and as a university teacher of drama and English in his own country.
Clause 4. *He* is also an accomplished writer of novels, stories and poetry.
Clause 5. *His background and his professional life* have made him uniquely able to write plays, etc.

In clause 5, the novelist is referred to in the possessive pronouns *his* and *his*, each standing in place of *Soyinka's*.

We can express the Theme + Rheme structure of a text diagrammatically to show the *thematic progression* in the text. In diagrams of this type, the letters (A, B, C, and so on) represent the person, thing, idea, or whatever is referred to by the wording. Thus any Theme or Rheme referring to the same entity will have this indicated by the same letter. Fig. 5.1 represents the thematic structure of Text 5B. The first Theme (labelled Theme A, referring to Soyinka by name or pronoun) is re-iterated in each clause, with additional elements in clause 5 (labelled B and C, 'background' and 'professional life'). The Rheme in the first clause is Rheme A because it too refers to Soyinka although indirectly, 'Nigerian' being an attribute of Soyinka. Each of the other four Rhemes represents New information and each is labelled with a fresh letter (B to E). The arrows in Fig. 5.1 indicate identity of reference.

Fig. 5.1 Example of the constant Theme pattern

The additional elements in the Theme of clause 5 (*background*, and *professional life*) are signified by the letters B and C) because the concepts are recoverable from the Rhemes in the previous clauses. However, this last point is not directly relevant to the main Thematic pattern of this text.

Daneš (1974) identified a number of models of thematic progression including the one in Text 5B, where the Theme does not change for a section of the text. This is usually known as the *continuous* or *constant Theme pattern*. We will use the term *constant* in this book.

The use of *he*, in clauses 2 and 4, is an example of the cohesive feature *reference*. Clause 3 fails to refer directly to Soyinka because the subject of the verb *has devoted* is omitted, but the reader understands that the person who has devoted his life to drama is the same as the person who *was born in 1934*. Here, the omission of any word (even a pronoun) to refer to Soyinka is an example of the cohesive feature named *ellipsis*. In clause 4, we find the word *also*, which is an example of a *conjunctive Adjunct*. Its function is to help the reader link the clause which refers to his general writings with the earlier clauses that refer only to dramatic writings.

In addition, Text 5B includes some clear examples of *lexical cohesion*. Lexical cohesion can occur between words which are members of the same semantic set, which is to say that they are associated in terms of meaning. The association concerned may be one of related or equivalent meaning or may be one of contrast. In Text 5B, the words listed in each of the four lines stand in a variety of meaningful relationships with each other, and each of these relationships helps the cohesive effect when they are used together in the same short stretch of written English:

1. dramatist – drama – theatre
2. writer – novels – stories – poetry – write – plays
3. scholar – university – teacher – professional
4. [Nigerian – country – African] – [English – Western]

Since each word in each line is joined in some meaningful relation to the following word, the words are said to form a *cohesive chain*. Any text may contain a number of cohesive chains. In the fourth chain given above, the lexical
items are all concerned with places and nationalities but since these fall into
two linked groups, the African and the English, we have separated them with
brackets.

Thus, Text 5B can be said to be *cohesive* because the logical progression of
the information through the text is helped both by the thematic structure and
the use of the devices: *reference*, *ellipsis*, *conjunction*, and *lexical cohesion*.

In the remainder of this chapter, we look first in more detail at patterns of
thematic progression and then at some of the uses of cohesive devices.

5.3   *Thematic progression*

As we have seen in Text 5B, thematic progression can be very straightforward. However, there are other types of thematic progression that are equally
common and equally cohesive although they tend to be more complex.

5.3.1   The constant Theme pattern

The constant pattern, where a common Theme is shared by each clause and
this Theme equates with Given information, as in Text 5B, is common in short
passages of biographical information and sometimes in narratives which focus
on the behaviour of one person. It is also frequently found in textbooks and
descriptions of factual information focusing on a particular thing or concept.

Text 5C, from a booklet on survival in tropical forests, provides a further
illustration of the constant pattern in use; here the Theme of each clause refers
wholly (*it*) or partially (*its* length) to the main topic of the text, the saw-scaled
viper.

> The saw-scaled viper is found in dry sandy areas where there is little
> vegetation. Its length is about two feet, and it is sandy in colour with darker
> spots. It is aggressive and very poisonous. It may be found in the full blaze
> of the sun or beneath hot stones and in crannies heated by the sun.

Text 5C   (Ministry of Defence pamphlet, *Jungle Survival*[3]).

5.3.2   The linear Theme pattern

The second type we look at in this chapter is the *linear pattern*. In this type, the Rheme of one clause is taken up as the theme of the subsequent clause. An example of this can be seen in Text 5D, which comes from a popular science book.

The stomach produces gastric juice, which contains dilute hydrochloric acid. The acid kills most of the bacteria in the food. The partly digested food passes next into the duodenum, the first part of the small intestine. This is a coiled tube about eight metres long, which is as wide as a man's thumb.

Text 5D   (Martin, Larkin and Bernbaum (eds), *The Penguin Book of the Natural World*[4]).

The first sentence in Text 5D contains two clauses. The Rheme of the first clause (*gastric juice*) becomes the Theme of the second clause (*which*, a relative pronoun, standing in place of *gastric juice*). The Rheme of the second clause (*dilute hydrochloric acid*) is taken up as Theme of clause 3 (*The acid*). The Rheme of clause 3 (*the food*) becomes the Theme of clause 4 (*The partly digested food*). Finally, the Rheme of clause 5 (*the duodenum, the first part of the small intestine*) is summarized in the word *This*, which is the Theme of the first clause in the final sentence. Diagrammatically, this pattern can be represented as in Fig. 5.2.

Fig. 5.2   Example of the linear Theme pattern

5.3.3   The split Rheme pattern

The third common type of thematic progression dealt with here is known as the *split Rheme pattern*. This pattern occurs when the Rheme of a clause has two components, each of which is taken in turn as the Theme of a subsequent clause. An example of this can be seen in Text 5E, which is taken from a chapter in a geography textbook discussing population distribution in 1970.

> The only other considerable region of dense population in the world lies in Japan. This country shows a remarkable fusion of both densely populated rural and urban communities. Japanese peasant farmers, who constitute 45 per cent of the total population, practise a typical monsoon Asian subsistence economy, whereas the millions of people living in vast industrial cities such as Tokyo and Osaka have much in common with counterparts in Europe and North America.

Text 5E   (Lowry, *World Population and Food Supply*[5]).

If we analyze this passage clause by clause and mark the Themes of the clauses in italics, as we did for Text 5B, we get the following:

Clause 1. *The only other considerable region of dense population in the world* lies in Japan.

Clause 2. *This country* shows a remarkable fusion of both densely populated rural and urban communities.

Clause 3. *Japanese peasant farmers* practise a typical monsoon Asian subsistence economy

Clause 4. *who* constitute 45 per cent of the total population

Clause 5. *whereas // the millions of people living in vast industrial cities such as Tokyo and Osaka* have much in common with counterparts in Europe and North America.

Clause 2 has two co-ordinated components in its Rheme, indicated by the word *both*: (1) *densely populated rural communities* and (2) (*densely populated*) *urban communities*. The first, referring to rural communities, is taken up as Theme of clause 3 (*peasant farmers*) and also as the Theme of clause 4 (*who*). The second, referring to urban communities, is taken up as topical Theme of clause 5 (*the millions of people living in vast industrial cities such as Tokyo and Osaka*). The Split Rheme Pattern can be represented diagrammatically as in Fig. 5.3.

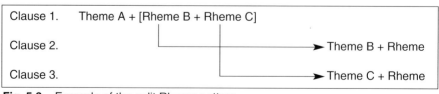

Fig. 5.3   Example of the split Rheme pattern

5.3.4 Derived Themes

We have looked so far at three common types of thematic pattern that help in the structure of coherent texts, but, as a glance at almost any book will show, they do not account for all the thematic patterns that can be identified.

In a longer text, a variety of topics for discussion might be introduced by an author at, say, the beginning of a chapter. Later in the course of the chapter, the author might refer back to any one of the topics or aspects of the topics and use it as Theme. As a result, we often find texts where two or more independent Themes alternate within the text. A straightforward, typical example of this type of thematic structure can be seen in Text 5F, which is a short narrative section from Ted Hughes' story *The Iron Man*. At this point in the story a farmer's son, a boy called Hogarth, meets the Iron Man for the first time.

> And now the Iron Man was coming. Hogarth could feel the earth shaking under the weight of his footsteps. Was it too late to run? Hogarth stared at the Iron Man, looming, searching towards him for the taste of the metal that had made that inviting sound.
>
> Clink, Clink, Clink! went the nail on the knife.
>
> CRASSSHHH!
>
> The Iron Man had fallen into the pit. Hogarth went close. The earth was shaking as the Iron Man struggled underground. Hogarth peered over the torn edge of the great pit.

Text 5F (Hughes, *The Iron Man*[6]).

In this text, with the exception of the interspersed representation of the sounds of clink and crash, we find an alternating pattern of Themes: 'The Iron Man' and 'Hogarth', both of which have been introduced to the reader earlier in the book. Here, *the earth* also appears as Theme, being picked up from the Rheme in the second quoted clause.

In many texts, it can be difficult to analyze thematic progression even where it is fairly straightforward unless we take into account the notion of *derived Themes*. The term is used to describe expressions in Theme position which are cohesively linked in meaning, but not necessarily in form, to a topic which has been stated earlier in the text.

In long educational texts, such as science and geography textbooks, elaborate structures can be signalled by the writer early in a section or chapter. These structures then serve as a way of introducing New information which can be taken up as Theme of subsequent clauses. In, for example, *The*

Penguin Book of the Natural World[4] (Section 112), there is a chapter on rodents. After the heading *The animal kingdom: the gnawing rodents*, the writer begins with the sentence:

> *Rodents, gnawing animals, usually of small size, are the largest order of mammals, making up two fifths of all mammal species.*

After a general description of the physical characteristics of rodents, the author continues by introducing as New information in Rheme position what are to become his subsequent Themes:

> *The order can be divided into three main groups: squirrels, rats and porcupines.*

Each of the groups (*squirrels, rats and porcupines*) then becomes a (derived) Theme in turn. The paragraph on rats is typical of many such paragraphs in the book and is given in Text 5G. The derived Themes in the paragraph are all subcategories of rat-like rodents. In fact, the author continues to describe this type of rodent in a continuation of the passage, beginning the next two sentences with *the spiny mouse* and *lemmings*.

The rat-like rodents include hamsters, lemmings, voles and gerbils, as well as rats and mice. The black rat is found in buildings, sewers and rubbish yards, but has been largely replaced by the bigger, more aggressive, brown rat. Voles are mouse-like rodents that live in the grasslands of Europe and Asia; water voles, or water rats, build complex tunnels along river banks. The house mouse often lives inside buildings and is a serious pest because it eats stored food. The field mouse, on the other hand, very rarely comes near human dwellings.

Text 5G   (Martin, Larkin and Bernbaum (eds), *The Penguin Book of the Natural World*[4]).

In this text the Themes chosen by the author relate closely to the overall topic of the paragraph: *the rat-like rodents*, which is also the Theme of the first sentence. In a similar way the Theme *the rat-like rodents* relates to the chapter heading *Rodents* (see Fig. 5.4).

Each of the subordinate themes here is said to be *derived* from the *hypertheme* 'rodents'. In this particular book, there is an even higher level of hypertheme, *the animal kingdom*, which is subsequently used by the authors to allow them to introduce as Theme such items as *sea mammals* and *flesh eaters*.

We now leave discussion of thematic progression and return to the cohesive features of text outlined in Section 5.2.

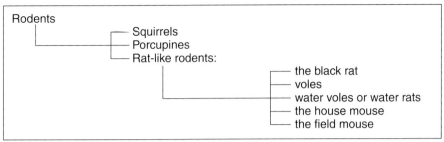

Fig. 5.4   An example of derived Themes

5.4   *Cohesive ties*

As we mentioned above, cohesive ties can be classified into four main types: reference, ellipsis and substitution, conjunction, and lexical cohesion. In Section 5.2, in Text 5B, we saw all four in operation simultaneously, working together with the thematic and information structure of the text, and this is how they are normally used by speakers and writers. Now, however, we deal briefly with each type of cohesive tie in turn.

5.4.1   Reference

As we have seen in the text examples above, reference can be cohesive when two or more expressions in the text refer to the same person, thing or idea. Thus, in Text 5B *Wole Soyinka, he, his* and *him* all refer to the same person, and in Text 5C *saw-scaled viper, its* and *it* all refer to the same creature.

A characteristic of cohesive reference is that, on second and subsequent mention, instead of being named, the person or thing referred to may be indicated by means of a pronoun, demonstrative (*this, these,* etc.) or a comparative. As we have seen in the sections on thematic progression, the repetition of nominals may also have a cohesive function, but there is a special characteristic that is produced by the use of unnamed reference. When readers or listeners come across a pronoun or a determiner, say, they are forced to mentally identify the linked nominal in order to make sense of the text. This has a very strong cohesive force.

The term *reference*, as used by Halliday and Hasan (1976), is an extension of the term as used in philosophy and some types of semantics to mean an act of referring to entities outside the discourse ('in the real world' as it were, although we need to remember that 'real world' can include imaginary worlds, such as we find in fiction or myth). Reference in this sense is not necessarily textually cohesive. For example, when out walking, a person might point to a bird in a tree and say to a companion, 'Look at that'. In this case, *that* refers to an entity which is identifiable in the situation of utterance. The word *that* here is an example of non-cohesive *exophoric reference* or reference *outside the text*.

If, on the other hand, the speaker says, 'Look at that bird' and the companion replies, 'I can't see it' or 'Where is it?', with *it* referring to the previously mentioned bird, co-referentiality is established between the pronoun *it* and the *bird*, and cohesion is established. The latter is known as *endophoric reference* or reference to something *within the text* (in this case the short exchange about the bird).

Strictly speaking, of course, it is speakers or writers who *refer* to entities, using expressions for the purpose, but as a shorthand device we often talk about words or expressions referring *to each other* and say that endophoric reference occurs when *two or more expressions* refer to the same entity.

Endophoric reference is classified into *cataphoric* and *anaphoric reference*. *Cataphoric* is 'forward pointing', in the sense that in a text the unnamed expression, usually a pronoun or demonstrative, appears first and the named expression appears second, as in example (1) from a computer manual, where the cohesive tie is indicated in bold type.

> (1) To see how it works, type VER and press ENTER. You will see **this** on your screen:
>   **MS-DOS Version 6.00**

This forms a cohesive tie with the message *MS-DOS Version 6.00*. In this case of cataphoric reference, the reader does not fully understand the sense of *this* until he or she has read on to the next line in the text.

The second type of endophoric reference, and by far the most common, is called *anaphoric* reference. This type is 'backward looking' in the sense that the named item appears first and the pronoun appears second. It is, therefore, similar to all the examples discussed in Text 5B above.

In terms of grammatical realization, there are three main types of cohesive reference: *personal reference*, *demonstrative reference* and *comparative reference*. What is known as *personal reference* (although it does not always involve people) is dependent on the use of personal pronouns (masculine, feminine and neuter). As we saw in Chapter 2, pronouns can be used anywhere in the clause that a nominal group can be found. Possessives are also commonly referential and can be used as Modifier or Head in a nominal group. *Demonstrative reference* is dependent on the use of determiners (*this*, *these*, *that* and *those*) and adverbs (*here*, *now*, *then*, *there*), and *comparative* reference uses adjectives like *same*, *other*, *identical*, *better*, *more* or their adverbial counterparts *identically*, *similarly*, *less*, and so on, to forge links with previously mentioned entities.

We end this section on reference with one example of each type of referential tie. In each of our examples, the tie operates across adjoining sentences, but referential ties can stretch over a number of sentences in a text and often do so both in conversation and in written texts.

(2) Personal reference
West African dwarf sheep are found roaming about the towns and villages in many southern parts of West Africa in small flocks. **They** thrive and breed successfully in areas of trypanosomiasis risk. **Their** coat colour is either predominantly white with irregular black patches, or black marked with white patches.

(3) Demonstrative reference
Be careful of **wasps, bees and hornets**. **These** are dangerous pests.

(4) Comparative reference
Beecher Stowe gives a **moving account** of the horrors of slavery. Clemens' treatment of the issue in the classic novel *Huckleberry Finn* is **lighter** but **more subtle**.

5.4.2   Substitution and ellipsis

Substitution is used where a speaker or writer wishes to avoid the repetition of a lexical item and is able to draw on the grammatical resources of the language to replace the item. In English, there is a set of words available for this purpose.

The main difference between reference and substitution is that, as we have explained, in the case of referential cohesion, the tie exists between two or more references to the same concept. With substitution we do not have co-referentiality, but rather a substitute for a *word* or *group of words*. The difference should be clear from (5) and (6).

(5) Reference
Would you like **this cake**? I bought **it** this morning.

(6) Substitution
Would you like **this cake**? Or do you prefer the other **one**?

In the case of reference in (5), *this cake* and *it* refer to the same object. In (6), however, *one* does not refer to the same object as the word *cake* in the question. *One* refers to a different cake. It replaces the word 'cake' so that the group 'the other one' means 'the other cake'. Nevertheless, in spite of the non-identity of referents, the receiver of the message can only interpret *one* in terms of the previous mention of *cake*, and this forms a cohesive tie.

There are three types of substitution in English: *nominal*, *verbal* and *clausal substitution*, and each type has its own set of substitute words.

In nominal substitutes, *one*, *ones* and *same* can stand in place of nominal groups and Head nouns (not necessarily the whole of a nominal group), as in (7), (8) and (9).

(7) 'Would you like **some sandwiches**?'
    'Please pass the **ones** with cucumber in.'
(8) 'I'm having **chicken and rice**.'
    'I'll have **the same**.'
(9) In an experiment, some children were given six cardboard **discs** each in a different colour. They were then asked to choose the colour they liked best. The majority chose **the blue one**.

The words *one* and to a lesser extent *same* resemble pronouns, but there are certain crucial differences between substitutes and other pronouns. First, *one* has a plural form in *ones* but only a third person form, unlike personal pronouns. Second, it can be used with Deictics (realized, for example, by articles and determiners) and Numeratives:

this one, a red one, the blue one, some old ones, five new ones

while ordinary pronouns cannot:

*this it, *the red it; *some old they

In verbal substitutes, a form of the verb *do* (plus, sometimes, additional words like *it* or *that*), can stand in place of the lexical verb in a verbal group.

(10) 'We met in Brazil. Do you remember?'
     'Yes, we must have done.'

Done here stands in place of *met in Brazil*.

The third type, clausal substitution, is extremely common both in speech and in written prose. Here, the words *so* and *not* can stand in place of an entire clause or part of a clause, and the reader or listener can only interpret the meaning of the substitute in terms of what has previously been expressed in full. In (11), a conversation between two people from the play *The Importance of Being Earnest*, there are two examples of *so* substitution, one in each response.

(11) 'I do mean something else.'
     'I thought so.'
     'And I would like to take advantage of Lady Bracknell's temporary absence [...]'
     'I would certainly advise you to do so.'

The equivalent negative expression to *so* is illustrated in (12).

(12) 'Well, I don't intend to get killed if I can help it.'
     'I suppose not.'

An interesting point about substitution is the grammatical distinction between the use of the substitute *not* following a verb like *think*, *suppose*, *guess* and the ordinary negative form of the verb, as in *I don't suppose*. Students of English as a second or foreign language can be easily confused by the distinction between *I think not* and *I don't think*, sometimes interpreting the former as an ordinary negative form.

In the same cohesive class as substitution, we find *ellipsis*, or the omission of words, groups or clauses (referred to by IFG as 'substitution by zero'). Ellipsis takes place in similar grammatical environments to substitution. Thus, we have *nominal, verbal* and *clausal ellipsis*.

The grammar of nominal ellipsis permits the omission of Head nouns in a nominal group as in (13) where *two* in the final clause means *two cucumber sandwiches*. The Classifier and the Head noun are not realized, leaving the Numerative as Head of the nominal group.

> (13) 'Have you got the cucumber sandwiches cut for Lady Bracknell?'
> 'Yes, sir.'
> (*Algernon inspects them and takes two [E]*)

Verbal ellipsis is common in all short form answers and responses as is exemplified in (14) where there are two examples of verbal ellipsis in responses (indicated with [E]). In both cases the tie is with *save you* in the first sentence of the verbal exchange. In these instances, it is the lexical verb that is omitted.

> (14) 'I'll help you. I'll save you.'
> 'You can't [E].'
> 'I can [E].'

In (14) the finite in the verbal group is realized both negatively and positively. It is also possible to omit the finite and realize the lexical verb as in (15).

> (15) The boys were filling the bags, the men [E] moving them to the dikes.

Example (13) also illustrates clausal ellipsis; where we understand the first response 'Yes' to mean 'I have got cucumber sandwiches cut for Lady Bracknell'. In (16) the clause *open the door* is omitted in the second sentence.

> (16) Get up quick and open the door. If you don't [E], they will break it down.

5.4.3 Conjunction

Conjunction is the term used to describe the cohesive tie between clauses or sections of text in such a way as to demonstrate a meaningful relationship between them. It is also possible to perceive this process as the linking of ideas, events or other phenomena. This 'linking' or 'joining' is achieved by the use of *conjunctive Adjuncts*, which are sometimes called *cohesive conjunctives* (for example, *then, for this reason, on the other hand*). These are words or expressions that have two textual functions: they indicate *conjunction* and, at the same time usually indicate the type of relationship that operates between the elements being joined (for example, relationships of *time, reason, cause, result, concession*).

In Chapter 3, we discussed the difference between conjunctive Adjuncts and *conjunctions* (*linkers* and *binders*), pointing out that, although they have a lot in common semantically, they have different grammatical characteristics. We can see this illustrated in (17), where a linking conjunction (*but*) points out a contrastive relationship between two propositions within one sentence, and (17a) (constructed) where a similar relationship is expressed in separate sentences with the use of a conjunctive Adjunct (*however*).

(17)   Over the last twenty years more than a third of a million compounds have been screened by pharmaceutical companies for their anti-cancer properties, but only twenty or thirty have shown any real promise.

(17a)   Over the last twenty years more than a third of a million compounds have been screened by pharmaceutical companies for their anti-cancer properties. However, only twenty or thirty have shown any real promise.

The nature of the relationships that can be expressed by the use of conjunctive Adjuncts are many, and lack of space prevents a full account here, but four classes of cohesive conjunction, each of these with numerous subclasses, were identified by Halliday and Hasan (1976), who provide a fuller account:

- additive
- adversative
- causal
- temporal

Some common types are illustrated in (18) and (19). In (18), an extract from an academic paper on management, there are two examples, the first additive-exemplification and the second adversative-contrastive.

(18)   It is easy to identify theoretical conflicts in management accounting. **For example**, contingency theorists argue that the type of management accounting system which is appropriate to an organization is dependent on a number of organization-specific variables. **By contrast**, the emphasis in much of the management accounting research published between the late 1950s and the mid-1970s was on the development of specific normative models which were allegedly suitable for use in a wide variety of organizations without any context-specific adaptation.

In (19), there is an example of a causal-result relationship as well as a cohesive reference in *this* and also an internal additive-sequential relationship. The conjunctive Adjuncts are indicated in bold type.

(19)   There is a severe shortage of mathematics teachers in Britain and America. **As a consequence of this**, far too many people leave school without any interest in pursuing the study of subjects like engineering that rely on mathematical concepts. Two possible solutions are available. **Firstly**, it should be a priority to train more teachers; **secondly**, teachers' salaries should be made competitive with other jobs in order to attract young people to the profession.

The causal-result relationship is indicated in *as a consequence*; the additive-sequential relationship in *Firstly* and *Secondly*. The latter is said to be 'internal' in this case because it is ideas within the text that are ordered in sequence. In contrast, in another text, an external temporal-sequential relationship might be signalled by the use of *firstly, secondly,* etc. to introduce the time sequence of specific events referred to.

It can be seen from (18) and (19) that conjunctive Adjuncts provide a useful guide to the rhetorical paths that a writer is following. They have been compared to signals or signposts that indicate the direction of argument.

5.4.4   Lexical cohesion

Lexical cohesion refers to the cohesive effect of the use of lexical items in discourse where the choice of an item relates to the choices that have gone before.

We have already seen in the analysis of Text 5B (Section 5.2) that words that are associated in meaning can form cohesive chains and, moreover, a text may well have more than one cohesive chain running through it. We now look in a little more detail at the types of associative meaning that are possible between lexical items.

One important type of lexical cohesion, probably the one with the strongest cohesive force, is repetition (or *reiteration*) of the same item. Thus, if a person's name is mentioned more than once (as is the name Hogarth in Text 5F), the reader will recognize the link in a chain of information connected with that person. Synonyms and near synonyms can have the same effect as can other words which refer to the same person. In other parts of the book from which Text 5F was taken, for example, Hogarth is referred to as *the boy* and *the farmer's son*. Where the cohesive chain has the same referent, it is termed *an identity chain*. This type of chain is arguably the strongest type of lexical cohesion and it has much in common with reference.

Nevertheless, for cohesion to occur, it is not necessary for each word in a chain to refer to the same entity or even to belong to the same word class. All the words related to the root *pollen* play a part in the cohesion of (20).

> (20) A flower cannot produce seeds until it is pollinated and its ovule fertilized. Pollination is the transfer of pollen from the male parts (stamens) to the female parts (stigmas) of a flower. If pollen is carried to the stigma of the same flower, it is called self-pollination.

Example (20) also includes examples of re-iteration of *flower* and *stigma*. Later in the same text, we find further use of the word *seeds* and also reference to *plants*, a word which stands in a superordinate relationship with *flower*, and then to *grasses*, a word in a subordinate relationship to *plants*.

Near-synonyms can sometimes be quite difficult to pin down in a text. However, a good example of how they are used came in a newspaper report of floods in France and Holland, which reported the fact that many families had been forced to leave their homes. This short piece contained the words *left, exodus, abandoned, deserted, evacuated, moved*, all of which entail the core meaning of *leave*.

As well as synonyms, words from mutually exclusive categories (such as *male* and *female* or *hot* and *cold*) or words with opposite and contrastive meanings (*antonyms*) can have a cohesive effect.

Another type of lexical relationship which is often cohesive is termed *collocation*. *Collocation* covers two or more words which can be said to 'go together' in the sense of frequency of occurrence. If words commonly occur in the same text and we are frequently exposed to their co-occurrence, we come to expect them together. Traditionally, for example, children's stories with a princess in them usually ended up with a prince in them as well, although the *prince and princess* collocation is an example of an association that may well be changing with more egalitarian approaches to children's literature.

One aspect of collocation that we need to remember is that words collocate differently in different registers. The word *cone*, for example, collocates with *angle, cross-section, base* and *circle* in a geometry textbook, but with *ice cream* in the context of a children's holiday. Similarly, the word *data* would collocate with *bank, processing*, and *storage* in the field of computer applications, but *spoken* and *written* in applied linguistics.

One of the most important types of lexical cohesion concerns the use of *general nouns*. These are nouns that have very general all-embracing meanings; they form a class of high level superordinates. Some extreme examples of words that can be used as general nouns (although they are not always used in this way) are the words *thing, person, people, place, plant*, and *idea*. With words such as these, a speaker or writer can create a cohesive link with almost any previously mentioned entity, as for example in (21) where *ideas* acts as an all-embracing word that coheres with much of the substance of the previous text.

> (21) The ideas outlined above should provide the basis for the practical analysis of texts.

A special class of general nouns called *anaphoric nouns* (*A-nouns*) are words that are used to talk about on-going discourse and sum up or refer back to sections in a text. Individual anaphoric nouns include such words as *accusation, criticism, account, analysis*, but there are many such words in English. These nouns are extremely important in academic writing where they can be used as a device to connect a previously discussed topic with either New information or a new topic in an argument, as we can see from the examples in (22).

(22a) This *explanation* has been challenged by [. . .]
(22b) The *controversy* outlined in the first section is [. . .]
(22c) However, serious questions have been raised about even the few *proposals* in the first chapter.

Nouns like these, which are used to refer to other sections of the current discourse (*metadiscoursally*), are often used together with pre-modifying anaphoric devices like Deictics (*the, this, these*) or post-modifying expressions which refer the reader to the text (such as *outlined above, in the previous chapter, given earlier*).

In short, lexical cohesion involves meaningful connections in text that are created through the use of lexical items and that do not intrinsically involve reference, substitution, ellipsis or conjunction.

Summary

This chapter has tried to make the case that texts have texture as a result of a complex interaction of linguistic resources which are used by writers and speakers to construct coherence. These resources include the information structure (organization of Given and New information) and the thematic structure (Theme and Rheme) at clause level and also the way in which thematic patterns (thematic progression) are built up from clause to clause through a text. The thematic structure of the text is supported by the cohesive component of the grammar, which consists of reference, ellipsis and substitution, conjunction and lexical cohesion. Although we may analyze each of these elements separately, there is likely to be a blending of many cohesive elements in any stretch of genuine discourse except in very short or abbreviated texts.

Further study

IFG, Chapter 9 provides a fuller account of text and texture, which makes explicit links to wider aspects of the grammar and introduces the theory that there are *logogenetic patterns* in text. These patterns relate not only to Thematic patterns such as we have examined in this chapter but also to mood, polarity, process type, etc., as well as other strata such as the phonological patterns in a spoken or poetic text, in fact the entire meaning potential of the language.

Eggins (1994) has an interesting discussion of Theme and includes a network representing the system choices for Theme that we have discussed in this chapter.

The major work in the area of cohesion is Halliday and Hasan (1976), which still provides the fullest account of cohesive ties in English. Halliday and Hasan (1989) deals with aspects of text and cohesion from an explicitly social semiotic perspective, and Halliday and Matthiessen (1999) – a difficult book to dip into – bring a broader theoretical perspective to the topic. Martin (1992) is the most detailed work on text analysis, introducing many factors that lack of space has forced us to neglect.

Hoey (1983, 1991) develops Halliday and Hasan's account to investigate how cohesive features combine to organize long stretches of text. In his earlier work, he considers cohesion in relation to some important patterns of rhetorical organization. In his later work, he looks in detail at cohesive chains and the significance of repetition. Hoey continues to make important contributions to functional theory, including ideas on the role of the sentence (as distinct from clause), which he suggests may be 'a part grammatical, part textual phenomenon', a view that is compatible with much of the literature on the topic.

For samples of text analysis, see Mann and Thompson (1992). This unusual book incorporates quite distinct analyses of the same text by twelve distinguished linguists, including Halliday. A further example of analysis by Halliday of a text from Charles Darwin, demonstrates how the interaction of Given and New with Thematic progression underpins the rhetorical value of the discourse (Halliday and Martin, 1993: Chapter 5). Two excellent monographs on lexical cohesion are Tadros (1981) and Francis (1986). A good introduction to general aspects of textuality, relating grammar to various registers, can be found in Hillier (2004).

Although much of what has been discussed in this chapter is applicable to spoken discourse, space has prevented any detailed discussion of spoken text, and most of the examples of spoken interaction have been taken from drama (Oscar Wilde) rather than natural conversation.

A good introduction to spoken discourse can be found in Coulthard (1985), which includes the role of intonation, and more advanced studies are reported in Coulthard (1992).

Much has been written on the question of how far cohesive elements can account for coherence in discourse, and how far linguistic description can help us understand it. Work on domain models and genre models of discourse provides increasing evidence for the importance of social expectation and rhetorical structures in text as factors in coherence. Some discussions in the areas of philosophy and pragmatics relate to the matters discussed in Chapters 4 and 5. Of particular interest is work on shared assumptions (*mutual knowledge*) and *frames* and *schemata*. Other work is concerned with the psychological processes involved in comprehension (for example, so-called *top-down* and *bottom-up text processing*) and the psychological conditions necessary for human communication to take place at all (*communicative principles* or *maxims*). Introductions can be found in Brown and Yule (1983) and Mey (1993). Jaworski and Coupland (1999) is a useful collection of articles, some of which relate to these matters.

Hewings' (1999) work on sentence initial structures in students' geography essays is relevant to work of Theme, and McCabe (1999) productively compared thematic structures in English and Spanish history textbooks. Comparisons of texts in different languages in terms of features of textuality are an increasing research area with applications to translation and teaching.

Gledhill's work (2000) on the genre of research articles focuses on the use of collocation and the unfolding of grammatical metaphor in science. Gledhill makes the interesting claim, based on his empirical research, that 'words are chosen not simply for the information they bring along, but also for their long-range ability to signal textual relations'.

Exercises

Exercise 5.1

(a) Identify the Themes in Text 5H and say whether each is marked or unmarked.
(b) Find two examples from the text of nominal groups with articles which do not have nouns as Head. Are these elliptical groups? Give reasons for your answer.
(c) Comment on the cohesive ties formed by the following pronouns: *she* (sentence 2); *they* (sentences 4 and 5).
(d) List two lexical chains in the text.

> Once upon a time, there lived a rich merchant who had three beautiful daughters. The youngest was the prettiest of the three and she was also good and kind to everyone. Her elder sisters were also quite attractive but they were neither good or kind. They were greedy and extremely selfish.

Text 5H

Exercise 5.2

Text 5I on the subject of time and the calendar has a somewhat complex thematic pattern. Try to identify the type of thematic progression used by the author. Is it constant, derived, linear or split Rheme or a combination of more than one pattern? (Note: Ignore the clause beginning *the earth*.)

The two basic periods upon which our system of time-keeping depends are the year and the day. These are determined by two quite distinct notions. The year depends upon the time the earth takes to travel round the sun in a circular path [...] The day depends principally upon the time taken for the earth to rotate around its axis.

Text 5I   (Land, *The Language of Mathematics*[7]).

Exercise 5.3

Identify cases of substitution or ellipsis in each of the following pairs of sentences:

1. Is the contract severable? If so, is the agreement valid?
2. In the recent national emergency, fifteen people were killed. Five are still missing.
3. The answer to this problem can be reached by two paths: the short one and the long one. Both in my judgement are satisfactory.
4. Outside, the sleet had turned to rain. The car radio said more was forecast.

Exercise 5.4

Read the following old joke about the man who visited his doctor and explain the cohesive ambiguity. Why is such a breakdown in communication unlikely in real life?

Man: Doctor, a crab bit my toe.
Doctor: Which one?
Man: I don't know, all crabs look alike to me.

Exercise 5.5

Find two short texts from different sources (for example, a letter and an introduction to an essay, or a report and a recipe) and compare the ways texture is created in each text.

Notes

1. Speight, K. 1943: *Teach Yourself Italian*. London: English University Press Ltd.
2. Lott, Bernard 1986: *A Course in English Language and Literature*. London: Edward Arnold.

3. Pamphlet 1967: *Jungle Survival*. PAM (AIR) 214. London: Ministry of Defence.
4. Martin, E., Larkin, S. and Bernbaum, L. (eds) 1976: *The Penguin Book of the Natural World*. Harmondsworth: Penguin.
5. Lowry, J.H. 1970: *World Population and Food Supply*. London: Edward Arnold.
6. Hughes, Ted 1986: *The Iron Man*. London: Faber & Faber.
7. Land, Frank 1960: *The Language of Mathematics*. London: John Murray.

6

Process and participant

Jerry took the money, picked up a hat from the table and strolled out. Half an hour later he returned and gave some of the bills to Thaler.
[. . .]
Presently something hit the door.
Jerry opened the door and we went down three steps into the back yard. It was almost full daylight. There were ten of us in the party.
'This all?' I asked Thaler.
He nodded.
'Nick said there were fifty of you.'
'Fifty of us to stand off that crummy force!' he sneered.
A uniformed copper held the back gate open, muttering nervously: 'Hurry it up, boys, please.'
I was willing to hurry, but nobody else paid any attention to him.
We crossed an alley, were beckoned through another gate by a big man in brown, passed through a house out into the next street, and climbed into a black automobile that stood at the kerb.
One of the blond boys drove. He knew what speed was.
I said I wanted to be dropped off somewhere in the neighbourhood of the Great Western Hotel. The driver looked at Whisper, who nodded. Five minutes later I got out in front of my hotel.
'See you later,' the gambler whispered.
The last I saw of it was its police department licence plate vanishing around a corner.

Text 6A   (Hammett, *Red Harvest*,[1] pp. 51–2).

6.1   *Meanings: the clause as representation*

Without getting bogged down in philosophical debate about the nature of reality, we can say for practical purposes that language is a means of representing the world. Or perhaps, more precisely, a means of representing 'worlds', perceived or imagined. Language encodes our experience, and thereby plays a crucial role in our involvement with other people, animal life in general, inanimate matter and, indeed, in Douglas Adams' memorable phrase, 'Life, the Universe and Everything'.

The extent to which language determines, rather than simply represents, experience is one of the major questions in philosophy and in linguistics, but we do not propose to go into it here. Suffice it to say that when we speak of language as 'representing' real-world events, or imaginary ones, we are not ruling out the probability that language itself has a central formative role in human experience, nor are we challenging the indisputable fact that it is also part of the reality which it is said to represent. (See the discussion of Whorf in Chapter 12.) It is purely for ease of discussion that we take the practical line of saying that we have, on the one hand, experience and, on the other hand, language, which symbolically represents it.

There is more than one kind of meaning present in language. The expression 'What does it mean?' can be a different question on different occasions. When we say that *Sint sa'at new?* means *What time is it?*, we are substituting one encoding for another, English for Amharic. We are, in effect, matching up the two and judging them to be in some sense equivalent. Something similar is going on when we say that (1) (below) means the same as (1a): we are claiming that one is a paraphrase of the other, though in this case instead of matching two expressions from different languages we are matching two grammatically distinct expressions from the same language, English. We are talking about their ideational function and ignoring textual and interpersonal considerations.

(1)   [We] were beckoned through another gate by a big man in brown [. . .]
(1a) A big man in brown beckoned us through another gate.

The difference between (1) and (1a) is that the first expression in the pair is in the passive voice and the second is in the active. We have touched on this relationship already in our discussion of Subject in Chapter 3. Let us look at it again in the context of this new example.

Some people have difficulty with the claim that two sentences like (1) and (1a) *mean* the same thing. They say that there is a difference; they are not precisely interchangeable. They are right. As we have seen in the discussion of Theme and Rheme (Chapter 4), with regard to the way that the text is being packaged, there is a big difference in the writer's actual choice of the passive version (1) and the grammatically possible choice which he did not take up (1a). In the actual text, the clause corresponding to (1) is elliptical. It occurs in a series of clauses with the same Subject (*we*), and so the Subject is omitted, as it is for all the clauses in the series except the first. We can say that *we* is 'understood' to be the Subject of each of the clauses in the series (2).

(2) We crossed an alley,
       [we] were beckoned through another gate by a big man in brown,
       [we] passed through a house, out into the next street,
       and [we] climbed into a black automobile that stood at the kerb.

Out of context, it might seem that the choice between the active and passive clauses is virtually unconstrained, but in context there is not the same freedom. The author could not have used the active voice here without making a number of other changes. To some extent, then, the choice is, as it were, determined for the author by his other choices; it is a consequence of his decision to present a series of closely linked, consecutive events in this particular form. It is tied up with his decision to make the group of which the narrator is a part the focus of the narrative at this point. In short, it is in large part a question of the textual metafunction and thematic choice (see Chapter 5).

It might be as well to stress here again that when we talk about 'choice' or the writer's 'decision' or 'opting' for something, we are not suggesting that this must be a conscious procedure. In the case of a professional writer, there is no doubt a great deal of explicit awareness of the merits of alternative forms of expression, frequently involving hesitation over a particular choice or the rewriting of a word, a phrase, a sentence or large chunks of text. To some extent, self-consciousness about language probably operates in all human beings in certain circumstances but for much of the time we speak without reflecting on questions of form, vocabulary, and so on. Our use of terms like 'choice' is neutral with regard to whether the language user is conscious of choosing or not.

So the kind of meaning we are concerned with in this chapter is the kind in which active and passive are seen as in some sense substitutable for each other. That is a very approximate way of putting it. It is rather that there is a systematic relationship between the active form and its passive counterpart, and part of that relationship is to do with the representation of 'real world' relationships mentioned above. This is the *ideational* metafunction, the *clause as representation* as Halliday puts it. Active–passive relations are far from being the whole picture; they simply provide a convenient jumping-off point.

In order to discuss these issues, it is necessary to bring into play a set of semantic technical terms distinct from the syntactic categories, SFPCA. Hence we have the term Actor (briefly mentioned in Chapter 2) and several more, which will be introduced in this chapter.

6.2 *Processes*

Text 6A is the end of a chapter recounting a shoot-out between corrupt police and a group of gangsters in whose predicament the narrator has become embroiled. In this extract, the police are then bribed to let the gang escape. In this short text, we have a linguistic representation of numerous human actions, including speaking, and a few other phenomena that are not exactly actions. As befits a thriller, there is a great deal going on, plenty of action.

Looking more closely at the linguistic representation of these imaginary events and the people and things involved, analyzing them in terms of what is represented, we shall use the terms *process* and *participant*. The process centres on that part of the clause that is realized by the verbal group, but it can also be regarded as what 'goings-on' are represented in the whole clause. The participants are the entities involved in the process. In the case of this text, they are mostly humans; they happen to be male, adult and American, but gender, age and nationality are less important for the particular processes involved than the fact that they are human, or at least animate. They include: *Jerry, you, he, Thaler, we, more men, us, ten of us, I, fifty of you, fifty of us, that crummy force, a uniformed copper, nobody else, a big man in brown, one of the blond boys, the driver, who, the gambler,* and (repeatedly) *I.* Of course, in many instances the same individuals are referred to by different forms; for example, *Jerry* and *he*; and in some cases the same item refers to different individuals; for example, in the second sentence, *he* refers to *Jerry*, but in the sentence *He knew what speed was, he* refers to *the blond boy*.

However, not all the participants are human or even animate. In the first clause in (3) below, there are two participants *something* and *door*, both inanimate.

(3)   Presently something hit the door.

Also, in other clauses we find inanimate participants: *the money, a hat, some of the bills, the office, the back gate, an alley, that* (referring to a black automobile), *the car, it, its police department licence plate* and even the abstract entities *any attention* and *speed*.

The term 'process' as a technical term in SFG has a slightly different meaning from its everyday meaning. As we have said, it is used in two senses: (i) to refer to what is going on in the whole clause, and (ii) to refer to that part of the proposition encoded in the verbal group. This is a little confusing perhaps, but that is how the terms are used. Processes can be subdivided into different types, and it is here that the difference between the technical and non-technical senses of the term is highlighted. For instance, not only is (4) described as a process but so are (5) and (6).

(4)   Jerry opened the door.
(5)   It was almost full daylight.
(6)   There were ten of us in the party.

In order to discuss this aspect of language satisfactorily, it is necessary to distinguish between these two types of process and several others and to label them accordingly. Different types of participant, too, have to be distinguished from each other with different labels. And different types of process mostly involve different types of participant.

In Chapter 2, we discussed the misleading practice of describing verbs as 'doing-words'. In the days when grammar was widely taught, teachers would use this term and illustrate it with examples like (4) above.

It is quite reasonable to describe *opened* in (4) as a 'doing-word', but to focus exclusively on such verbs leaves out of account many structures where the term could not reasonably be applied: for example *was* and *were* in (5) and (6). It is also potentially misleading to apply the term 'doing-word' to *saw* or *was* in the last sentence in the text, repeated here as (7).

> (7) The last I saw of it was its police department licence plate vanishing around a corner.

One implication of this too-narrow labelling is that all clauses represent physical actions, which is plainly false. It is evident that it is not the case, even in our text, which is selected from a genre in which action is highly prized. Clearly, although *What did Jerry do?* is a question which might trigger the response *Jerry opened the door* (or, more probably, *He opened the door*), there is no similar question involving *do* that could be the trigger for *It was nearly daylight*; *There were ten of us in the party*; *I saw the last of it*; or *He knew what speed was*. SFG distinguishes carefully between these different processes.

6.3   *Material process*

The prototypical action-type clause beloved of traditional school grammars is classified in our grammar as a *material process clause* (labelled as **Process: material**). Most material processes could reasonably be said to involve 'doing-words'. In an action-oriented narrative such as the one from which this text fragment is taken, such processes tend to occur frequently, though they are by no means the only type.

The first sentence in the text consists of three clauses, (8), (9), (10), with ellipsis of the Subject (*Jerry* or *he*) in the second and third clause. There are three processes and all three are material.

> (8)   Jerry took the money,
> (9)   [Jerry] picked up a hat from the table
> (10) and [Jerry] strolled out.

6.3.1   Actor and Goal

In (8) *Jerry* is explicitly the performer of an action represented by the Process (*took*). We therefore label *Jerry* as Actor. In the imaginary world of this narrative, Jerry did something to the money; he *took* it. It is Jerry who performs the action, and it is the money that undergoes the action. The label we give to *the money* in this clause is *Goal*. Unfortunately, this term is not as self-explanatory as the label *Actor*, but it is one that is in widespread use in semantics. IFG describes Goal as 'the point of impact'; the term does not refer to the destination of motion through space. A similar analysis applies to (9); the elliptical Subject *Jerry* is Actor; *a hat* is Goal. (*From the table* is not a participant but a Circumstance, which is briefly discussed later in this chapter.)

However, (8) and (9) differ grammatically from (10) and from (11) (below) in one important respect.

(11)   Half an hour later he returned.

In (10) and (11) we have a material process again, but this time there is only one participant in each: the elliptical *Jerry* in (10) and *he* in (11). (The expression *Half an hour later* is Circumstance.) Here there is no Goal involved in the process. The Process realized by the verb *returned* is not extended from the Actor *he* to any other entity. In Chapter 3, we introduced the notion of *transitive* and *intransitive* clauses. Examples (10) and (11) are intransitive. *Transitive* clauses involving material processes include, among others, (3), (4) and (8), repeated here, and (12).

(3)   Presently something hit the door. (Actor: *Something*; Goal *the door*)
(4)   Jerry opened the door. (Actor: *Jerry*; Goal: *the door*)
(8)   Jerry took the money. (Actor: *Jerry*; Goal: *the money*)
(12) A uniformed copper held the back gate open. (Actor: *a uniformed copper*; Goal: *the back gate*)

The choice between active and passive voice is significant for SFPCA functions since the item which is Complement in the active is Subject in the corresponding passive, but the items retain the same functions of Actor or Goal regardless of voice. This is evident in Fig. 6.1, where (3), (4) and (8) and their passive equivalents are labelled for SFPCA and also for participant functions.

In the original text, the clauses analyzed above are in the active voice. We have supplied the corresponding passive form. Example (1) is passive in the original; we supply the corresponding active form in Fig. 6.2.

Intransitive clauses in a material process include (13), (14) and (15).

(13) We went down three steps into the back yard. (Actor: *we*)
(14) One of the blond boys drove. (Actor: *One of the blond boys*)
(15) Five minutes later I got out in front of my hotel. (Actor: *I*)

Active

Presently	something	hit	the door.
	Jerry	opened	the door.
	Jerry	took	the money.
A	**S**	**F/P**	**C**
	Actor	**Process: material**	**Goal**

Passive

Presently	the door	was	hit	by something.
	The door	was	opened	by Jerry.
	The money	was	taken	by Jerry.
A	**S**	**F**	**P**	**A**
	Goal	**Process: material**		**Actor**

Fig. 6.1

Passive

We	were	beckoned	through another gate	by a big man in brown.
S	**F**	**P**	**A**	**A**
Goal	**Process: material**			**Actor**

Active

A big man in brown	beckoned	us	through another gate.
S	**F/P**	**C**	**A**
Actor	**Process: material**	**Goal**	

Fig. 6.2

Half an hour later	he	returned.
	Jerry	strolled out.
	One of the blond boys	drove.
A	**S**	**F/P**
	Actor	**Process: material**

Fig. 6.3

Intransitive clauses have no corresponding passive clauses and in the examples considered have only the Actor as Subject (compare Fig. 6.3).

6.3.2   Beneficiary

In (16) we have a material process with three participant roles.

(16) [he] gave some of the bills to Thaler.

The Process, in the narrow sense of the term, is realized by the verbal expression *gave*. The elliptical Subject *he* is Actor; it is not expressed in the clause but it is plainly understood, carried over, as it were, from the first clause. This is a straightforward case of ellipsis as it is 'fully recoverable'; that is, we know exactly what the referent of the 'gap' is. It has to be *he*. By now, it should be clear that *some of the bills* is Goal. So what is the third element: *to Thaler*?

The label for this participant is *Beneficiary*. In Chapter 3 we discussed clauses of this type, which are called ditransitive clauses. In the SFPCA dimension, they typically feature two Complements, more delicately distinguished as direct and indirect object Complements (C^{do} and C^{io}). These involve verbs such as *give*, *send*, *offer*, *buy*, *take*, and so on. In terms of our present interest, the process involves two participants other than the Actor.

There is an optional alternative sequencing for the Goal and Beneficiary in such clauses. With no significant change of ideational meaning, (16) could take the form of (16a).

(16a) He gave Thaler some of the bills.

The label Beneficiary is self-explanatory with regard to the example we are talking about. The character Thaler in the story literally benefits from the process (though admittedly the money was his in the first place). The label cannot always be interpreted so literally, however. If the proposition is negated, it does not affect the label given to the participant. In the invented clauses (16b) and (16c), the Beneficiary label still attaches to Thaler.

(16b) He didn't give some of the bills to Thaler.
(16c) He gave no money to Thaler.

Moreover, in the real world – or in fictional worlds – you can give things to people that they benefit from and things that are of no benefit at all; they may even be harmful. You can promise someone a punch on the nose, hand them cigarettes, give them an earful of abuse, or offer them a poisoned chalice. As far as the labelling of the participants is concerned, the relative benefit or damage is of no significance; the receiver is still labelled Beneficiary. A similar analysis applies to the parental admonishment *I'll give you something to cry about*, and comparable threats.

The term Beneficiary is not unusual in having a different range of application from its non-technical sense. Within the framework of the grammatical description, these are technical terms and must be used with the meanings ascribed to them for the purpose of the analysis. This is no stranger than the fact that in the register of computers the word *window*, though it shares something of the meaning of the everyday term, has a more specific technical meaning limited to the computer.

In active voice clauses the Beneficiary is usually the indirect object Complement, but in passive clauses it is often the Subject (see Fig. 6.4).

Active

he	gave	Smith	some cash.
S	F/P	C^{io}	C^{do}
Actor	Process: material	Beneficiary	Goal

Passive

Smith	was	given	some cash.
S	F	P	C^{do}
Beneficiary	Process: material		Goal

Fig. 6.4

6.3.3 Scope

English (together with some other languages) has a tendency to nominalize (that is, to express in noun form) certain events which might be seen as essentially processes and which often have a non-nominal synonym (see Chapter 11). Sometimes these nominalizations are coupled with a verb which has little lexical meaning, a verb which is semantically almost empty in this context, usually *take* or *have*. Such verbs are sometimes said to be *delexicalized* because they have lost their full lexical content and become almost 'dummies'. Thus we can say *I dined before I came* or, nominalizing, *I had dinner before I came*, and in informal conversation we would usually prefer the second expression. Similarly, we have *bathe* versus *take a bath* or *have a bath*; *wash* versus *have a wash*; *swim* versus *have/take a swim*; *drink* versus *have/take a drink*; *look* versus *have/take a look*; *rest* versus *have/take a rest*, and so on. The members of each of these pairs may not be exactly synonymous, and there are often stylistic/register differences, but you will probably agree that up to a point they mean the same thing. You will perhaps also agree that, functionally speaking, there is a difference between the role of *the money* in *Jerry took the money* and the role of *a bath* in *I took a bath*. English encodes them in a grammatically similar way, but it seems desirable at the semantic level of process and participant to make some distinction between them. The term used in IFG for items like *a bath* in *I took a bath* is *Scope*.

There is a very close similarity between Scope and Goal. As with many other categories in grammar, this is no clear-cut distinction with a sharp dividing line between the two categories; instead, one merges into the other. Since the examples in the text are peripheral rather than clear cases, we will postpone discussion of them and go outside for our first examples.

The most clear-cut example of Scope, as we see it, is where the process and the participant are blended together, as in the expressions already mentioned. Of course, in a more literal use of the words *I took a bath* (for example, as uttered by a burglar whose larceny extends to ripping out the plumbing), *a bath* would be analyzed as Goal. In the case of the burglary situation, the verb *take* retains its lexical meaning of 'seize, transfer to one's possession' instead of being a delexicalized dummy. This time it does resemble *Jerry took the money*. The rule-of-thumb probe seems to be to ask whether the utterance in question can be roughly paraphrased as 'What X did to Y was Z it.' In the second case, where the thief is talking about his crime, his meaning could be expressed as 'What I did to the bath was take it.' In the first case, where the speaker is referring to his or her personal hygiene, no such paraphrase is conceivable.

A similar sort of role to that of *a bath* in the personal hygiene example seems to attach to *a song* in *She sang a song*, and also to *a terrible death* in *Don Giovanni died a terrible death*, or *the good fight* in *Fight the good fight*. These too are classified as Scope. In these instances, we find not 'empty' verbs like *have* or *take* but verbs which share key semantic features with the Head noun in the Scope element: *die* has a lot in common with *death*; *sing* with *song*.

This is a fairly limited set of items, however, and the relationship still holds for items which are not so obviously related. For example, the italicized items in the following are all Scope: she sang *the national anthem*; she hummed *a tune*; the band played *'Waltzing Matilda'*; run *the straight race*; he counted off *a hundred or two;* did Pele play *football?*

One example of Scope, in the Hammett extract is *any attention* in (17).

(17) Nobody else paid any attention to him.

Lexically and grammatically, the structure resembles a clause with a Goal, but the semantic evidence suggests that *any attention* is Scope; on either analysis, *to him* is Beneficiary.

In the extract, we also find the clause: *We crossed an alley*. In the IFG model, *an alley* is classed as Scope. This seems to us a more peripheral case than the ones we have already considered. Again the question test, rough though it is, seems to bear out this decision. It does not seem to be quite right to say *What we did to the alley was cross it.* The argument is that *an alley* is not so much the recipient or sufferer of the action as the scope of the action, hence we label it Scope. And even less likely is *What we didn't do to any attention was pay it.* The first type where the Scope is an identifiably existing entity (*the alley*) can be subclassified as *Scope: entity*. The second where the Scope is essentially an expression of the process itself (*attention*) is subclassified as *Scope: process*. Examples of Scope: entity are: *cross the alley*; *climb a mountain*; *run a mile*; *play a piano*. Examples of Scope: process are *take a bath*; *die a death*; *sing a song*; *play football*; *hum a tune*. However, we shall not be making further use of this subclassification in this book. Scope is a sort of subcategory of a broader functional category known as Range and in some publications the term Range is used instead; Scope is Range occurring in material processes. Other forms of Range occur in other processes as discussed below.

A rather rare participant in material process is *Initiator.* This shows up in such structures as *He marched them up to the top of the hill* in the satirical folk rhyme, *The Grand Old Duke of York.*

> The grand old duke of York
> He had ten thousand men
> He marched them up to the top of the hill
> And he marched them down again.

Here *he* is not Actor; the actual marching is done by *them. He* is the prime instigator of the action, which he initiates; hence Initiator.

6.4   *Mental process*

Some processes involve not material action but phenomena best described as states of mind or psychological events. To these we give the label *mental processes*. Mental processes tend to be realized through the use of verbs like *think, know, feel, smell, hear, see, want, like, hate, please, disgust, admire, enjoy, fear, frighten.*

In (18), we cannot construe the process as an action and so we can deduce that it is not a material process.

(18) He knew what speed was.

The clause could not serve as an answer to the question *What did he do?* In this respect it differs from the clause immediately preceding it: *One of the blond boys drove.* (What did one of the blond boys do? He drove; but not: What did he do? He knew what speed was.) Knowing is not doing.

Another example of mental process is *wanted* in (19).

(19) I wanted to be dropped off somewhere in the neighbourhood of the Great Western Hotel.

Simpler examples (20 to 24) can be found elsewhere in the same book.

(20) He didn't see me.
(21) I heard the shots.
(22) I knew the number.
(23) You didn't want it this morning.
(24) I dislike your manner.

6.4.1   Senser and Phenomenon

In all these examples the Subject is the one who experiences the process. For obvious reasons, this participant is labelled *Senser*. That which is experienced is given the label *Phenomenon*. The examples cited all have the same participant roles in the same order: Senser, Process: mental, Phenomenon, as demonstrated in Fig. 6.5.

He	didn't see	me.
I	heard	the shots.
I	knew	the number.
You	didn't want	it.
I	dislike	your manner.
Senser	**Process: mental**	**Phenomenon**

Fig. 6.5

It happens that in all these examples the Senser conflates with Subject and the Phenomenon conflates with Complement, but this is not always the case. Firstly, even with the same verbs, a change from active to passive would make the Phenomenon the Subject. For textual reasons, passive counterparts of these clauses are not very plausible, at least in this context, but they are hypothetically possible. For example, *he didn't see me* has the passive counterpart *I wasn't seen by him*; and *I heard the shots* could be paraphrased as *the shots were heard by me*. This reverses the order of the participants as seen in Fig. 6.6.

I	wasn't seen	by him.
The shots	were heard	by me.
Phenomenon	**Process: mental**	**Senser**

Fig. 6.6

In fact, we would be more likely to come across these structures with the Senser omitted (*I wasn't seen*; *the shots were heard*) because one common motivation for using the passive voice is that it permits us to omit certain participants. Thus in a different context it might be possible to find the clauses in Fig. 6.7.

I	wasn't seen.
The shots	were heard.
The number	was known.
It	wasn't wanted.
Phenomenon	**Process: mental**

Fig. 6.7

It is largely coincidental that all the Sensers in the examples above are realized as personal pronouns. The grammar permits nominal groups of any degree of complexity to function as Senser. Thus *he* in *He didn't see me* could be replaced with *Donald, the person I mentioned, my husband,* or many another nominal groups, without affecting the fact that it is still Senser.

There is one constraint that you should be aware of, however. The Senser is by definition a sentient being: a human or at least animate creature (except in metaphorical or fantastic uses). The Senser has to be animate since only animate beings (people and animals) can think, feel or perceive, though, of course, in metaphor and in fairy stories and the like such processes may be attributed to inanimate entities; computers are frequently talked about in this way. The Phenomenon may be animate or inanimate.

It is not only in passive clauses that the Phenomenon may show up as Subject. The situation worded as (24) *I dislike your manner* could be represented without too much change of meaning as (25).

(25) Your manner displeases me.

Both clauses express a mental process, and in both we have two participants: a Senser and a Phenomenon. One difference is that in (24) the role of Senser is realized as Subject (*I*) and the role of Phenomenon as Complement (*your manner*), whereas in (25) the roles are reversed. Similarly, the clause *I like it* has the potential alternative *It pleases me* (see Fig. 6.8).

There are several pairs of verbs in English which permit rough 'parallel' representations of this type. In Fig. 6.9, assuming an active voice clause, with verbs on the left, the Senser is Subject and the Phenomenon is Complement; with verbs on the right, the Phenomenon is Subject and the Senser is Complement.

Phenomenon in a mental process has a function similar to that of Scope in a material process. In fact, both are subcategories of the more general category: *Range*. Hence, you might find either Scope or Phenomenon labelled as Range.

I	dislike	your manner.
I	like	it.
S	F/P	C
Senser	**Process: mental**	**Phenomenon**

Your manner	displeases	me.
It	pleases	me.
S	F/P	C
Senser	**Process: mental**	**Phenomenon**

Fig. 6.8

like	please
dislike	displease
enjoy	amuse, delight
pity	move, touch (emotional sense)

Fig. 6.9

6.4.2   Phenomenon realized as clause

One example of Phenomenon realized as a clause can be found in (18), *He knew what speed was*, where *he* is Senser, *knew* is Process and *what speed was* is Phenomenon.

There are numerous examples of clause as Phenomenon in the source novel, usually involving the verb *know*. The fragment in Text 6B exploits *know* to breaking point.

Noonan knows that Thaler knows about the cheque. He knows that Thaler came here while Willson was here, but didn't get in. He knows that Thaler was hanging around the neighbourhood when Willson was shot. He knows that Thaler and a woman were seen bending over the dead man.

Text 6B   Hammett, *Red Harvest*,[1] p. 32).

In all but one of these instances, the Phenomenon is realized by a full clause. This is fairly common in the type of mental process that involves 'knowing' (with verbs like *know, guess, suspect, deduce, calculate*). The clause complex *He knows that Thaler came here* can be analyzed as in Fig. 6.10, where it is compared with (18) and a simpler example.

He	knows	that Thaler came here.
He	knew	what speed was.
He	knew	everything.
Senser	**Process: mental**	**Phenomenon**

Fig. 6.10

Since the Phenomenon *that Thaler came here* is a clause in its own right, it too expresses a process, this time a material process with *Thaler* as Actor. Of course, all clauses realizing Phenomenon have their internal process and participant functions, as do all other clauses. We will not pursue this here, but we return to complex structures in Chapters 9 and 10.

6.5   *Relational process*

Relational processes are typically realized by the verb *be* or some verb of the same class (known as *copular verbs*); for example, *seem, become, appear* (as in *She appeared cheerful*) or sometimes by verbs such as *have, own, possess*. In SFPCA terms, they typically have a Subject and an intensive Complement. The semantics of relational processes is very complicated, and different sets of participant functions can be associated with different, more delicate categories of relational process. Out of context, it is often difficult, frequently impossible, to subclassify relational processes precisely.

6.5.1   Attributive process

A common type of relational process ascribes an attribute to some entity as in (26).

(26) She was hungry again.

In (26) we have an Attribute (*hungry*) and a Carrier of the attribution (*she*); the Process is locally focused on *was* (past tense form of the verb *be*, the most typical copular verb). Text 6C is made up entirely of relational processes.

> She was in a ward on the third floor, alone. The other four beds were empty. She could have been a girl of twenty-five or a woman of fifty-five. Her face was a bloated spotty mask.

Text 6C   (Hammett, *Red Harvest*,[1] p. 83).

These are analyzed in Fig. 6.11.

She	was	in a ward on the third floor.
The other four beds	were	empty.
She	could have been	a girl of twenty-five or a woman of fifty-five.
Her face	was	a bloated spotty mask.
Carrier	**Process: relational**	**Attribute**

Fig. 6.11

We find two examples of relational process in (27). Both are instances of attribution.

(27) I would rather have been cold sober, but I wasn't.

The Carrier (*I*) and the Attribute (*cold sober*) are the same in both clauses, but in the second clause the Attribute is 'understood' instead of being explicit; that is to say, it is another instance of ellipsis: *but I wasn't [cold sober].*

Also classed as attributive relational process are certain possessive structures, such as (28).

(28) I had a little money.

Here *I* is the **Carrier: possessor** and *a little money* is the **Attribute: possessed**.

Other copular verbs which appear in attributive relational processes include the following:

feel   as in   *I feel sick.*
look   as in   *He looked the picture of misery.*
remain as in   *Kyoto remained the capital for many years.*
smell   as in   *The durian fruit smells disgusting.*
sound   as in   *You sound a little strange.*
taste   as in   *The coffee tasted delicious.*

6.5.2 Identifying process

An additional function for relational processes is *identifying,* as in (29). The key roles here are Identified and Identifier.

(29) Quint is his name.

Here the participants are respectively *Quint* (Identifier) and *his name* (Identified). It is clear from the context that these are the functions. The speaker could have reversed the sequence without changing the functions.

(29a) His name is Quint.

Example (29a) would be the more usual ('unmarked') order: *Identified*, *Identifier* respectively.

Since *Quint* can scarcely be anything but a personal name in English, the structure is fairly unambiguous with regard to the participant functions. However, with a hypothetical, decontextualized sentence such as *Carpenter is his name*, we could have either a parallel structure to the real one about Quint or a reversed structure with *Carpenter* as the Identified and *his name* as Identifier (as in *Carpenter is his name not his profession*). However, in spoken English the intonation, as well as the context, offers clues to which participant function is intended and so the ambiguity is usually removed.

6.6　*Verbal process*

Speaking is certainly a kind of action, and to some extent it would not be unreasonable to treat it as material process. On the other hand, it has some features of mental process, especially if we believe that verbalization of thoughts is a kind of inner speech. A case can be made for postulating a new category of process: *verbal process* (labelled as **Process: verbal**.) Consider (30).

> (30)　I said: 'If there isn't, I'll have to take him down to the City Hall.'

In this example, we have the person who produces the utterance, to whom we give the self-explanatory title of *Sayer*; the verbal process itself, realized here as *said*; and the representation of the words actually spoken, which in this context we label *Quoted*. The function *Quoted* is realized as direct speech. The wording is identical to that initially uttered by the Sayer, or at least, it is presented as though it were identical.

Somewhat different from this is the verbal process where the words of the Sayer are transposed in line with the perspective of the speaker or writer who is reporting the speech. This involves reported (i.e. indirect) speech, as in (31).

> (31)　I said I wanted to be dropped off somewhere in the neighbourhood of the Great Western Hotel.

Here *I* is Sayer and *I wanted to be dropped off somewhere in the neighbourhood of the Great Western Hotel* is *Reported*. (The reported element itself contains one clause or more and so it could in turn be analyzed in terms of process and participant, but we will not go into that here. Strictly speaking, since Quoted and Reported are separate clauses from the clause containing Sayer and Process, they are not participants in that clause.)

There are various ordering possibilities with this type of process, particularly with the direct speech form. The most neutral ('unmarked') ordering is

Sayer–Process–Quoted, but we can have Sayer following Quoted, as in (32), or even interrupting Quoted, as in (33).

> (32) 'That's nice,' the grey-moustached sleuth on my left said.
> (33) 'I don't think I meant to kill him,' he repeated, 'though I took the gun with me.'

In some texts, we find the sequence Quoted–Process–Sayer as in (34).

> (34) 'Must be another march,' grumbled the taxi-driver.

In modern English, with the sequence Quoted–Process–Sayer, Sayer must be a full nominal group with a noun as Head (often a proper noun) and not a pronoun. Only in more old-fashioned or whimsical texts will you find Sayer realized as a pronoun in this sequence, as in (35), from an eighteenth-century novel, *Tom Jones*.

> (35) 'And a good riddance, too,' answered he.

In addition to the Sayer and the Quoted or Reported, there is a third participant in some of these examples: the person to whom the verbalization is addressed. In material process terms, this would be the Beneficiary, but since we have set up a separate system for verbal process, we call this participant the *Receiver*. An example of this is *her* in (36).

> (36) I asked her if she had heard him.

The typical verb for verbal processes is *say*, but there are many others. Probably the most important are *ask* and *tell*, for, although *say* can be used with all types of Quoted (statements, questions, orders), we need to distinguish among these when the speech is Reported. Thus, with (37), the author might easily have substituted *said* for *asked*.

> (37) 'Where did the shots come from?' the chief asked.

However, in reported questions (indirect speech) such as (36), we cannot use the reporting verb *say*. Direct speech equivalents of (36) include (36a) and (36b).

> (36a) 'Did you hear him?' I asked (her).
> (36b) 'Did you hear him?' I said (to her).

Example (36c) is not a valid option, however.

> (36c) *I said to her if she had heard him.

In fact, there is an additional area of meaning open to the writer/speaker who produces a verbal process clause, particularly one involving Quoted; this is in the choice of the lexical verb selected to encode the verbal process. In contradistinction to the neutral *say*, a large number of verbs can be exploited, each carrying some extra element of meaning.

Sometimes this meaning can relate to the *speech act* realized. Just as we can have *ask* to indicate a question or *tell* to indicate a command, so we can use such verbs as *urge, explain, remind, challenge, beg, promise, grumble, agree, report* to convey other subtleties of what speech act theorists call *illocutionary force*. All these verbs are exploited in Quoting structures in the source novel.

Incidentally, as well as expressing a question (eliciting information), with Reported (but not normally with Quoted), *ask* can also serve to realize a request for goods or activity. In such cases the Reported often takes the infinitive form; see (38) (italics added).

(38) I went to the phone and asked the girl *to send the house copper up.*

In Text 6A, we find (39).

(39) 'See you later,' the gambler whispered.

This typifies another kind of meaning that can be conveyed by the choice of lexical verb, a meaning connected with the nature of the actual delivery of the speech: such things as the tone, quality or volume of voice. Other examples in the same text fragment are *sneer* and *mutter* in (40) and (41).

(40) 'Fifty of us to stand off that crummy force!' he sneered.
(41) [. . .] muttering nervously: 'Hurry it up, boys [. . .]'

From many other examples in the same novel, we might mention: *lisped, growled, snarled, barked, bawled, babbled on, gasped.* Sometimes this aspect of the meaning overlaps with the illocutionary force already mentioned. For example, whereas *whisper* (in this text, at least) comments only on the voice quality, the choice of the word *sneer* tells us something of the Sayer's intention as well as of the manner of his delivery. The choice of *babble*, on the other hand, does not indicate illocutionary force, but rather, as well as commenting on the manner of delivery, conveys something of the narrator's judgement on the quality of what was being projected.

Another way of adding such extra information is by an Adjunct, as in the example *muttering nervously*, where the writer conveys more than a plain use of *saying* could achieve not only by choosing a non-neutral verb, *muttering*, but also by adding a circumstantial Adjunct *nervously*. Adjuncts usually (not always) conflate with the function *Circumstance*, which is discussed below.

Finally, in this section on verbal process, we will mention two other potential participants: *Verbiage* and *Target*. The term Verbiage is used in this context to label items like *the truth* in (42):

(42) I told her the truth.

Here the expression *the truth* represents what the Sayer said but instead of representing it as a quotation of the actual words used (Quoted) or a report of the proposition expressed in those words (Reported), it rather refers to what is said by classifying it in terms of its character as an expression. In fact, just as Sayer is a specialized form of Actor, so Verbiage in verbal process is similar to Scope in material process and Phenomenon in mental process. Hence, it is a further example of the broader category of Range. This similarity can be readily seen in such expressions as *ask a question, state your case, talk my language, speak English, tell (someone) the facts.*

Verbiage can also be a clause that is not a projection of speech or thought, as in (43) (italics added).

(43) He told me *what I wanted to know.*

Target is a fairly peripheral participant and does not occur with direct or indirect speech, except incidentally. It is the person or thing which is 'targeted by the process' (IFG Chapter 5), as with *party leadership* in (44).

(44) Former party officials criticized *party leadership.*

Lexical verbs which accept a Target include: *describe, explain, praise, flatter, blame, condemn, castigate.*

6.7   *Other processes*

Halliday classes the processes Material, Mental and Relational as major processes and the others as minor. In addition to verbal process, already discussed, the minor processes include *existential process* and *behavioural process.*

Existential process (**Process: existential**) has only one participant, the *Existent*. This type of process has two main forms of grammatical realization: (i) with a copular verb and an empty *there* as Subject: (45) and (46).

(45) There were ten of us in the party.
(46) There were fifty of you.

(ii) with a copular verb, the Existent as Subject and usually a circumstantial Adjunct: (45a).

(45a) Ten of us were in the party.

The latter looks very similar to a relational process, and indeed the same wording in a different context could be relational. For example, in describing a group of twenty people, half of whom were members of the Socialist Party, one might say *Ten of us were in the party* where *Ten of us* would function as Carrier and *in the party* as Attribute (compare *Ten of us were party members*; or *Ten of us were Socialists*).

When we have only the Existent without any explicit circumstance, the semantically empty Subject *there* is almost obligatory. This is not a participant since it is simply a sort of place-holder or syntactic marker. An exception is the unusual type of structure typified by the second clause in the well-known proposition of the French philosopher, Descartes (mentioned earlier): *I think*; *therefore I am*. Similarly, *Ghosts do not exist* is a negative existential process: *Ghosts* (Existent) *do not exist* (Process: existential). As with most other grammatical phenomena, negation does not affect the participant function label.

As far as clear definition and discrete classification is concerned, the bottom of the barrel is *behavioural process* (**Process: behavioural**). This is the grey area between material and mental processes. As with existential process only one participant is normally required, but this one is labelled *Behaver*.

Example (47) could be a candidate for the label Process: behavioural, but it could equally be argued that it is a material process.

(47) [...] the car slid away.

A more straightforward example of behavioural process (though not a finite clause) is (48).

(48) [...] its police department licence plate vanishing around a corner.

Rarely, a further participant occurs, namely *Behaviour* as with *salty tears* in (49).

(49) I could cry salty tears.

Other examples are *a sigh* in *breathe a sigh*, *blood* in *sweat blood*, and *sweet dreams* in *dream sweet dreams*. Like Scope in material process and Verbiage in verbal process, Behaviour is a subcategory of Range. A number of processes that we analyzed as material earlier in this chapter border on behavioural and might well be analyzed as such. For example: *sing a song, hum a tune, rest/take a rest, swim/have a swim*. On this analysis, *a song, a tune, a rest, a swim* would realize the function Behaviour.

6.8   *Grammatical metaphor*

6.8.1   Experiential grammatical metaphor

Expressions involving nominalization (*take a bath, have a look*, and so on) are identified in SFL as examples of *grammatical metaphor*. In essence, we perceive bathing as 'doing'. The usual way of encoding such phenomena in English is to opt for material process with an Actor; hence, we have the possibility of saying: *I bathed, I looked*, and so on. This choice, where the process matches our perception of bathing as 'doing' rather than a thing, is said to be *congruent*. The nominalized form is designated *non-congruent* or more usually **grammatical metaphor**. In *The driver looked at Whisper*, the form *looked* has been chosen; the author might have used the non-congruent grammatical forms *took a look* or *had a look*, but chose not to. Similarly, he might have written *gave a nod* in place of *nodded* (in *The driver looked at Whisper, who nodded*) but again opted for the congruent expression with the process realized as a verb.

In its usual sense, the term *metaphor* applies to a figurative use of language where something is implicitly suggested as having the qualities of something else; one thing is seen in terms of another. Simple examples are *Life was a song; Our birth is but a sleep and a forgetting; He is a real pussy-cat.* Slightly more complicated examples are *The fog comes / on little cat feet; epidemics wiped out the population; a fat salary.* In fact, metaphor permeates the language in everyday expressions such as *lower your guard; open your heart; break a promise; retreat from the world; build up a relationship; drop a hint, a sharp tongue,* and, less obviously, in such expressions as *raise the price, a fall in temperature, a full life, waste one's time.* The antithesis of 'metaphorical' in this sense is 'literal'. *My life was a song* is metaphorical; *I was happy* is literal.

Grammatical metaphor resembles traditional metaphor (mainly lexical) in that it involves a choice between a more straightforward and a more oblique realization of meaning. But the choice is made within the available grammatical options rather than the lexical options – not so much one word/idea instead of another as one grammatical form instead of another, though, of course, this will usually entail more extensive differences of 'meaning'. And just as there is no suggestion that literal expression is intrinsically better or worse than metaphorical expression, there is also no suggestion that congruent forms are better or worse than grammatically metaphorical ones. Nor is the congruent form necessarily the more frequently used form. Sometimes the grammatically metaphorical form may be more usual in current usage. *I had a bath* is more usual in contemporary English than *I bathed*, but *I listened* is more usual than *I had a listen*. *Pay attention* is a fairly clear example of a metaphorical expression which has become idiomatic. It combines traditional metaphor with grammatical metaphor: the lexical item *pay* suggests that we are treating the process of attending as if it were currency; the nominalization of the process as the abstract noun *attention* exploits the grammatical metaphor option. The clause *Life was a song* also combines literary and grammatical metaphor, and the literal paraphrases *Life was happy* and *I was happy with my life* retain the grammatical metaphor. More congruently, but less efficiently, we might say: *I was alive and I was happy (to be so).*

In fact, different contexts may demand different alternatives, and here register and genre are crucial. Situational and textual factors have a considerable bearing on which options are preferred in any particular instance. We may have seemed to suggest sometimes that congruent and grammatically metaphorical alternatives are simply variant ways of saying the same thing, but the truth is that any difference in expression means a difference in meaning of some kind. Even the choice between *bathe* and *take a bath* has situational or stylistic significance. Most English speakers are more likely to feel comfortable with writing *Cleopatra is said to have bathed in ass's milk* (in literary-historical register) than with saying *I think I'll bathe before I go to bed* (in informal conversation register).

One way of looking at nominalization is to say that it involves an alternation within the experiential metafunction: instead of being realized by a verb (*bathe, think, explain, destroy*), a process is realized as a thing (*bath, thought, explanation, destruction*). This is a very imprecise formulation, but it may help us to see what is going on. The expressive possibilities available to a nominalized process form are different from those available to processes realized as verbs. For example, a nominalization can be succinctly modified with adjectives: *the recent deplorable destruction of villages* has a brevity that is hard to achieve with the more congruent use of the verb *destroy* in place of the noun *destruction*. Moreover, the nominal group expressing the process is available for use as Subject or Complement or part of an Adjunct: *the recent deplorable destruction of villages cannot be justified on these grounds; the spokesman condemned the recent deplorable destruction of villages; this intransigent attitude has been strengthened by the recent deplorable destruction of villages.*

For these reasons, among others, this type of grammatical metaphor is particularly important in formal written style, appearing frequently in such genres as university textbooks and academic journals, and in what is loosely known as scientific writing. The following extract is from a popular science book:

> . . . . if the water is magnified a few million times, there will be revealed a strongly expressed granular structure formed by a large number of separate molecules closely packed together. Under the same magnification it is also apparent that the water is far from still, and that its molecules are in a state of violent agitation moving around and pushing one another as though they were people in a highly excited crowd. This irregular motion of water molecules, or the molecules of any other material substance is known as *heat (or thermal) motion.*

Text 6D   (Gamow, *One Two Three . . . Infinity,*[2] p. 185)

In the first sentence, we have the verb *is magnified,* the process being realized by a passive voice verbal group. The circumstances of the process are spelled out too: it is a massive magnification of a few million. Subsequently this same process is referred to using the grammatical metaphor (nominalization): *the same magnification*. The nominalization enables the writer to avoid the stylistically clumsy repetition of the group *a few million times*. In the next sentence we find the verb *moving* realizing a process, which is picked up in the final sentence as (*This irregular*) *motion*. The modified nominalization cohesively encapsulates all the information conveyed in the previous embedded clauses *that the water .... crowd*. (See *cohesion* in Section 5.4 of this volume.) It also makes this information available to be presented as Theme, thus contributing to the continuing unfolding of the text as message (see Chapter 4).

Sometimes, though, the grammatically metaphorical form can be more unwieldy than a more congruent counterpart, as in the metaphorical (50) from the same source and our slightly more congruent (50a):

(50)   the evaporation of liquids takes place at different temperatures for different materials
(50a) different liquids evaporate at different temperatures for different materials

Of course the co-text must be taken into account, and generally, texts which make heavy use of nominalization are able to pack in a lot of information economically; as a result, they tend to be denser and are sometimes more difficult to process. At its worst, inept or inappropriate use of nominalization may create an impression of pomposity or pretentiousness, but it is a valuable and even essential part of language use.

Example (51) is part of a sentence from a published medical research abstract.

(51)   The GDP counts contributed to intraoperative decision making in three patients, ... by localisation of tumour not identified by inspection of palpation .....
       [GDP = Gamma detecting probe; palpation = feeling with the fingertips]

This is comprehensible to readers from outside the medical profession only with considerable effort. But if we try to paraphrase it with more congruent forms (51a), the result is far from satisfactory.

(51a) Someone used a GDP and, by using the figures which came up, surgeons could decide what to do while they were operating on three patients. They could do this because they could find precisely where a tumour was even though this had not been found out by palpating the patients' bodies.

No doubt a better rendering than (51a) could be constructed, but there is nearly always something lost when such attempts are made – and, as in this case, there is often something added that may be unnecessary, undesirable or simply wrong. For one thing, the paraphrase uses 51 words to the original's 21, and, since the genre here is an abstract (a brief account where space is limited), that is a serious disadvantage. For another, the rewrite is more specific about the agents than the original is. We can't be sure that the decisions are all made by surgeons. It may, for example, be anaesthetists who are helped in this way. It is redundant to say that 'someone' used a GDP, and in this context it doesn't matter; all that matters is what was found out by using it. True, the original is hard for a lay reader to process, but for a specialist it presents no problems, and this is communication between specialists. It is not necessary for outsiders to understand it. People sometimes argue that all writing should be comprehensible to any reader, but this is unrealistic. No doubt writers are sometimes deliberately and unnecessarily obscure for sinister reasons, but interaction is determined, among other things, by the nature and relations of the interactants. If the authors had been writing for a lay audience they would certainly have expressed themselves differently though it is unlikely that they would have completely avoided grammatical metaphor; nor is such avoidance necessary or desirable.

Nevertheless, it is often useful for an analyst or a critical reader to attempt to rephrase a structure in order to get at the way the language is being used or to identify the author's intentions and effects. Such a procedure is sometimes called 'unpacking', and it can shed light on the manipulation of the reader or listener by a writer or speaker, among other things.

6.8.2   Logical and interpersonal metaphor

The *Collins Cobuild English Grammar* tells us: 'When you want to indicate the reason for something, you use a reason clause' (p. 355), and their examples include the following (52):

> (52) I couldn't feel anger against him because I liked him too much.

Well, yes, up to a point, Cobuild! But there are other ways of achieving the same broad effect (and presumably the authors of the grammar did not intend to suggest otherwise). One way is to use the noun *reason*, as in our reconstruction (52a).

> (52a) The reason I couldn't feel anger against him is that I liked him too much.

In this instance, the noun *reason* conveys a meaning more congruently expressed by the conjunction *because*. You may recall from Chapter 1 that the ideational metafunction divides into experiential and logical and that relations expressed by conjunctions fall within the logical metafunction. So (52a) can be described as a logical metaphor. Instead of two clauses, the second dependent on the first, which have the pattern **X because Y**, we have the pattern **X is Y**, involving two embedded clauses (see Chapters 8 and 9). In our rewrite, we have replaced the more congruent use of two mental process clauses bound by a logical sign (*because*) with a relational process clause containing two embedded mental process clauses. (Arguably, this explanation suggests an overlap between logical and experiential metaphor.)

IFG also claims that grammatical metaphor is involved in the alternation between, on the one hand, the use of modal verbs (*may, might, must*, etc.), and, on the other, modal adverbs (*probably, possibly, necessarily*, etc.), adjectives (*probable, possible, necessary*, etc.) and nouns (*probability, possibility, necessity*). Thus (53) is perceived as a more congruent version of the grammatically metaphorical (53a).

(53)   There may be three major indicators of generic integrity.
(53a) Possibly there are three major indicators of generic integrity.

Because modality is regarded as being located within the interpersonal metafunction, this is classed as interpersonal metaphor. Other grammatical metaphors relating to (53) include (53b) and (53c).

(53b) Three possible major indicators of generic integrity . . . .
(53c) The possibility of three major indicators of generic integrity . . .

There are further grammatical metaphors involved in these examples, for grammatical metaphor permeates the language and can be fearsomely difficult to pin down. Hence, it is often very hard for analysts to reach agreement about specific instances. However, especially in the case of experiential metaphor, the concept can often go some way towards explaining how the language works.

6.9   *Circumstance*

We have already mentioned in passing the third component of the clause as representation: *Circumstance*. This is the name given (in the context of this dimension of analysis) to those elements which carry a semantic load but are neither process (in the narrow sense) nor participant. In some respects, Circumstance, as the name suggests, is more peripheral than participants, being concerned with such matters as the settings, temporal and physical, the manner in which the process is implemented, and the people or other entities accompanying the process rather than directly engaged in it. Typically, but not exclusively, Circumstance conflates with Adjunct and the grammatical realization is adverb or prepositional phrase.

In the first clause in our main source text, the Circumstance is realized by the adverb *Presently*. This tells us something about the timing of the process in relation to the other events described previously. In *we went down three steps into the back yard*, there are two Circumstances *down three steps* and *into the back yard*, both telling the reader about the location of the process. In the elliptical, non-finite clause *muttering nervously: 'Hurry it up boys'*, the

Circumstance is realized by the adverb *nervously*, a circumstantial Adjunct, telling us about how the Sayer performed the verbal process.

In subsequent clauses, *out into the next street, into a black automobile that stood at the kerb* (and, in the embedded clause within that, *at the kerb*); *somewhere in the neighbourhood of the Great Western Hotel*; and *around a corner* are all Circumstances which give information about the spatial location of the process. *Five minutes later* is a Circumstance concerned with location in time.

In IFG, Circumstances fall into nine types: *Extent, Location, Manner, Cause, Contingency, Accompaniment, Role, Matter and Angle*, all discussed in great detail, but considerations of space preclude further discussion here.

Summary

In this chapter, we have dealt with the semantics of the clause: the process and participant, and, very briefly, the circumstance. Processes can be subclassified into the major ones: material, mental and relational; and the minor ones: verbal, existential and behavioural.

The participants identified with the various processes are as follows in Fig. 6.12.

material	Actor, Goal, Beneficiary, Scope, Initiator (rare)
mental	Senser, Phenomenon
relational	Carrier, Attribute, Identified, Identifier
verbal	Sayer, Quoted/Reported, Verbiage, Target, Receiver
existential	Existent
behavioural	Behaver, Behaviour (rare)

Fig. 6.12

The VOICE system (active–passive) allows us to choose among certain participants for the Subject function. For example, in a material process, the active voice has Actor as Subject whereas the passive voice allows Goal or Beneficiary to be Subject. Similarly, in mental processes, Senser and Phenomenon may alternate as potential Subject, depending on voice. Different lexical verbs (for example, *fear/frighten*) also affect the choice of Senser or Phenomenon as Subject. Passive voice also allows us to omit participants that would be stated in the active voice; for example, Actor in material processes; Senser in mental processes.

Circumstances are typically Adjuncts, but not all Adjuncts are Circumstances. For example, in passive voice material processes, Actor may conflate with Adjunct. In some instances, the distinction between participant types is very subtle, one notable case being Goal versus Scope, and another the participants in relational processes. Also there are some overlaps: in particular, behavioural process overlaps considerably with other processes. Scope, Phenomenon, Verbiage and Behaviour are all types of Range.

The notion of grammatical metaphor attempts to explain some apparent anomalies in the area of process and participant analysis and can be extended to the logical and interpersonal metafunctions. Grammatically metaphorical forms are contrasted with congruent forms, which are closer to the typical modes of expression. For example, process is more congruently realized by verbs than by nouns.

Further study

The classic work on the topic of this chapter is Halliday's 'Notes on transitivity and theme in English' (1967, 1968). It is interesting to compare Halliday's account with that of Fillmore (1968), which has striking similarities although it emerges from a very different linguistic tradition. Fillmore's account treats as a single phenomenon the two perspectives separated out by Halliday as *transitivity* and *ergativity* and deals with data from a wide range of languages. A later, major treatment of these and related issues can be found in Halliday and Matthiessen (1999). Some additional participant roles are posited in that volume and in IFG Chapter 5; see also Martin *et al.* (1997: Section 4.2.2) for *Assigner, Inducer* and *Attributor.* The latter is particularly good in providing probes for distinguishing the processes.

IFG Chapter 5 also includes an extensive account of the Circumstance function, which we have treated in a cursory manner. Occasionally, a material process clause may be better described as 'happening' rather than 'doing'. For example, we analyze *Shakespeare died in 1616* as material Process with *Shakespeare* as Actor, but arguably this is not so much an action which Shakespeare carried out as something which happened in which he was the key player. IFG and Halliday and Matthiessen (1999) analyze such structures as material, but add 'another interpretation' of transitivity and voice: the 'ergative interpretation' (IFG Section 5.8), which explains the semantics of the clause in terms of causative relations. Here the problem of processes like dying is addressed – the grammatical problem, that is!

Both these books also deal with another way of looking at relational process involving the participants Token and Value. See also Thompson (2004).

Simon-Vandenbergen *et al.* (2003) is a collection of papers on grammatical metaphor by SFL linguists. Grammatical metaphor in general and nominalization in particular are dealt with in Martin's chapter in Halliday and Martin (1993) 'Life as a noun: arresting the universe in science and humanities', part of which also appears under the title 'Nominalization in science and humanities' in Ventola (1991). Halliday and Matthiessen (1999, p. 273ff.) discuss and develop Lakoff's (1992) demonstration of how metaphor is used to manipulate public opinion in time of war. Applying the notion of grammatical metaphor, they unpack a military text, showing that it avoids mentioning human participants and represents the business of killing people in terms of impersonal abstractions.

Exercises

Exercise 6.1

The following are all material processes. Label the process (Process: material) and label participants as Actor, Goal, Scope (one only), Initiator (one only) or Beneficiary.

1. Neurotoxins will kill the insects.
2. You can write him a note.
3. Sufficient water should be added.
4. Standing crops can be trampled by wild animals.
5. Dylan sang a few of his classic numbers.
6. They might swim the pack-horses across the river.
7. Someone had found the fugitives a suitable hiding-place.
8. The prisoners were given small concessions.

Exercise 6.2

The following are all mental processes. Label the process (Process: mental) and label the participants as Senser and Phenomenon.

1. He saw the whole room.
2. Perceptual relationships were seen correctly.
3. I loved her in the springtime.
4. They were also noticed by the researcher.
5. Must we envisage the question in a purely intellectual sense?
6. Considerable discomfort may be experienced.
7. Does this explanation convince anyone?
8. The next report fascinated all of us.

Exercise 6.3

For each of the following: (a) identify the type of process as Process: material, Process: mental, or Process: relational; (b) identify the Subject and assign its participant label.

1. The transoms are carved from massive cypress blocks.
2. The patient experienced the usual side-effects.
3. Hormones can be injected into animals.
4. Mary had a little lamb.
5. The castle was built in 1603.
6. This was definitely bad news.
7. I want results.
8. Chemicals are spread on the land.
9. He absolutely hated the large formal dinners.
10. Why was he so anxious?
11. Herbivores can digest fibres.
12. People didn't like it.
13. Such a man would see enemies everywhere.
14. One of the witnesses before the committee was Nobel-winning economist Paul Samuelson.
15. I eventually fascinated reporters.
16. Hunt became a special projects man.
17. They could be rotated independently.
18. Not a sound was heard.
19. The only important risk is the moral one.
20. I remember the humorous aftermath of our first formal state banquet.

Exercise 6.4

(a) Analyze the following examples of verbal processes, labelling the process and participants (Sayer; Quoted; Reported; Verbiage; Receiver).
(b) Rewrite example (1) as direct speech and label your rewrite as in (a).
(c) Rewrite example (2) as reported (indirect) speech and label as in (a). Do not analyze the quoted or reported clauses.

1. He asked me if the money was traceable.
2. Dean said, 'That's the good news.'
3. Then he said, 'Can we meet again soon?'
4. Someone suggested we should do it differently.
5. The informants told the police everything.

Exercise 6.5

Some of the following are existential processes; some are not. Identify the existential processes. Identify the Existent in each.

1. There was little understanding of acoustics.
2. On either side of this structure are beige curtains.
3. There they heard further stories.
4. There is no ventilation.
5. There will not be many traitors.
6. There we come to a new dilemma.

Exercise 6.6

Explain the following old joke in terms of process and participant.

Comedian A: My dog's got no nose.
Comedian B: Your dog's got no nose? How does he smell?
Comedian A: Terrible.

Exercise 6.7

Open-ended question. Suggest a more congruent way of expressing the following examples:

1. ... her announcement that her husband's spirit had contacted her ...
2. ... a decision years ago that no patent for such a device would be considered ...
3. ... the possibility of the publication of a similar book ...
4. Our interest in crystals is understandable.
5. The reason a keel boat will lean much more easily is that she presents no resistance in the shape of a hard bilge.
6. The success of the *I-Ching* lies largely in its rather flattering and generally non-threatening messages.
7. The search for the elusive substance has led to the discovery of several processes of merit.
8. A better crumb structure gives the soil more stability.

Exercise 6.8

Open-ended question. Consider the following two sentences, one of which actually occurred in a popular science book, and one of which is our rewritten version.

(1) The higher the melting point of a substance, the higher the boiling point.

(2) If a substance melts at a high temperature, it will boil at a high temperature.

(a) Which one seems to you the more congruent form?

(b) Which one do you think is the original? Why?

Exercise 6.9

Consider the following sentence, which could be seen as a grammatical metaphor (experiential). What kind of process does it seem to be at first sight? How might it be expressed more congruently? What would the process be on this reading?

1. India has many such dams.

Notes

1.   Hammett, Dashiel 1975: *Red Harvest*. (Originally published by Cassell and Co., 1950). London: Pan Books.

2.   Gamow, G. 1947: *One, Two, Three ... Infinity*, New York: Mentor Books.

7

Structure of the nominal group

7.1 *Head and Modifier revisited*

In Chapter 2, we looked briefly at the make-up of groups. To recapitulate with new examples, let us begin by looking at (1).

(1)   Electricity is supplied to most homes through an underground cable.

The first nominal group here is *electricity*. It is made up of a single word, a noun. The noun stands alone without modification of any kind, and so we have a nominal group consisting of only a Head. This is the simplest kind of nominal group.

The second nominal group, *most homes*, is only slightly more complicated, with a Head, *homes*, and a Modifier *most*. Since the Modifier comes before the Head, we can call it a *Premodifier*.

The third, *an underground cable*, also has a Head, *cable*, and is premodified, this time by the determiner *an* and the noun *underground*.

Modification does not always precede the Head, however. Consider the first nominal group in (2):

(2)   In houses thirty or more years old it is still possible to find two or more fuse boxes.

The nominal group *houses thirty or more years old* has *houses* as Head and *thirty or more years old* as Modifier. Since the Modifier follows the Head this time, we can label it *Postmodifier*.

Take another example:

(3)   In modern homes the mains switch and the fuses are contained in a box called a consumer unit.

You will perhaps have identified the nominal groups here as *modern homes*, *the mains switch*, *the fuses* and *a box called a consumer unit*. The Heads are respectively *homes*, *switch*, *fuses* and *box*. The Modifiers are, in order of occurrence: *modern*, *the*, *the mains* and *called a consumer unit*, the last being a Postmodifier. More on this last structure is in Chapter 8.

The function of Modifier can be realized by various word classes, most frequently by determiners, numerals and adjectives as Premodifier. In (4) with the nominal group *these two unusual botanical specimens*, we have a determiner followed by a numeral followed by two adjectives all serving to modify the Head, which is realized by the noun *specimens*.

(4)   These two unusual botanical specimens proved invaluable.

In (5) we find a prepositional phrase, *from lower socioeconomic classes*, as Modifier of the Head *people*, this time a Postmodifier.

(5)   Poor health is more common in people from lower socioeconomic classes.

As we can see from the examples already given, however, the function of Modifier can often be realized by a noun (*fuse* in *fuse boxes*, and *mains* in *mains switch*). Common examples of noun as Modifier are found in such everyday expressions as: *art gallery, biology book, football field, history lesson, telephone number*; but they seem to be particularly characteristic of scientific and technical terminology: *accelerator pedal, animal husbandry, claw hammer, data base, socket outlet.*

Since no mad dictator has turned up to ban them (see Chapter 2), the field of mechanical engineering is especially rich in expressions of this kind. In a car manual or a website for vehicle maintenance, we frequently meet samples of three-word or four-word combinations: *the distributor drive shaft, the crownwheel centre line, the distributor clamp plate, the cylinder head bolts, stub axle bearings*, as well as the occasional four-item term (not counting the determiner), such as *the scuttle panel grille sealing*, and occasionally even longer items like *the timing chain tensioner cylinder retaining bolts.*

The problem of deciding what exactly constitutes a word creeps in at this point. The terms just listed are the names of specific identifiable items in a car engine. One might argue that these are, in effect, unanalyzable terms like *wheel* or *brake*; it just happens that in English we write them as separate words. In the text where we found these terms, *crownwheel* is written as one word though it clearly combines the two elements *crown* and *wheel*. This might have been written as two words just as, in the same text, *clamp plate* or *drive shaft* are. Obviously, it is sometimes difficult to draw a hard and fast line between words and groups of more than one word. This difficulty is reflected in the uncertainty in written English about whether to write *word processor, word-processor* or *wordprocessor*; *ball game, ball-game* or *ballgame*; and so on. We shall not pursue this particular conundrum, but, as far as convenient, we shall continue to treat items as words on the basis of whether or not they are written as separate items.

The scope of these modifiers is not always predictable from their form. We often have to fall back on specialist knowledge to interpret the items. Is *the cylinder head gasket*, for example, *the gasket* relating to *the cylinder head* or *the head gasket* relating to the *cylinder?* Or doesn't that distinction mean anything? Without some knowledge of internal combustion engines, we might be at a loss for answers, though a thoughtful examination of the rest of the text in which the nominal group occurs usually helps. In fact, in this case, it is the first interpretation that is right, and, once you are aware of that, you can see that there is a hierarchical relationship in which *cylinder* modifies *head* and *cylinder head* modifies *gasket.*

7.2   *Logical and experiential metafunctions*

In the nominal group *these two new light switches*, the items *these, two, new* and *light* are all classed as Modifiers in relation to the Head *switches*, and are to that extent functionally similar. However, you can probably see that, from other points of view, we need to treat them as significantly different from each other. One way in which they differ is in the sorts of things they say about the switches; or, that is, in their *experiential* roles.

We can divide the ideational metafunction into two: *logical* and *experiential*. IFG describes logical and experiential as *sub-functions* or *modes* of the ideational metafunction (see our Section 1.7.3) but here, for convenience, we call them *metafunctions.* Head and Modifier fall within the logical metafunction, concerning dependency relations, but we continue this chapter by considering the nominal group in terms of the experiential metafunction.

7.2.1   Deictic

The function of the word *these* is, in a manner of speaking, to point out, and the label we give to such items is *Deictic*, a term derived from the Greek for *pointing.* In nominal groups, the Deictic function is realized by determiners: for example, demonstratives *this, that, these* and *those*, and also the article *the*, which Halliday identifies as a weak form of demonstrative. In such cases the function is fairly literally one of 'pointing', but, as always with technical terms of this kind, you should not take the label too literally. Deictics can also be possessive nouns or pronouns: for example, *Sony's* in *Sony's latest model; your* in *your home.* Further, they can be non-specific items such as the indefinite article *a/an, some, each, every, neither, both, all.*

7.2.2   Numerative

The item *two* is a Numerative. Numeratives can be realized by numerals such as *two* or *second* (in *the second switch*) or by such expressions as *many, several, few,* and *lots of.* In Example (2), the electricity manual data discussed above, we have *two or more fuse boxes,* where *two or more* functions as Numerative.

7.2.3   Classifier and Epithet

The items *new* and *light* (in *these two new light switches*) realize two other functions: *Epithet* and *Classifier.* The function of a Classifier is to put the modified item into a subclass of such items: for example, in *bus station* the Classifier *bus* puts the item *station* in a subclass of stations, distinguishing it from *train station* (or *railway station*), or more broadly from such things as *petrol station* (or *gas station*); *supply* in *supply cable* distinguishes the type of cable from other types, and the same is true of *fuse* in *fuse box.* These are Classifiers. Hence, in *these two new light switches*, we can label *light* as Classifier. (Note: this is not the adjective *light* relating to weight, colour or brightness as in *a light load* or *a light colour* but the noun *light*.)

When you speak of *a noisy station, a new cable* or *the wrong box*, the items *noisy, new* and *wrong*, though they may help to define the scope of the terms *station, cable* and *box* respectively, do not identify a subcategory of stations, cables or boxes in the same sense that *railway* or *supply* or *fuse* do. The Classifier identifies a subclass: *bus* in *a bus station* pinpoints something that is distinctive and classificatory. *Noisy* or *new* indicate features or characteristics of the station that do not put it into a subset of types of station; they just tell us something about the characteristics of this particular station. Hence our decision to find a different label, and the label used is Epithet. Thus, *new* in *these two new light switches* is Epithet.

Out of context, many expressions are ambiguous with regard to this functional distinction between Classifier and Epithet. Take the nominal group *some dancing girls*, for example. This string of words can be used to refer to some girls who earn their living by dancing (*dancing* as Classifier) or some girls who happen to be in the process of dancing (*dancing* as Epithet). In the motor-vehicle maintenance text already referred to, we find such terms as *retaining bolts*, which are grammatically comparable to the first sense of *dancing girls*, but not the second. Here *retaining* realizes the function Classifier; retaining bolts are bolts which have the permanent task of retaining, that is, holding something in place. Compare from the same source: *blanking pieces, cooling system, connecting rod, locking disc, steering axis.*

An example from a less specialized register is the well-known 'ambiguous' nominal group, *a Spanish teacher.* Where this means a teacher who has Spanish nationality, *Spanish* is Epithet; but where it means a teacher of Spanish, *Spanish* is Classifier. In the first sense, we are speaking about a teacher who has the characteristic or quality of being Spanish; in the second, we refer to a teacher belonging to a subclass of teachers, namely teachers of Spanish (language), as distinct from science teachers, mathematics teachers, and so on. Thus it is not illogical to talk about *a German Spanish teacher,* where German is Epithet and *Spanish* is Classifier. Of course, when such 'ambiguous' expressions occur in real utterances, there is rarely any confusion about meaning. The context usually provides sufficient information to make it clear what is intended. Furthermore, in spoken English, the distinction between Epithet and Classifier is often reflected by differences in stress and intonation. With neutral emphasis, (*Classifier*) **danc**ing girls has similar stress to **butter**cup; (*Epithet*) dancing **girls** is more like *yellow rose*.

Incidentally, there is a further grammatical distinction between the two meanings of the word *Spanish* in these two different uses. In the Epithet instance, *Spanish* is an adjective; in the Classifier instance, *Spanish* is a noun (the name of the language). As we have already said, however, the adjective versus noun distinction does not necessarily correspond to that of Epithet versus Classifier. Indeed, in our previous example *some dancing girls*, the item *dancing* is a form of verb in both the Classifier and the Epithet uses though it is arguably more nominal as a classifier than as an epithet. Adjectives can certainly function as Classifiers: *electric* in *electric light, electric cable, electric shock*, for example; or *fast* in *fast food*.

In so far as there is a simple criterion for distinguishing Epithet from Classifier, it is that the structure with Epithet can normally be paraphrased in a clause with *be*, for example, *the switches are new*, whereas the Classifier cannot – *the switches are light* has no connection with light switches in this sense. *The teacher is Spanish* can only apply to the Epithet reading of *the Spanish teacher* and not to the Classifier interpretation (compare: **the teacher is chemistry*). As is often the case, though, the test is not absolutely watertight.

7.2.4   Thing

In *these two new light switches*, the main item with regard to the experiential metafunction is *switches*. This rejoices in the undistinguished name of *Thing*. This is the experiential label that SFG assigns, and the usual warning applies against taking technical terms too literally. In this sense, Thing may be a material inanimate thing, an animal, a person, a substance or even an abstract concept. It is simply the name given to one of the six possible functions in the experiential structure of the nominal group. It specifies the class of the item referred to. As we have said, Classifier specifies the subclass, and this is why it is sometimes difficult to say whether certain combinations should be treated as one word or two; for example, *word processor*: Classifier + Thing, or *wordprocessor*: Thing. We apply the label Thing not only to the inanimate noun *cable* in *supply cable*, but equally to the animate *girls* in *some dancing girls* or *teacher* in *a Spanish teacher*, as well as the abstract noun *wizardry* in *statistical wizardry* or *beliefs* in *eighth-century religious beliefs*.

7.2.5   Qualifier

The sixth function in the nominal group is *Qualifier*. This is the experiential label for the Postmodifier in, for example, *the electrical resistance of the insulation*, where *resistance* is Thing, and *of the insulation* is Qualifier. We can say that Qualifier conflates with Postmodifier.

Very frequently in English, the Qualifier function is realized as a prepositional phrase (as in all but one of the Qualifiers in Fig. 7.1). In *The Wind in the Willows*, the Thing is *Wind* and the Qualifier is *in the Willows*; in *the square on the hypotenuse*, the Thing is *square* and *on the hypotenuse* is Qualifier. Further examples of nominal groups containing prepositional phrases as Qualifiers are as follows (the Thing is printed in bold and the Qualifier is in italics): a **fire** *with an under-floor air supply*, the **packing** *between the hearth and the surround*, a **light** *over the front door*.

By far the most frequent preposition in Qualifiers is *of*. For example: the centre **line** *of the crownwheel*, **adjustment** *of the bearings*, **rotation** *of the differential*, an **area** *of up to 20 square metres*, the most economical **use** *of cable*. This structure is by no means restricted to technical texts, as witness: a **bill** *of sale*, the probable **owner** *of the car*, the **capital** *of Romania*, the **price** *of coal*.

Fig. 7.1 represents a number of nominal groups analyzed for logical and experiential functions.

Premodifier				Head	Postmodifier
Deictic	Numerative	Epithet	Classifier	Thing	Qualifier
these	two	new	light	switches	
the	two		domestic	flights	available
the	many	large	oil	companies	in operation
	several	dirty		ones	
the		complete		dismantling	of the gearbox
the			keyboard	layouts	
a		careful		study	of this matter
an		effective	prediction	scheme	

Fig. 7.1

Prepositional phrases in nominal groups are an instance of *embedding*, where one structure is, as it were, enclosed in another; in this instance the embedded element is the prepositional phrase. (In Chapter 8, we look at another form of embedding within the nominal group, namely, that of the clause.)

7.3 *Postmodifier/Qualifier versus Adjunct*

A prepositional phrase has two major roles: as Postmodifier/Qualifier in a nominal group and as Adjunct in a clause. In example (6) the prepositional phrase with *for* is a Postmodifier; in example (7) the prepositional phrase with *for* is an Adjunct.

  (6)   Nearby is Chendor Beach, a popular nesting ground *for the giant leatherback turtles.*
  (7)   [...] a section of the road is closed from 7.00 p.m. to midnight *for the Saturday Night Market.*

In (6) the nominal group *a popular nesting ground for the giant leatherback turtles* is in apposition to the proper noun *Chendor Beach*. The ideational make-up is in Fig. 7.2.

a	popular	nesting	ground	for the giant leatherback turtles
Deictic	**Epithet**	**Classifier**	**Thing**	**Qualifier**
Premodifier			**Head**	**Postmodifier**

Fig. 7.2

However, in (7) the prepositional phrase is operating at a different rank. Instead of being an embedded element in a nominal group, it realizes a function at the rank of clause, namely Adjunct. It provides information about the Circumstance of the Process. It does not postmodify *midnight*.

In (7) we have further examples of prepositional phrases both as Postmodifier (*of the road*) and as Adjunct (*from 7.00 p.m. to midnight*).

A crude probe for distinguishing between Adjunct and Postmodifier depends on the fact that usually the Adjunct can readily be moved whereas the Postmodifier cannot. Hence, (6a) is not a possible paraphrase of (6) but (7a) is a paraphrase of (7).

  (6a)   *For the giant leatherbacked turtles* nearby is Chendor Beach, a popular nesting ground.
  (7a)   *For the Saturday Night Market*, a section of the road is closed from 7.00 p.m. to midnight.

Sometimes ambiguities can arise as a result of these two potential functions for the prepositional phrase. Indeed, this type of ambiguity has been a favoured example for those grammarians who are preoccupied with such matters. Examples like (8) (an invented example) are often adduced to illustrate this point.

(8)   Michael reads books on trains.

On one interpretation, we have as Complement of the clause a nominal group *books on trains*, where *books* is Head and *on trains* is Postmodifier (paraphrasable as *books about trains*). On the other interpretation, we have as Complement a nominal group consisting of an unmodified Head *books* and a Circumstantial Adjunct *on trains*, which tells us where Michael does his reading. We can represent this as in Fig. 7.3.

Michael	reads	books on trains.
		Head + Postmodifier
S	F/P	C

Michael	reads	books	on trains.
S	F/P	C	A

Fig. 7.3

Sometimes this structural ambiguity exists but without any significant pragmatic effect.

(9)   Malaysia Airlines (MAS), the national carrier, operates an extensive network of domestic routes within the country.

Whether we interpret *within the country* as Postmodifier of *routes* or as a circumstantial Adjunct telling us where MAS operates its routes has no significant effect on our understanding of the situation.

7.4   *Embedding*

We have said that a prepositional phrase is composed of a prepositional group and a nominal group. The prepositional group is usually a simple preposition, that is to say an unmodified Head (*in, on, of,* etc.), though it can be modified (*right in,* etc.). With maximal information, the nominal group *the square on the hypotenuse* can be represented in tree diagram form as in Fig. 7.4.

Often a prepositional phrase postmodifying a Head noun in a nominal group contains within itself another prepositional phrase postmodifying a Head noun, as in *the solution to the problem of inflation*. This is a nominal group with the noun *solution* as Head. The Postmodifier is the prepositional phrase *to the problem of inflation*. The preposition here is *to* and the nominal group is *the problem of inflation*. But this nominal group (*the problem of*

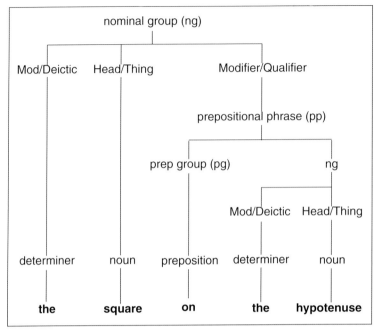

Fig. 7.4

inflation) is also analyzable in the same terms: the Head is the noun *problem* and the Postmodifier is the prepositional phrase *of inflation*. This prepositional phrase can in turn be analyzed into preposition *of* and nominal group *inflation*. Represented as a tree diagram (omitting the experiential functions), this gives Fig. 7.5.

Sometimes the embedding goes beyond the two levels seen in the previous example. In (10), there are three stages of embedding.

(10) It proved to be the first of many steps on the road to ruin.

In this example, the Complement of *be* is the nominal group *the first of many steps on the road to ruin*. Using brackets [ ] to show the prepositional phrase boundaries, you can represent the nominal group in question as (10a):

(10a) the first [of many steps [on the road [to ruin]]]

7.5   *Nominal group complexes*

Sometimes two or more groups combine as a single constituent to jointly fulfil a function such as Subject or Complement. We discussed an example of one such structure in Chapter 3, curtailed and renumbered here as (11) with italics added.

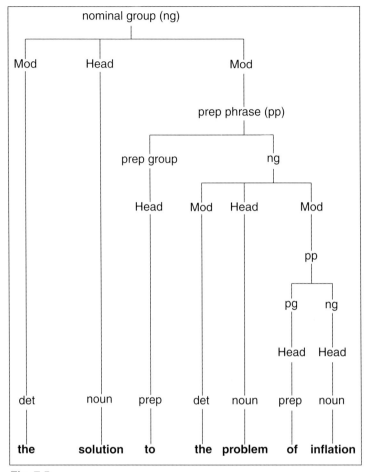

Fig. 7.5

(11) The night before Easter Sunday, 1920, *Otto Loewi, an Austrian physiologist*, awoke in the night [. . .]

At that point we contented ourselves with describing *an Austrian physiologist* as a nominal group in apposition to *Otto Loewi* and pointing out that the whole bundle realized the function of Subject. This implies that these two nominal groups are in some sense a single item, a super-nominal-group, as it were. The term we use for this type of combination is a *nominal group complex*.

A nominal group complex can also be formed by explicitly linking two or more groups together with a binding conjunction (*and*, *or*). Example (12) provides three instances of this.

(12)   For lunch and dinner, plain or specially prepared rice is often eaten with side
       dishes of delicious chicken curry, 'rendang' and a variety of others.

In (12), *lunch and dinner* constitute a nominal group complex in a prepositional phrase as Adjunct; *plain or specially prepared rice* realizes the function
of Subject, and in *delicious chicken curry, 'rendang' and a variety of others*,
three nominal groups make up a group complex in a prepositional phrase.

Group complexes of this kind are described as *paratactic*. Parataxis
involves the linking of equal units and is discussed further in Chapter 9.

In Halliday's model, groups with adjective as Head are classed as nominal
groups; there is no such construct as an adjectival group. Not all Systemic
Functional linguists accept this point, but we are not going to debate it here.
Thus a group complex such as those italicized in (13), and even (14) and (15),
is classed as a nominal group complex. (Of course, in the IFG model, adjectives realizing Modifier are not groups of any kind but only dependent
elements in the nominal group.)

(13)   Such publicity positioned Chang as the surgeon chosen by Australia's *rich-
       est and most famous*.
(14)   My position in this debate is *enthusiastic, cautious and sceptical*.
(15)   Exhortations to the public to avoid heart disease by exercise, avoiding smok-
       ing, and making dietary changes are *banal, dull, often depersonalized, and
       frequently tinged with moralism and puritanism*.

7.6   *Other kinds of group complex*

Although this chapter is about the nominal group, it is worth mentioning
here that complexes exist in groups other than nominal. For example, (16)
contains an adverbial group complex (italics added) realizing the function
of Adjunct.

(16)   The affected eye should be bathed *regularly and carefully*.

Example (17) has a verbal group complex, and (18) prepositional group complexes, both being paratactic.

(17)   He neither *seeks nor assumes* formal leadership.
(18)   *Up and down* the City Road; *In and out of* the Eagle [...]

Prepositional phrases (which you must remember are not classed as groups in
Halliday's model) can also form complexes as in (19).

(19)   He decided that *with no children of his own and with no position on the staff
       of a major hospital* his ideas might not outlive him.

Note that linked nominal groups in a prepositional phrase (i.e., with a single
preposition) are examples of a nominal group complex and not of a

prepositional phrase complex. See, for example, (12) above, which contains two nominal group complexes in prepositional phrases: *for lunch and dinner* and *of delicious chicken curry, 'rendang' and a variety of others*. A preposition which frequently takes a nominal group complex to complete the phrase is *between*: for example, *between you and me, between the devil and the deep blue sea*. It can also take a simple nominal group, of course, for example *between them, between the two extremes*.

Prepositional phrases can be linked with adverbial groups to realize Adjunct as in (20). This is a little embarrassing for us because it shows up an inconsistency in our categories. The two structures have in common the fact that they could each independently realize Adjunct, but this grammar assigns them crucially different labels: group and phrase. There does not appear to be any obvious label for this particular type of complex.

(20) Data are often presented *partially and without proper analysis.*

Summary

In this chapter, we have looked in some detail at the nominal group. After recapitulating the logical structure of the Head-Modifier analysis, we moved on to outline the experiential metafunctions that are realized in the nominal group: Deictic, Numerative, Epithet, Classifier, Thing and Qualifier. Qualifier and Postmodifier conflate; they are frequently realized by a prepositional phrase. A prepositional phrase may have another prepositional phrase embedded within its nominal group (as Postmodifer/Qualifier of the nominal group) and this phenomenon can be repeated with multiple embeddings. Groups can be combined as paratactic group complexes by explicit linking or by apposition.

Further study

Verbal group

In (21) we see a different kind of *verbal group* complex from that in (17). Verbs such as *want, like, begin, continue, pretend* combine with other verbs in what can be analyzed as a single clause. Such a group is *hypotactic* not *paratactic*: see Chapters 9 and 10.

(21) She *began to practise* medicine on her own in a small way.

We return briefly to such structures in Chapter 10.

Thing and Head

IFG (Section 6.2.6) has a detailed discussion of the relation between Thing and Head. Although these two usually conflate, there are exceptions, that is instances where Head is not Thing. The most usual is Epithet as Head in relational clauses like *you're very lucky*. Various experiential functions can conflate with Head in elliptical constructions, for example, Epithet: She took the *yellow* and left the *white*. Numerative: The *second* is more interesting. Deictic: *This* is my story; *This* is my song. However, IFG discusses examples of mismatch between Thing and Head even when Thing is present, in such constructions as *a pack of cards* where *pack* is Thing and *a pack of* is Numerative, but the Head is *cards*; see Fig. 7.6. Why is *pack* analyzed as Head here? It is because it determines the agreement of the verb: *a pack of cards was lying on the table* (singular), and not *a pack of cards were lying on the table* (plural).

a	pack	of	cards
Premodifier	**Head**	**Postmodifier**	
Numerative			**Thing**

Fig. 7.6

IFG (Section 6.2.7) also discusses the logical and experiential structure of the verbal group. In experiential terms, a multi-word verb like *may have been working* contains the functions Finite, Auxiliary 1, Auxiliary 2, and Event. What Thing is to the nominal group, Event is to the verbal group, i.e. the key experiential element. But in terms of the logical metafunction, it is the Finite that is Head or α (alpha) and each of the others is analyzed as dependent on what precedes it: see Fig. 7.7. The dependency moves from left to right.

may	have	been	working
Finite	**Aux 1**	**Aux 2**	**Event**
α	β	γ	δ

Fig. 7.7

In terms of dependency, then, the verbal group operates in the opposite direction from the nominal group, where the Thing tends to be Head or α (alpha) and the dependent item immediately preceding it β (beta), and the one before that γ (gamma), and so on (i.e. from right to left).

a	popular	meeting	ground
δ	γ	β	α

Fig. 7.8

See Chapters 9 and 10 for dependency labelling (of clauses) with Greek letters.

Exercises

Exercise 7.1

Explain potential ambiguities in the following (invented) sentences in terms of Epithet and Classifier.

1. He loved the Japanese teacher.
2. Ingrid is a Swiss German teacher.
3. The road was blocked by working men.

Exercise 7.2

Analyze the italicized nominal groups in the following examples in terms of the experiential functions: Deictic, Numerative, Epithet, Classifier, Thing and Qualifier.

1. *The three red wires* will have been joined in *one terminal*.
2. *Car factories* produce *millions of cheap vehicles*.
3. *Domestic manufacture of goods* underwent *several significant changes*.
4. *Rapid, extensive technical development* replaced *older concerns*.
5. *The disastrous slump* was caused by *three unforeseen factors*.
6. There has been *much economic dislocation*.
7. *The available financial statistics* do not support *the many optimistic claims made*.
8. *The first dam on the Indus* was completed in 1932.
9. *This vast forested river basin* extends over some 700 million hectares.
10. *A broken brake cable* can easily be repaired.

Exercise 7.3

Label the italicized prepositional phrases in the following examples as either Postmodifier in a nominal group or as Adjunct in a clause.

1. Hit the new pin *with a hammer*.
2. Jung also rejected his view *of childhood amnesia*.
3. Kandinsky took great pains to elucidate his artistic system *in theoretical terms*.

4. The genes located along a DNA module are present *at all times*.
5. His approach *to this action* was based on two basic dominant ideas.
6. The downturn was caused by over-investment, the result of imperfections *in the investment process*.
7. They were tired of the woman *with the handbag*.
8. Don't come *between me and my work*.
9. The distinction *between factives and nonfactives* is significant for prediction.
10. You can take a horse *to water*, but you can't make him drink.

Exercise 7.4

Identify the group complexes (and prepositional phrase complexes) in the following and label them according to type (nominal group complex, verbal group complex, etc.)

1. In this sense, there is no past and no future.
2. He failed utterly and completely.
3. This may be a result of low pay or poor working conditions.
4. Low carbohydrate diets and low protein diets are especially detrimental.
5. I neither criticize nor condone this behaviour.
6. Equally exciting is Chinese New Year, a major festival.
7. Attach the frame above and below the aperture.
8. The money went on the payment of debts and as gifts to relatives.
9. It seemed to shrink and grow alternately.
10. I want an answer here and now.

Exercise 7.5

Read the fragment in Text 7A from a do-it-yourself manual and answer the questions which follow it.

Window Choices
Replacement windows and patio doors can be timber (softwood or hardwood), aluminium or plastic (unplasticized polyvinyl chloride – uPVC). All are available made-to-measure to fit exactly into an existing opening, but wooden made-to-measure windows are less easy to come by than aluminium and uPVC ones.

Text 7A   Thomas and Holloway, (*Which? Book of Home Improvements and Extensions*[1]).

(a) List all the nominal groups in the first sentence.
(b) In two places the writer has used brackets to separate a nominal group from another nominal group. How do you analyze the bracketed group in relation to the other one?
(c) Comment in general on the group complexes in the first sentence.
(d) How do you perceive the relation between *unplasticized polyvinyl chloride* and *uPVC*?
(e) In the first sentence of the text, the author introduces the types of materials that can be used for replacement windows and patio doors. Later in the text, he uses the names of these materials as Classifiers. Identify all the Classifiers in the text and indicate which are introduced (as Thing) in the first sentence.
(f) From your reading of Chapter 5 you will know that *ones* (the last word in the text) is a substitution. Comment on the way it functions in this text.

Note

1. Thomas, Jill and Holloway, David (eds) 1983: *Which? Book of Home Improvements and Extensions.* London: Consumers' Association and Hodder & Stoughton.

8

Embedded clauses

8.1 Embedded clause as Postmodifier/Qualifier

In Chapter 7 we looked at some forms of modification of the Head in nominal groups (and, briefly, other groups). In this chapter we consider, among other things, the way in which clauses can fulfil a similar function. In (1), you will find a nominal group *a sealed unit that holds the service fuse*. Here the functions Thing and Head are simultaneously realized by a single noun (in bold print in the example). The Qualifier and Postmodifier functions are simultaneously realized by a clause (in italics).

> (1) The main supply cable goes to a sealed **unit** *that holds the service fuse*.

What we see here, then, is a clause which is functioning as part of a nominal group inside another clause. This is a further example of *embedding* (discussed in Chapter 7 in connection with prepositional phrases). In systemic terminology it is also known as *rankshift* because, in terms of the rank scale (see Chapter 1), an item of one rank (clause) is being used as the whole or part of an item of a lower rank (group). *That holds the service fuse* retains its intrinsic qualities as a clause (with its own SFPCA functions), but it is also a Postmodifier in a nominal group inside another clause.

- We call the clause which is inside another clause the *embedded* (or *rankshifted*) clause.
- We call the clause which contains the embedded clause the *superordinate* clause.

Because, in this particular case, the embedded clause is part of a constituent of another clause, it can be treated (as in Fig. 8.1) as though it were a simple element in that clause without regard to its internal structure.

Ignoring any further subtleties, an analysis of the superordinate clause in terms of SFPCA is shown in Fig. 8.2.

However, because the Adjunct contains a nominal group whose Postmodifier is also a clause, this clause too can be analyzed in terms of the

a	sealed	unit	that holds the service fuse
Deictic	**Epithet**	**Thing**	**Qualifier**
Premodifier		**Head**	**Postmodifier**

Fig. 8.1

The main supply cable	goes	to a sealed unit that holds the service fuse.
S	F/P	A

Fig. 8.2

criteria we have just applied to the superordinate clause. Without regard to the fact that it functions as part of another clause, it can be examined in terms of its own SFPCA structure, or other characteristics, and the groups within it can be analyzed in terms of their own structures.

An analysis of the embedded clause in (1) gives us the labelling in Fig. 8.2a.

[[that	holds	the service fuse]]
[[S	F/P	C]]

Fig. 8.2a

Putting the two together in one diagram, we have Fig. 8.3. (The use of double square brackets [[ ]] enclosing a clause is a convention symbolizing an embedded clause.)

The main supply cable	goes	to a sealed unit	[[that	holds	the service fuse]].
			[[S	F/P	C]]
S	F/P	A			

Fig. 8.3

What we have done here first is analyze the superordinate clause in terms of its functions, represented on the third line of Fig. 8.3. We then shift to a more detailed stage of analysis (second line of the figure) to analyze the rankshifted clause embedded within the nominal group.

Let us now look at another example.

(2)   The circuit should be tested with some device which reliably indicates the presence of mains voltage.

Here, the embedded clause is (2a):

(2a) which reliably indicates the presence of mains voltage

In analyzing for clause structure, example (2), like the first example, needs to be treated as having two depths, as indicated in Fig. 8.4, where the labelling of the superordinate clause is represented on the third and sixth rows and the labelling of the embedded clause is represented on the fifth line of the figure.

The circuit	should	be tested	with some device
S	F	P	A
[[which	reliably	indicates	the presence of mains voltage.]]
[[S	A	F/P	C]]
Adjunct continued			

Fig. 8.4

Analyzed for its experiential and logical structure, the nominal group *some device which reliably indicates the presence of mains voltage* can be represented as in Fig. 8.5. This time we are not considering the internal structure of the embedded clause.

some	device	[[which reliably indicates the presence of mains voltage]]
Deictic	**Thing**	**Qualifier**
Premodifier	**Head**	**Postmodifier**

Fig. 8.5

8.1.1   The defining relative clause

All the embedded clauses discussed so far are known as *defining relative clauses* (also known as *restrictive relative clauses*). Full defining relative clauses contain a *relative pronoun* or *relative adverb*. A relative pronoun may be a Wh-word (*who, whom, which, whose*) or it may be *that*. In some relative clauses, however, the relative pronoun can be omitted entirely, and sometimes other elements are omitted. (A different type of relative clause, called a non-defining – or non-restrictive – relative is discussed in Chapter 9.) The relative adverb *where* is not usually interchangeable with *that* and is not omitted, but the relative adverb *when* sometimes is.

Two significant considerations in the grammar of relative clauses are: the grammatical function of the group in which the clause is embedded; and the grammatical function of the relative pronoun inside the embedded clause itself.

In English, any common noun, and some pronouns, can be modified by a defining relative clause. The nominal group which contains the relative clause may realize any function normally open to nominal groups: for example, it may be Subject, direct object Complement, intensive Complement, part of an Adjunct or part of a prepositional phrase functioning as Modifier in a nominal group. In (3), (4), (5) and (6), the nominal group containing the relative clause is italicized and its grammatical function given in parentheses; the relative clause itself is enclosed in double brackets.

(3) *Any circuit* [[*that is to be worked on*]] must be dead. (Subject)
(4) Soil variations greatly affect *the plants* [[*which can be grown*]]. (Direct object Complement)
(5) The circuit should be tested with *some device* [[*which reliably indicates the presence of mains voltage*]]. (Complement of preposition in an Adjunct)
(6) It's *a job* [[*that can be done all in one go*]]. (Intensive Complement)

More significantly, perhaps, within the relative clause, the relative pronoun can realize any of the functions open to a nominal group. In the previous examples, although the nominal groups containing the relative clause have different functions, the relative pronoun is the Subject of the embedded clause in every example. It does not always have to be so, however.

In (7), (8), (9) and (10) the relative clause is in double brackets and the relative pronoun is in italics; the function in parentheses is that of the relative pronoun **within** the embedded clause:

(7) The men [[*who* founded modern science]] had two merits. (Subject)
(8) Suddenly, the work [[*that* the Greeks had done from pure love of theory]] became the key to warfare and astronomy. (Direct object Complement)
(9) In 1900, de Vries finally brought out the book [[in *which* he put forward his 'mutation theory']]. (Complement of preposition in Adjunct)
(10) It is most passionate in those [[*whose* lives are most exposed to catastrophe]]. (Possessive Premodifier of Head in Subject)

In (10) the nominal group *whose lives* is Subject of the relative clause, but the relative pronoun itself, *whose*, is Modifier, not Head of its group.

This is not the complete range of possible functions for the relative pronoun, but it gives some idea of the possibilities. The relative word itself can function as Adjunct (realized as *where* or *when*). We refer to these as relative adverbs, but they too are sometimes called relative pronouns. In (11) the relative clause is bracketed and the relative italicized.

(11) I remember those first days [[*when* Kissinger was in the White House]].

In a non-relative clause the function of the direct object Complement is usually signalled by its position in the clause. The relative clause in (8) corresponds to the (constructed) nonrelative clause (8a).

(8a) The Greeks had done the work from pure love of theory.

In (8a) the direct object Complement is in its normal place after the Predicator. When this same proposition is expressed as a relative clause, as in the actual example, (8), the relative pronoun *that* comes at the beginning of the clause even though it is the Complement: *that the Greeks had done from pure love of theory*. The requirement for the object Complement to follow the

Predicator is overridden by the requirement that wh-words and *that* come at the beginning of the clause. Of course, there are other reasons why we do not always place the Complement after the Predicator, as we have indicated in the discussion of Theme and Rheme in Chapter 4, and it is arguably for thematic reasons that the relative or interrogative pronoun or adverb always comes first in its clause.

In sentences of this kind, some languages (unlike English) permit a pronoun in the Complement position as well as the relative marker at the beginning. This is why we sometimes find foreign speakers of English saying (or, in this case, more probably writing) such things as (12).

(12)   *The work that the Greeks had done *it* from pure love of theory became the key to warfare and astronomy.

To speakers of such languages, English seems to miss out a crucial element. English teachers who condemn this error as 'illogical' are mistaken. True, there is a kind of logic in the omission, but the inclusion is no less logical. To understand this is not, of course, to recommend the practice.

8.1.2   Contact clauses

Even more tricky for the foreign learner is the relative clause which omits the relative pronoun entirely (but without any further ellipsis). We cannot omit the relative pronouns from (13) and (14).

(13)   The men [[*who* founded modern science]] had two merits [. . .]
(14)   Here they met the woman [[*whose* ideas were to change their lives]].

However, instead of writing (8) (repeated below), the author (Bertrand Russell) could, if he had wished, within the options offered by English grammar, have written (8b).

(8)   Suddenly, the work [[*that* the Greeks had done from pure love of theory]] became the key to warfare and astronomy.
(8b)   Suddenly, the work [[the Greeks had done from pure love of theory]] became the key to warfare and astronomy.

In fact, in (15) (brackets added), the same author did take this zero-pronoun option when he chose to write:

(15)   Socrates was guilty of not worshipping the gods [[the State worshipped]].

Similar examples (brackets added) from our other sources are (16) and (17).

(16)   The nerves [[we have just discussed]] are efferent nerves.
(17)   The sorts of improvements [[you might want to make to an existing system]] include adding sockets, installing fixed equipment and re-organizing lighting.

Here there is no relative pronoun *which* or *that*, but the meaning is the same as if *which* or *that* had been included. Such clauses are often called *contact clauses*. Even in written English contact clauses are not particularly rare, but in spoken English they are much more common than clauses with a relative pronoun. The following example is from a recording of a group discussion in a hospital.

(18) Is there anything else [[you'd like to do]] – before you go on to order any barium investigations?

In the exercises at the end of this chapter, you are asked to think about the *grammatical* limits to the possibility of omitting the relative pronoun.

8.1.3   Relative with preposition

We now return to an example that we discussed earlier, (9), repeated here.

(9) In 1900, de Vries finally brought out the book in which he put forward his 'mutation theory'.

In this example, the relative pronoun *which* is the complement of the preposition *in* in a prepositional phrase functioning as Adjunct. The corresponding nonrelative clause would be: *he put forward his 'mutation theory' in the book*.

In principle, the grammar offers four choices here. Example (9) is the choice that the author made, where the preposition is placed before the relative pronoun. The others, which he did not choose, are as follows.

(9a) In 1900, de Vries finally brought out the book [[*which* he put forward his 'mutation theory' in]].

(9b) In 1900, de Vries finally brought out the book [[*that* he put forward his 'mutation theory' in]].

(9c) In 1900, de Vries finally brought out the book [[he put forward his 'mutation theory' in]].

In fact, it is an over-simplification to suggest that the author had all these possibilities open to him. In practice, the one that he chose is most likely because it is the preferred option for text in a formal register. So, although the grammar contains all these possibilities, stylistic norms tend to determine which one is chosen. All the choices are available to the language user, but statistically there are strong preferences according to the domain.

In another register, for example, in informal spoken text, the push might well be in the direction of one of the other possible forms, for example, in the following utterances (from transcripts of classroom discourse by Sinclair and Coulthard, 1975, pp. 67, 71).

(19) Can you think of anything [[that they would be put on]]?

(20) [...] further along up the road [[you're driving on]] there are some workmen.

This time, stylistic norms push the teacher who made these utterances away from the formal options (*on which they would be put* and *on which you're driving*) towards the less formal choices. (This happens even though classroom discourse is far from being the most informal of registers.) In fact, the most significant stylistic choice here is between the preposition occurring at the beginning and the preposition occurring at the end. The difference between keeping and omitting the relative pronoun is less striking, and both occur in this discourse.

It must be borne in mind that the criteria for stylistic choices are subtle and that crude generalizations are dangerous. There may be good reasons why in specific instances the chosen form might not correspond with the spoken/written, formal/informal dichotomy suggested here. For example, in casual conversation the more formal option may be selected for humorous effect. Also, there are constructions which militate against putting the preposition first even in formal registers; hence, the well-known story that, when reprimanded for ending his written sentences with prepositions, Churchill (or some other wit) satirically replied: 'This is the kind of pedantry *up with which I will not put. . .*'. There is, of course, no basis for the prescriptive view that 'fronted' prepositions are preferable in all circumstances. In fact, 'with which I will not put up' would avoid the final preposition shibboleth with less comic effect since *up* is not a preposition here but an adverb particle, but the sort of pedant who insists on this so-called 'rule' is not likely to appreciate the difference, and anyway the satire on misguided pedantry is justified.

When we speak of the omission of the relative pronoun or 'fronting' of prepositions, these are only convenient metaphors to facilitate discussion of varying but related structures. Some linguists have suggested in the past that relative structures without relative pronouns are best explained as structures resulting from so-called 'deletion transformations' operating on underlying forms which do contain nominals (see the discussion of Chomsky in Chapter 12); this seems to give a sort of precedence to the so-called full relative form. Similarly, the alternation between a preposition at the front or at the end of the clause can be described as a movement from one position to the other. Although in this book we use such terms as 'omission' and 'fronted', the terms are used loosely and metaphorically and there is no suggestion intended of any such transformational account. In SFG, the various structures discussed are seen rather as the outcome of differing paradigmatic choices.

8.1.4   Non-finite relative clauses

In the previous chapter, we considered an example which we renumber here as (21).

(21) In modern homes the mains switch and the fuses are contained in a box called a consumer unit.

The nominal group *a box called a consumer unit* can be analyzed as in Fig. 8.6. In discussing this earlier, we avoided discussing one way in which it differs from the other examples we were considering. This difference centres on the fact that the Postmodifier/Qualifier *called a consumer unit* is itself a clause, for, although it lacks the functions Subject and Finite, it does contain a Predicator (realized by the non-finite verbal group *called*) and a Complement (realized by the nominal group *a consumer unit*). This is represented in Fig. 8.7.

a	box	[[called a consumer unit]]
Deictic	**Thing**	**Qualifier**
Premodifier	**Head**	**Postmodifier**

Fig. 8.6

In modern homes	the mains switch and the fuses	are	contained	in a box	[[called	a consumer unit.]]
					[[P	**C]]**
A	**S**	**F**	**P**	**A**		

Fig. 8.7

The term *reduced relative* is widely used for such structures, that is for non-finite clauses which have the same function as 'full' relative clauses. Note that this is not the same as a contact clause, where only the relative pronoun is omitted. Examples (22) to (26) are further illustrations of non-finite relatives. As before, the nominal group containing the relative clause is in italics and the relative clause is enclosed in double brackets.

(22) Hot water taps draw their water from *a pipe* [[*connected to the top of the hot water cylinder*]].
(23) *Most of the arguments* [[*presented in favour of this position*]] had little impact [. . .].
(24) *All pipes* [[*drawing water from a cold water cistern*]] should be fitted with a stop valve.
(25) Take off *the circlip* [[*holding the shaft control lever*]].
(26) [. . .] fit a new oil seal into *the clutch housing* [[*protecting the oil seal lip*]].

In these examples, then, the italicized structures have no Subject or Finite but they are clauses nevertheless: non-finite clauses. There is an obvious systematic relationship here to clauses with a relative pronoun as Subject and a Finite *be*. Try inserting *that is/are/was/were* at the start of each of the five relative clauses above. In some cases, you find a neat fit, and in others the result is a little clumsy; but roughly speaking there is a correspondence. It works better with the first two than with the rest.

Analyzed in SFPCA terms, these clauses, lacking S and F, are *moodless*, but they all have Predicators, three have Adjuncts and two have Complements. Since the missing Subject would be the relative pronoun in a corresponding full relative clause, obviously there is no relative pronoun present. Otherwise, they are just like 'full' relative clauses and, as with full relatives, they function as Postmodifiers in nominal groups.

8.2   *Multiple embedding of clauses*

In Chapter 7 we saw how prepositional phrases can repeatedly recur one within another. This is the phenomenon of *recursion* in grammar. The examples we analyzed there were of nominal group within prepositional phrase within nominal group. When this recurs repeatedly, we have *multiple embedding*.

Repeated recursion can also happen with relative clauses, and, as with prepositional phrases, the repetition may go on indefinitely, though in naturally occurring, unselfconscious text, it is fairly limited. Example (27) has two stages of embedded clause, a relative clause within a relative clause.

(27) This is the malt that lay in the house that Jack built.

In (27) everything after the word *is* realizes the Complement, but this contains an embedded clause modifying the Head noun *malt,* and this in turn contains a nominal group containing a further *embedded* clause modifying *house.* This gives us the bracketing in (27a) or, with SFPCA labels, Fig. 8.8. The nominal groups containing embedding are: *the house that Jack built* and *the malt that lay in the house that Jack built.*

(27a) This is the malt [[that lay in the house [[that Jack built]]]].

This	is	the malt	[[that	lay	in the house	[[that	Jack	built.]]]]
						[[C	S	F/P]]
			[[S	F/P		A		]]
S	F				C			

Fig. 8.8

Another structure with more than one embedded clause is one where two or more linked clauses are embedded. The first example below, (28), contains two linked 'full' relative clauses; the second, (29), contains two linked moodless clauses ('reduced' relatives). (Italics and brackets have been added. The symbol ‖ indicates a boundary between two clauses without embedding, discussed in Chapter 9).

(28) This presents Plato's ideal of *a man [[who is both wise and good in the highest degree ‖ and who is totally without fear of death]]*.

(29) *A radial circuit [[run in 2.5mm² cable ‖ and protected by a 20A fuse]]* can supply an area of up to 20 square metres.

Sometimes, we find two linked relative clauses with only one relative pronoun, as in (30).

(30) but *cables [[that run through insulation ‖ or run next to one another for a considerable distance]]* should be bigger.

Occasionally, we find complicated combinations of linking and embedding as in (31).

(31) A technological leader has to engage in expensive research and development activities which may lead nowhere, or which may lead to new inventions which have to be protected through patents [. . .]

Here we have two relative clauses linked by *or*:

(i) *which may lead nowhere*
(ii) *which may lead to new inventions which have to be protected through patents*

Within the second clause is a further embedding:

(iii) *which have to be protected through patents.*

Clauses (i) and (ii) jointly postmodify the Head *activities*, and clause (iii) postmodifies *inventions*. The embedding here can be represented by bracketing as in (31a).

(31a) expensive research and development activities [[which may lead nowhere ‖ or which may lead to new inventions [[which have to be protected through patents]]]]. . . .

Children's games and folk literature often exploit such characteristics of the language, pushing structures beyond normal limits. This happens in the folk poem 'This is the house that Jack built', cited above, where each successive step builds on the previous one by converting part of the previous utterance into a relative clause postmodifying a new Head:

This is the house that Jack built. (1 embedded clause)
This is the malt that lay in the house that Jack built. (2 embeddings)
This is the rat that ate the malt that lay in the house that Jack built. (3 embeddings)
This is the cat that killed the rat that ate the malt that lay in the house that Jack built (4 embeddings)
and so on . . . and on . . . and on.

8.3   *Embedded clause as Subject or Complement*

The examples of embedding that we have looked at so far are clauses as Postmodifiers in a nominal group. It is also possible for an embedded clause to function as the whole of the Subject. You can see two parallel examples in 32.

(32) [...] what is beautiful is also, in some respects, ugly; what is just is, in some respects, unjust.

Before we get down to the embedded element, we can identify in each of the two superordinate clauses a fairly straightforward relational clause on the relational pattern *X is Y* plus one or two Adjuncts:

(i)   [something] is [...] ugly;
(ii) [something] is [...] unjust.

In a different text, the constituents here represented as [*something*] might be realized by such nominal groups as, for example, *the picture* and *this law*. This suggests that whatever fills that slot has much in common with a nominal group since it fulfils one of the potentials of a nominal group: that of realizing the Subject function. In each of these two parallel clauses, however, this Subject is itself a clause with a full clause structure. Thus the analysis is as in Fig. 8.9. (Double vertical lines ‖ indicate a clause boundary without rankshift.)

[[what	is	beautiful]]	is	also	in some respects	ugly; ‖
[[S	F	C]]				
S			F	A	A	C
[[what	is	just]]	is	in some respects		unjust.
[[S	F	C]]				
S			F	A		C

Fig. 8.9

Once again, we have analyzed the superordinate clause (represented in Fig. 8.9 two lines below the text), and then, at a greater degree of delicacy, we have broken down the Subject into its own clause structure (represented as the line immediately below the text). Apart from the additional Adjunct (*also*) in the first, the two have identical structure: in both, the embedded clause is the Subject of the superordinate clause; in both embedded clauses, the Subject is the pronoun *what* (meaning *that which*).

Another example of an embedded clause as Subject is (33), analyzed in Fig. 8.10.

(33) That Aristotle appealed to such principles is not surprising.

[[That	Aristotle	appealed	to such principles]]		is	not surprising.
[[	S	F/P	A	]]		
S					F	A C

Fig. 8.10

The word *that* looks at first glance as if it might be the relative pronoun that we find in a sentence analyzed earlier as (1), repeated here.

(1)   The main supply cable goes to a sealed unit *that* holds the service fuse.

However, a closer examination reveals that, whereas the word *that* in (1) is a crucial part of the embedded clause (the Subject), the item *that* in the 'Aristotle' sentence (33) has no such function. Indeed, it is not part of the SFPCA structure of the clause at all, but rather has a textual function akin to that of a binding conjunction. It signals the rankshifted nature of the clause but is not a participant and has no SFPCA function. In other words, it has no 'content'; it does not refer to any person, thing, or concept; it is not a nominal group or any other kind of group. Some linguists call this second type of *that* a *complementizer*. (It should not be confused with the SFPCA function of Complement.) When *that* is a relative pronoun, it can be paraphrased by *who*, *whom* or *which*; the complementizer *that* has no such correspondence. We return to structures of this kind in Chapter 10.

As well as functioning as Subject, embedded clauses can also function as Complement as in (34), analyzed in Fig. 8.11.

(34) They took what they wanted.

They	took	[[what	they	wanted]].
		[[C	S	F/P]]
S	F/P	C		

Fig. 8.11

8.3.1   Non-finite clauses as Subject or Complement

Just as embedded non-finite clauses can realize the Qualifier/Postmodifier functions, they also realize the Subject or Complement function, as in the following examples. Again, the embedded clauses are presented in double brackets.

(35) [[Cutting plaster]] is not difficult.
(36) You will enjoy [[meeting your fellow members]].
(37) [[To err]] is human; [[to forgive]] divine.

An SFPCA analysis of these three gives us Fig. 8.12.

[[Cutting	plaster]]	is	not	difficult.
[[P	C]]			
S		F	A	C

You	will	enjoy	[[meeting	your fellow members.]]
			[[P	C]]
S	F	P	C	

[[To err]]	is	human;	[[to forgive]]	divine.
[[P]]			[[P]]	
S	F	C	S	C

Fig. 8.12

Example (37), a well-known quotation from the eighteenth-century English poet Alexander Pope, offers two instances of a minimal embedded clause consisting of only a Predicator. The second non-embedded clause *to forgive divine* is unusual in that it possesses a Subject and Complement, but no Finite or Predicator. This is possible because the presence of the preceding clause with its similar structure permits the ellipsis of the Finite in the second clause (see Chapter 5). Traditional grammarians would say that in the second clause *is* is 'understood'. In fact, it is so well understood that the line is often misquoted as: *To err is human; to forgive is divine.*

8.4   *Postposed clause*

The utterance analyzed above as (33), repeated here, originally occurred in a written text, a history of biological scientific discovery.

(33) That Aristotle appealed to such principles is not surprising.

Imagine a scenario where you are engaged in high-flown philosophical chat with a friend; or, if you find that difficult to imagine, pretend that you are participating in a philosophy seminar in which a spontaneous discussion of a paper on Aristotle is taking place. It is possible that you might come up with the utterance (33) as quoted. However, it is more likely that you would say (33a):

(33a) It isn't surprising that Aristotle appealed to such principles.

There is no significant difference in the experiential content of these two utterances, yet stylistically they differ considerably. The first typically belongs to a register at the formal end of the formality cline, whereas the second is nearer the informal end. There are also implications for Theme–Rheme and Given–New assignment (see Chapter 4). What is going on here syntactically?

Instead of being placed in the unmarked position for Subject, the embedded clause *that Aristotle appealed to such principles* is placed at the end, but, because English requires an explicit Subject in full declarative clauses, the so-called 'empty' pronoun *it* stands in, as it were, and holds the fort until the real 'content' of the Subject comes along in the shape of the embedded clause. In Chapter 3, we referred to it as a 'dummy subject', on the grounds that although it functions in some sense as a Subject, it has no content and is merely a grammatical place-holder.

In this, it differs from the personal pronoun *it*, which normally co-refers with some nominal group in the text (providing a cohesive tie) as in (38) and (39), or refers exophorically to some referent outside the text, as in example (40) (italics added).

(38) [...] there is a unity in the world, but *it* is a unity resulting from diversity.
(39) Remove the lower suspension arm hinge pin by withdrawing *it* towards the front of the vehicle.
(40) Is *it* a bird? Is *it* a plane?

In the first two examples, *it* refers to some item mentioned in the text, namely *a unity* and *the lower suspension arm hinge pin*, respectively. In the third, presumably, *it* refers exophorically to some object in the sky, visible to speaker and hearer.

The structure with the 'dummy' *it* in Subject position and the embedded clause placed later is often known as *extraposition*, on the grounds that the embedded clause is 'extra-posed' (literally 'placed outside'). It may also be described as *postposition* on the grounds that it is 'placed after'; and SFL linguists tend to use this term. As we said in Chapter 3, this structure is analyzed as a discontinuous Subject starting with *it* and continuing with the embedded clause. Hence we have the analysis in Fig. 8.13.

It	isn't	surprising	[[that	Aristotle	appealed	to such principles]].
			[[	S	F/P	A]]
S	<F	C>	Subject continued				

Fig. 8.13

Thus, Pope might have written *It is human to err; it is divine to forgive*, though, if anyone had suggested it, as a poet of some distinction, he would no doubt have rejected the idea since it would hardly have met the strict requirements of his metre, and the conciseness and thematic force of the original would have been lost.

As we have already said, we must be wary of crude generalizations about register. It is true that the use of the embedded clause without postposition is more typical of formal written language and the postposed version is more typical of informal spoken language, but these are tendencies and not absolutes. It is perhaps more common to find postposed Subject clauses in formal language than to find the non-postposed form in casual speech. Although it seems grammatically less straightforward than its counterpart, the postposed form is much more frequent in English and is found in a wider range of registers. In the wrong context, the structure without postposition can easily sound stilted. The length of the Subject clause is also a factor: other things being equal, the longer and more complicated the clause, the more likely it is to be postposed.

Non-finite embedded clauses can be postposed as in (41) to (43).

(41) It is difficult to disentangle them.
(42) It is impossible to say how far.
(43) It is important to keep all hose clips tight and occasionally to inspect the hoses.

Example (43) has two linked clauses in the postposition: (i) *to keep all hose clips tight*; (ii) *and occasionally to inspect the hoses*. (See Chapter 9 for further discussion of such structures.)

In spite of their similar appearance, infinitival clauses of this kind should be distinguished from infinitival clauses which have the meaning 'in order to [. . .]', as in (44) (italics added).

(44) Follow the same procedure *to shorten an old chain*.

Clauses of this last type are not postposed continuations of the Subject and so are analyzed quite differently; they are not embedded. We return to this point in Chapter 9, where you will learn to distinguish between embedded and dependent clauses.

8.5   *Other embedded clauses*

Some adjectives systematically permit clause embedding:

ready [[*to die for the cause*]]	*able* [[*to concede a point*]]
quick [[*to reply*]]	*glad* [[*to oblige*]]
eager [[*to help*]]	*happy* [[*to be of service*]]

(Recall that groups with adjectives realizing Head are classed in IFG as nominal groups: see Chapter 7.)

However, embedded clauses do not operate only as part of or in place of nominal groups. They can be placed as Postmodifiers in comparative adverbial groups, such as:

more easily [[*than anyone had imagined*]]
faster [[*than any of his rivals could manage*]]

and also in:

as thoroughly [[*as time permits*]]
as fast [[*as you can*]]

Embedded clauses can also postmodify adverbs and adjectives that are pre-modified by *too* or *so*:

too cleverly [[for anyone to imitate]]   *so soon [[that no one was ready]]*
too hot [[to handle]]   *so clever [[that you hate him]]*
too young [[to really be in love]]   *so sad [[that I cried]]*

Summary

In this chapter we follow up the issue of the structure of the nominal group (and, briefly, of other groups) by examining the phenomenon of embedded clauses. Like the prepositional phrase (see Chapter 7), the embedded clause can function as Qualifier, which usually corresponds to the Postmodifier in Head-Modifier terms. Because an embedded clause is one which is used as a unit of lower rank or as part of such a unit, it may also be referred to as a rankshifted clause.

In the case of defining relative clauses, the embedded clause functions experientially as Qualifier and Postmodifier within a nominal group, and as such can be treated as a simple constituent of the group. However, because it is a clause, it has the elements of clause structure within itself, and can be analyzed as a clause in its own right. The relative words (*that, who/m, which, whose, when*) may be omitted in certain circumstances to give a 'contact clause'. Also, relative clauses may be non-finite (that is, moodless, lacking Subject and Finite), in which case they may be known as 'reduced relatives'.

Multiple embedding (as well as linking) can occur in embedded clauses (as in prepositional phrases) and permutations of embedded prepositional phrases, relative clauses and linking may occur.

Embedded clauses can occur as Subject or Complement; these too can be finite or non-finite. Subject clauses can occur straightforwardly in the normal Subject position or they may be discontinuous with a dummy pronoun *it* holding the usual Subject position and the embedded clause postposed. The choice between these alternatives has implications for thematic meaning and may be influenced by register.

Finally, we list some examples of embedded clauses in adverbial groups and nominal groups with adjective as Head.

Further study

In this chapter, we mentioned 'The house that Jack built'. This is a great favourite not only of countless generations of children but also of introductory linguistics books. It can be used to demonstrate among other things that this potential for recursion is unlimited so long as it is 'right-branching' (the term relates to tree-diagram constituent analysis). That is to say, we can go on adding items at the end. Inserting a clause inside a clause which is inside another clause (known as 'nesting') is more difficult. In (45) from a philosophy journal, three levels of embedding occur but only one is not right-branching: *what is communicated in an utterance*.

(45)   No one disputes that there are various ways in which what is communicated in an utterance can go beyond sentence meaning.

The inserted brackets in (45a) indicate the embedding. We have numbered the pairs of brackets to show which belongs with which.

(45a)   No one disputes [[₁that there are various ways [[₂in which [[₃what is communicated in an utterance]]₃ can go beyond sentence meaning.]]₂]]₁

Clause no. 1 is Complement of the superordinate clause, clause no. 2 is a defining relative clause postmodifying *ways*, and clause no. 3 is Subject of clause no. 2. The limits on centrally embedding can be shown by the difficulty of processing (45b), a hypothetical paraphrase of (45).

(45b)   No one disputes [[₁that various ways [[₂in which [[₃what is communicated in an utterance]]₃ can go beyond sentence meaning]]₂ exist.]]₁

Exercises

Exercise 8.1

Identify the Qualifiers in the following examples and label them as prepositional phrase (pp), defining relative clause (rel), or 'other'.

1. a result of this discovery
2. an emphasis on re-investment
3. the problem that must be addressed
4. domestic consumption of grain
5. any routes open
6. pens in hand
7. the quest for oil
8. a nation which is self-reliant
9. the funding available
10. conditions they cannot operate in

Exercise 8.2

Identify the relative clauses in the following examples and label them as 'full', 'contact' or 'reduced'.

1. This is an area where livestock grazing predominates.
2. Settlements linked by a network of narrow roads lack certain advantages.
3. These trucks resemble the monsters now destroying our highways.
4. The dedication they bring to the work pays dividends.
5. Accept this in the spirit in which it is intended.

Exercise 8.3

Analyze the examples in Exercise 8.2 in terms of the clause functions SFPCA, indicating embedded clauses in the usual way.

Exercise 8.4

Analyze the following in terms of clause functions (SFPCA), indicating embedding:

These are men who always serve the faction that is in power.

Exercise 8.5

(a) Analyze the following for SFPCA, indicating embedding.
   1. It is clear that there is always a difference.
   2. That she had an appointment is easily verifiable.
(b) Rewrite (a)1. without postposition of the Subject clause, and rewrite (a)2. with postposition.

Exercise 8.6

(a) Try to specify grammatically when you *cannot* omit the relative pronoun or adverb. One way of proceeding would be to collect a sample of sentences containing relative clauses with and without a relative, and analyze them.
(b) Using a similar procedure, try to determine the grammatical conditions when a wh-relative pronoun is possible but *that*-relative is not.

9

Clause complexes: expansion

9.1 *Ways of combining clauses*

In Chapter 8, we mentioned the folk poem – or word-game – 'The house that Jack built'. This plays on the recursive potential of defining relative clauses, which are rankshifted clauses functioning as Postmodifier/Qualifier in a nominal group. In such instances, one clause is embedded within another as part of that other's constituent structure.

There are, essentially, two further ways in which sentences can incorporate more than one clause. The first involves simply linking the clauses together on an equal footing, as in (1) below. The second involves binding one clause to another in a dependency relationship, where one clause, in a manner of speaking, dominates the other, as in (2).

(1) We are here 6,000 feet above the sea, and the equatorial sunshine is immensely hot and bright.
(2) [. . .] the Blue Nile grows steadily wider and warmer as it advances at a slower pace into the desert [. . .]

Where clauses are joined together in either of these ways, we have a *clause complex*.

9.2 *'Equal' clauses*

When young children tell stories, they make heavy use of the conjunction *and*. This is perhaps the most basic way of combining clauses, and here too the potential is exploited in oral folk literature, where the device is used repeatedly to produce an interminable sentence.

In one such story, a cruel king with an insatiable appetite for narrative offers marriage to any girl whose storytelling can make him say, 'Enough!' As is usual in such tales, the price for failure is death. The astute young woman who wins this implausible competition achieves her goal by adding identical clauses to each other:

... and a locust came and took away another grain of corn, and another locust came and took away another grain of corn, and another locust came and took away another grain of corn. ...

Obviously, it would not take long for even the most enthusiastic listener to reach satiation point with such a story. Small wonder that the king in the tale admitted defeat and married the girl. In narratives composed by young children, the clauses linked together in this way are not usually identical repetitions, but the effect can be almost as monotonous if repeated too often.

Nevertheless, used with more discretion, this means of combining clauses is extremely common even in the most sophisticated writing, as shown by the first example in this chapter, (1) (from a popular history book), or the following text fragment (from a car manual).

(3) Lever the rear of the gearbox/transmission unit over towards the exhaust pipe and free the lefthand drive shaft from the sunwheel. Push the unit in the opposite direction and free the other drive shaft.

This text features two clause complexes. Each is in the imperative mood and consequently has no Subject. They are analyzed as in Fig. 9.1. The SFPCA labels are also given. Since conjunctions do not play an integral role in the SFPCA functions, they are unlabelled here. (Double vertical lines (‖) indicate a clause boundary. Triple vertical lines (‖‖) represent a clause complex boundary but are often omitted.)

‖‖ Lever	the rear of the gearbox/transmission unit	over towards the exhaust pipe ‖
P	C	A
1		

and	free	the lefthand drive shaft	from the sunwheel. ‖‖
	P	C	A
2			

‖‖ Push	the unit	in the opposite direction	‖ and	free	the other drive shaft. ‖‖
P	C	A		P	C
1			2		

Fig. 9.1

Apart from the fact that the last clause has no Adjunct, these four clauses are virtually identical in structure. The author might have chosen to present them as four separate sentences, but no doubt there were good reasons for linking the two pairs in this way. In terms of the real-world activity referred to here, the second proposition (*free the lefthand drive shaft from the sunwheel*) is logically linked to the first, and the fourth has a similar logical relationship to the third. The author chose to reflect these parallel relationships in two parallel clause complexes, each containing a pair linked by *and*.

When two clauses are linked in this way, we number the first clause 1 and the second 2, as shown in Fig. 9.1.

The possibility of going beyond two clauses in a complex is illustrated in the examples below, taken from a telephone company's information brochure, where we have a complex of three such clauses. In the locust story and the children's narratives we mentioned, we have a number of clauses with *and* occurring before each new clause. However, most registers of English feature only one occurrence of the conjunction *and* in multiple linked clauses, and this occurs before the last in the series. In written English, the clauses are usually separated by commas, though the comma is often omitted before *and*.

(4)   Your calls will be put through quicker with your new exchange, the lines will be clearer, and there will be fewer faults.

Without indicating the SFPCA structure, we can label the clauses as in Fig. 9.2. The numerals 1, 2, 3 indicate clauses of equal status in the order in which they occur; thus, we cannot have a sequence of clauses numbered *2, 3, 1 or *3, 2, 1. The numbers have no significance other than indicating the actual order in a series of linked clauses. In the story about the locusts, of course, the numbers would continue far beyond 3.

||| Your calls will be put through quicker with your new exchange, ||	
1	
the lines will be clearer, ||	and there will be fewer faults.|||
2	3

Fig. 9.2

From the same source as (4), in example (5), analyzed in Fig. 9.3, we have a complex of three imperative clauses linked by *and*.

(5) Just pick up the handset, tap in the code and enter the time you want to be contacted.

|||Just pick up the handset, ||	tap in the code ||
1	2
and enter the time you want to be contacted. |||	
3	

Fig. 9.3

Example (5) contains a rankshifted clause embedded in the third linked clause. Since it is embedded, it does not count as a separate element in the clause complex, and so it does not affect our analysis of the three linked clauses in any way except that in a more detailed analysis we could analyze the clause in its own terms as demonstrated in Fig. 9.4, and, by putting all this information in one diagram, we have Fig. 9.5.

enter	the time	[[you	want to be contacted]]
		[[S	F/P]]
P		C	

Fig. 9.4

||| Just	pick up	the handset, ||	tap in	the code ||
A	P	C	P	C
1			2	

and	enter	the time	[[you	want to be contacted]].|||
			[[S	F/P]]
	P		C	
3				

Fig. 9.5

In the following short text, (6), we find the repeated use of linking of paired parallels using the conjunction *and*; then a further clause is linked to the second pair by *but*.

(6) The planets came out of the sun, and the sun came out of a nebula. It has lasted some time, and will last some time longer; but sooner or later – probably in about a million years – it will explode, destroying all the planets.

As we have said already (see Chapter 2), these conjunctions (*and*, *but*) belong to a subcategory of conjunctions called *linking conjunctions* or *linkers*. They are also known as 'co-ordinating conjunctions'. They do not have a role in the SFPCA structure of the clause.

The semantic distinctions among *and*, *but*, *or*, and *so* can be very roughly summarized as follows: *and* is additive, indicating addition and sometimes chronological or logical sequence; *but* is adversative indicating a contrast of some kind; *or* is disjunctive, signalling alternation; *so* is consequential, indicating a cause-effect type of relation. In fact, the semantics of these words can be very subtle and shades of meaning can often be distinguished only in context.

The phenomenon of such linking is called *parataxis*, and clauses linked in this way are said to have a *paratactic* relation to each other. The term derives from two Greek words: *para* meaning 'by the side of' and *taxis* meaning 'arrangement'. (Compare *paramedic*, a term used to refer to someone who works alongside a doctor; *syntax* meaning literally 'arrangement with', which is the way grammatical forms combine together to make grammatical structures.) Clauses in a paratactic complex are numbered 1, 2, etc. as they occur.

9.3   *Dependent clauses*

The second way in which a clause complex can be formed is to combine the clauses in such a way that one is dependent on another. This is known as *hypotaxis,* and the clauses are said to have a *hypotactic* relation. Etymologically, this derives from the Greek *hypo* meaning 'below' plus *taxis* meaning 'arrangement'. (Compare: *hypodermic* 'below the skin', which is from *hypo + derma* 'skin'.) The rationale for this term is that one clause is attached to the other but with a lower status, hence it is, as it were, arranged below. A more usual term for this is *dependency,* and we shall normally use the term *dependent clause* to label a clause which is bound to another in a hypotactic relationship. The clause to which it is bound is called the *dominant clause.*

The example we gave of a dependent clause at the beginning of this chapter involved the conjunction *as.* The example is repeated here for convenience.

> (2) [...] the Blue Nile grows steadily wider and warmer as it advances at a slower pace into the desert [...]

Here the second clause (*as it advances at a slower pace into the desert*) is bound in a hypotactic relation to the first clause (*the Blue Nile grows steadily wider and warmer*). The conjunction *as* signals this relationship. We have already said that *as* and other words that belong in the same class make up the subclass of conjunctions known as *binding conjunctions* or *binders* (traditionally, 'subordinating conjunctions'). A complete list of these would be very long, but it would include such items as: *when, while, until, before, after, if, unless, since, because, where, whereas, so that.* This is not to say, of course, that some of these words (or rather phonologically and graphologically identical forms) cannot show up in different word classes or realize different functions.

In the previous section, we indicated that clauses in a paratactic (equal) relation can be labelled with the numerals 1, 2, etc. Hypotactic (dependent) relations are conventionally labelled using the Greek alphabet symbols: α Alpha; β Beta; γ Gamma; δ Delta, ε Epsilon, etc. The use of the Greek alphabet avoids the confusion that would arise from using the symbols A, B, C, etc., some of which are already in use as grammatical labels; for example, A means Adjunct and C is used for Complement.

So we can analyze (2) simply as: α, β or, by adding the SFPCA labels, as in Fig. 9.6.

||| The Blue Nile	grows	steadily	wider and warmer ||
||| S	F/P	A	C

α

as	it	advances	at a slower pace	into the desert. |||
	S	F/P	A	A

β

Fig. 9.6

9.3.1   Sequencing of clauses: Theme and Rheme revisited

One striking way in which hypotactic clause relations differ from paratactic ones is that the sequence of labels can vary. In paratactic clauses, as we have already said, the sequence 1, 2, etc., cannot be altered. Or to put it another way, if we change around the sequence of the clauses, then the numbers will reflect the new sequence. In one of the clause complexes quoted earlier, we had the sequence:

||| The planets came out of the sun || and the sun came out of a nebula. |||

1   2

In this complex, we hear first about the more recent event in pre-history, and then about an event preceding it. The effect of this is that we perceive pre-history from our present standpoint, seeing first the event which is closer to us in time and secondly the event which is further back in time. Suppose that the author, Bertrand Russell, had decided to put this the other way round, as he might well have done to achieve a somewhat different effect, placing the events in their chronological order. The clauses in first and second place would be different in content, but in our analysis the first would still be numbered 1 and the second 2.

||| The sun came out of a nebula || and the planets came out of the sun. |||

1   2

This is self-evident in view of what the numbers signify, namely the sequence (the order of occurrence) of the *clauses*. The numbering has nothing to do with the sequence of the real-time events being recounted.

However, the labels α, β, and so on, used to label clauses in a hypotactic relationship of dependency, do not say anything about clause ordering. They indicate rather the hierarchical relationship whereby one clause depends on – 'hangs from' – another.

|||As it advances at a slower pace into the desert || the Blue Nile grows

β   α

steadily wider and warmer.|||

A corollary of this is the fact that whereas the linking conjunction (*and, but, or, so*) never occurs at the beginning of the complex which it links, the binding conjunction (*as, because, when,* and so on) *can* occur at the beginning of the complex which it binds.

The decision to put the dependent clause before or after the clause on which it depends (the *dominant* clause) is not an arbitrary one. There are significantly different meanings attached to such choices, notably those identified with the functions of Theme and Rheme discussed in Chapters 4 and 5. As we indicated there, the functions of Theme and Rheme are most significant *within* the clause, as reflected by the sequencing of S, F, P, C, and A. Clearly, however, placing a clause at the beginning of a clause complex suggests a thematic role for that clause as a whole in relation to the other clause(s) within the complex.

- The thematically *unmarked* sequence is: dominant clause followed by dependent clause: α, β.
- The thematically *marked* sequence is: dependent clause followed by dominant clause: β, α.

So far we have been discussing a hypothetical alternative to an actual unmarked utterance, but let us now consider some authentic examples of thematically marked clause complexes.

We begin with an example from our well-thumbed motor-vehicle manual.

(7) Unless wear or damage is apparent, further dismantling of the rocker shaft is unnecessary.

This example has the sequence β, α, that is a dependent clause followed by a dominant clause. Example (7) can be analyzed as in Fig. 9.7, giving the clause complex labels and the SFPCA labels.

||| Unless	wear or damage	is	apparent ||
	S	F	C
β				

further dismantling of the rocker shaft	is	unnecessary. |||
S	F	C
α		

Fig. 9.7

The fact of making the dependent clause the starting point has meaning for the message conveyed. The dependent clause expresses a contingency, constraining the proposition expressed in the dominant clause. In (7), by placing the condition first, the author signals that this is the 'peg' on which the clause complex hangs. The same is true of the time clause in (8).

(8) When the gap is correct, the feeler blade should just fall by its own weight.

The starting point (the Theme) is *when the gap is correct*; the Rheme is the dominant clause *the feeler blade should just fall by its own weight*. Of course, each clause has its own internal thematic organization. In these clauses, the binder may be classed as *structural Theme*, a sub-type of textual Theme (IFG Section 3.4). So the analysis for Theme and Rheme in these two complexes can be shown as in Fig. 9.8.

Unless wear or damage	is apparent,
Theme	**Rheme**
Thematic clause	

further dismantling of the rocker shaft	is unnecessary.
Theme	**Rheme**
Rhematic clause	

When the gap	is correct,
Theme	**Rheme**
Thematic clause	

the feeler blade	should just fall by its own weight.
Theme	**Rheme**
Rhematic clause	

Fig. 9.8

The Themes of the first clause in both complexes are multiple Themes and so they could be more delicately analyzed, as in Fig. 9.9.

Unless	wear or damage	is apparent
When	the gap	is correct
structural Theme	*topical Theme*	
Theme		**Rheme**

Fig. 9.9

Although dependent clauses of this type usually begin with a binder (*when*, *if*, *unless*, *because*, and so on), they are not always signalled in this way. Consider (9).

(9) Should the crankshaft sprocket teeth be worn, remove the sprocket with a suitable extractor.

An alternative to this, without any striking change of meaning, would have been (9a).

(9a) If the crankshaft sprocket teeth are worn, remove the sprocket with a suitable extractor.

In the authentic version, (9), instead of using the binding conjunction *if* to signal a condition, the author has chosen the less frequently used possibility of Subject-Finite inversion with *should*.

Sometimes we find the binder *if* in the dependent clause used in connection with *then* in the dominant clause. In such cases, *if* goes with the dependent clause and *then* with the dominant clause. This can happen only when the dependent clause precedes the dominant as in (10).

(10) If an argument is valid, then it is consistent.

This example comes from a textbook on formal logic, which is a field that exploits the *if ... then* combination a great deal since it is a basic formula in logic. However, we can find frequent examples of it in fields other than logic and in genres other than the textbook. In (11), we find *then* following a dependent (condition) clause which, instead of using *if*, uses Subject-Finite inversion as in (9). This suggests that *then* is tied to the condition-consequence relation rather than to the actual word *if*.

(11) Should the tests prove the pump is functioning correctly, then obviously other causes for fuel starvation must be sought.

Then, used to express this consequence relation, seems to be semantically unnecessary since its function is only to 'underline' a semantic relation between the two clauses that is already explicit in the use of *if* or in the inversion with *should*. Of course, there may well be cases where such 'underlining' serves a useful textual purpose (see Chapter 5 on cohesion).

9.3.2   Non-finite dependent clauses

All the examples of hypotaxis that we have so far considered have involved finite clauses. However, dependent clauses are frequently non-finite, as in the following examples. The dependent clauses are in italics.

(12) Remove the fan and the water pump pulley and the drive belt *after slackening off the generator securing bolt and strap bolt.*
(13) Refill the cooling system *as previously described in this chapter.*
(14) *Hearing these words*, even an amateur mathematician would trot out Laplace's equation.

(15) *Looking down from the top*, one sees far below a narrow gorge filled with water.

In examples (12) and (13), the dominant clause precedes the non-finite dependent clause; in (14) and (15), they are the opposite way round. In (12) and (13) there are binders (*after* and *as*, respectively) to signal the dependency relation, but (14) and (15) do not have any. The Predicators in (12), (14) and (15) are present participles (V-ing forms) and in (13) the Predicator is a past participle (passive). Paraphrasing with finite clauses, we might recast the examples as:

(12a) Remove the fan and the water pump pulley and the drive belt after you have slackened off the generator securing bolt and strap bolt.

(13a) Refill the cooling system as the process was previously described in this chapter.

(14a) If (or When) he/she heard these words, even an amateur mathematician would trot out Laplace's equation.

(15a) When one looks down from the top, one sees far below a narrow gorge filled with water.

There are obvious strong correspondences between the authentic non-finite versions and the constructed finite ones, but they are not entirely straightforward, and so it would be rash to argue that they carry exactly the same meaning. (13a) involves some rather clumsy readjustment; the choice of *when* and *if* is in doubt in (14a) and perhaps (15a), and so on. Even so, there are strong resemblances. Sometimes, however, there is no obvious corresponding finite clause, as in (16).

(16) *Using a micrometer*, measure the dimension across two splines on the final drive pinion.

Non-finite clauses in a clause complex with a finite clause are always dependent. Earlier, *so* was mentioned as a linking conjunction (for example, *I have started so I'll continue*, where the two clauses are in a paratactic relation). However, in (17) we have a different *so*, an adverb functioning as Adjunct with a meaning similar to *thereby* or *in this way*. The two clauses are in a hypotactic relation, with the first clause dominant and the second dependent.

(17) Electric light simulates daylight, so inducing the fowl to lay more frequently.

Present and past participles are not the only Predicators to appear in non-finite dependent clauses. Infinitives are also common, as in (18), (19) and (20).

(18) *To remove the skin*, cut off the tail and scrape towards the head.

(19) An RCD can be fitted as a separate unit between the meter and main switch *to protect the whole house*.

(20) [. . .] the laws of perspective were first studied by the geometer Agatharcus *in order to paint scenery for the plays of Aeschylus*.

The examples we have considered in this chapter so far all have a similar function: they expand on the proposition in the dominant clause, indicating some contingency relating to that proposition: of condition, time, purpose, means, manner, and so on. For example, the infinitive clauses in (18), (19) and (20) all express purpose. In fact, the functions of these dependent clauses have much in common with those of Adjuncts and Circumstances within the clause, and in traditional grammar they are called 'adverb clauses' and sub-classified as adverb clauses of time, manner, condition, purpose, and others.

We label this class of dependent clauses *expansion clauses*. The expansion function cuts across the paratactic/hypotactic dimension so that both hypotactic and paratactic clauses can realize that function. The counterpart to the expanding function is that of *projection*, which is dealt with in Chapter 10. First, we take a look at a somewhat different dependent clause, also with an expanding function: the non-defining relative.

9.3.3   Non-defining relative clauses

In Chapter 7, we discussed the defining relative clause (also known as the restrictive relative clause), demonstrating that this is a form of embedded clause functioning as Qualifier/Postmodifier in a nominal group. This function involves the limiting of the scope of reference of the Head. Thus, when we read the example from Chapter 7,

Any circuit that is to be worked on must be dead,

we understand that the predication 'must be dead' applies not to just 'any circuit' but only to any 'that is to be worked on'. The defining relative clause is part and parcel of the nominal group and it narrows down the potential meaning of the Head.

Non-defining relative clauses (also known as 'non-restrictive' relative clauses) are less intimately bound up with the item that they relate to and are analyzed not as embedded clauses but as dependent clauses.

(21) [...] he then measured the shadow of the pyramid, *which was of course equal to its height.*

(22) This general rejection was mainly due to Hipparchus, *who flourished from 161 to 126 BC.*

(23) There is even a slight note of derision from Fanny Burney, *who also met Bruce at this time.*

The relative clauses italicized in (21), (22) and (23) are non-defining: they do not pinpoint their antecedents in the way that defining relatives do, their function is rather to provide additional information about the antecedent. Their function is not to restrict the scope of reference of a Head, but, almost parenthetically, to comment further. Such a clause is grammatically dependent on the dominant clause, but it is not an integral part of it. We could roughly paraphrase (21) by saying:

(21a) he then measured the shadow of the pyramid, *and it was of course equal to its height.*

However, we could not paraphrase the defining clause example by saying:

Any circuit must be dead, and it is to be worked on.

However, non-defining relatives are analyzed not as paratactic but as hypotactic structures. They are not integrated into the clause that contains the antecedent in the way that rankshifted clauses are, but they are dependent. Example (21) is analyzed as in Fig. 9.10.

||| he	then	measured	the shadow of the pyramid,||
S	A	F/P	C

α

which	was	of course	equal to its height.|||
S	F	A	C

β

Fig. 9.10

Along with this difference in meaning between defining and non-defining clauses, there are some additional implications for the grammar, as well as for intonation (in the spoken mode) and for punctuation (in the written).

In the construction of defining relative clauses, speakers of English usually have the option of using either wh-pronouns or *that.* In non-defining clauses, the relative pronoun is always – or nearly always – a wh-pronoun. Also, the frequent simple omission of the relative pronoun that occurs with defining clauses (in contact clauses such as: *the book ^ you lent me*) is not paralleled in non-defining clauses. However, 'reduced' non-defining relatives do exist (that is, moodless, non-finite relative clauses) as in (24).

(24) The citadel, *built by Saladin in the twelfth century,* was a fine complex of dun-coloured battlements.

There is a striking difference in the intonation of defining and non-defining clauses that is reflected in the practice of setting apart non-defining clauses with commas. Of course, punctuation is not always practised consistently enough for this to be a sure way of distinguishing the two clause types, but it is the norm in careful writing, and can often prevent potential ambiguity. Without the commas, and out of context, we might read the relative in (24) as a defining clause, inferring a distinction between this citadel built by Saladin and other citadels that were built by other people. In fact, when we look at Text 9A, we can see that this has to be a non-defining clause.

Cairo, on the other hand, was a flourishing place [. . .]. It lay a little distance from the right bank of the river under the cover of the Mokattam Hills, and was ringed by high walls and dominated by a citadel.

The skyline, seen from a distance, had romantic aspects: the domes and minarets of 300 mosques rose from the smoke of cooking fires, and the palm trees and cultivated fields along the river bank gave the place a placid and rather rural air. The citadel, built by Saladin in the twelfth century, was a fine complex of dun-coloured battlements, and in the desert beyond, on the opposite side of the river, one descried the pyramids.

Text 9A   (Moorehead, *The Blue Nile*,[1] p. 73).

The citadel is mentioned twice in this text fragment; the first time it is '*a* citadel'; the second time it is '*the* citadel'. We already know by the time of the second mention which citadel is being referred to here. There is therefore no need for a defining clause. For the purposes of this fragment of discourse, there is only one citadel. The fact that it was built by Saladin in the twelfth century is an expansion, a further piece of information that the author chooses to express as a non-finite dependent clause, a non-defining relative. He might have expressed it in a separate sentence or in a 'full' finite dependent clause (*which was built by Saladin in the twelfth century*), but, without more drastic changes, he could not have expressed it as an embedded clause modifying *citadel*.

There is a moral here. Although, for the purpose of exposition in this book, we frequently deal with isolated examples torn from their setting, we do not wish to suggest that sentences are constructed without regard to the sentences around them. We can say a great deal about the structure of clauses by looking at clauses in isolation, but language is produced and understood not as individual clauses but as text. What happens in any clause is determined by the rest of the text in which it occurs. We have made this point already, but it is important to bear it in mind, and we feel justified in repeating it from time to time.

There is another difference in the work done by defining and non-defining relative clauses. A non-defining clause may have as its antecedent not just a nominal group or its Head but an entire clause or clause complex. To look at it in another way, non-defining relatives sometimes express a comment on a whole proposition or set of propositions. This is exemplified in (25) and (26).

(25) She also had to tell her parents, which was not easy for her.

(26) (He then told me) he would postpone his remunerations till then, to which I
      agreed.

In (25), the antecedent of *which* is the whole clause, *she also had to tell her
parents.*

In (26) the antecedent of the relative pronoun (*which*) is the clause *he would
postpone his remunerations till then.* As with defining relatives, the relative
pronoun itself in a non-defining clause may be Subject, Complement or
Adjunct, or, as in this example, part of an Adjunct. Here the relative pronoun
is part of the prepositional phrase *to which*, realizing the function Adjunct.

You will recall that *proper noun* is the label given to nouns which refer to
the individual names of people, places, institutions, and so on; for example,
Hipparchus, Fanny Burney, Tokyo. Obviously, when a relative pronoun has a
proper noun as its antecedent, the relative clause is likely to be a non-defining
relative. The reason for this is that a proper noun defines its referent by virtue
of the fact that it uniquely names it. Of course, there may be more than one
person called Fanny Burney, or city called Tokyo, but that is not a factor that
is usually taken into account when we use the name *Fanny Burney* or *Tokyo;*
we speak as though only one existed. For example:

Oenopides, *who was slightly later than Anaxagoras*
Aristarchus of Samos, *who lived approximately from 310 to 230 BC*
Cicero, *in whose time there was probably no Latin translation*
Einstein's General Theory of Relativity, *from which the conception of
force in the Newtonian sense has been banished.*

In the above examples, the assumption is that there is only one Oenopides,
one Aristarchus of Samos, one Cicero and one Einstein's General Theory of
Relativity, or at least that we don't need to specify them any more precisely.
The relative clause is an expansion of the dominant clause; it is non-defining.

The exception to this is where an item which is normally a proper noun is
treated as a common noun, as in the following example.

(27) This was the Maria whom he had toasted at the source of the Little Abbai.

Here, the author treats *Maria* as though it were a common noun. There is a
determiner (*the*) before it (not usual with people's names in English), and the
clause which follows is a defining relative; it tells us which Maria he is talking about. Here the assumption is that there are many Marias – or at least
more than one – and some modification is needed to pin down the reference;
hence the embedded clause. *Maria* in this example is not a name for a unique
individual but stands rather for any one of the class of individuals called
'Maria', just as the noun *woman* potentially stands for any of the class of adult
female humans. The Modifier *whom he had toasted at the source of the Little
Abbai* serves to make the expression refer more precisely. In the same way,
some nostalgic native of Birmingham might speak of *the Birmingham where*

I grew up, opposing this by implication to *the Birmingham of today* or, conceivably, to some other city or cities called Birmingham. (Incidentally, you may be relieved to know that *toasted* in (27) refers to the custom of drinking to the health of someone and not to basic culinary techniques.)

In this particular example, (27), far from being an optional expansion, the defining relative clause is the main focus of information. The clause in which it is embedded has an identifying function (see Chapter 6). The sentence which comes before it in the original text is Text 9B.

> The real reason, however, was that he had discovered, like so many soldiers returning from the wars, that his girl had abandoned him for another man.

Text 9B   (Moorehead, *The Blue Nile*[1]).

Therefore, the pronoun *This* in (27) refers to the same person as *his girl*. The Deictic as Head word *this* (referring to *his girl*) functions as Identified and *the Maria whom he had toasted at the source of the Little Abbai* is the Identifier. We can be sure of these grammatical facts, however, only if we have read another section of the narrative (nine pages earlier), which runs as in Text 9C and describes the behaviour of the Scottish explorer, Bruce, at what he thought was the source of the Nile. Here again is evidence of the fact that grammatical choices emerge from factors outside the clause itself, often at considerable distance in the text.

> There was still another toast. 'Now, friend,' Bruce said, '[. . .], here is to – Maria!' [. . .] We are to hear more of this lady later, on Bruce's return to Europe.

Text 9C   (Moorehead, *The Blue Nile*,[1] p. 34).

9.4   *More complicated complexes*

Real text in English can – and usually does – contain very complicated grammatical structures. Most of the examples we have looked at in this chapter are relatively straightforward cases of complexes of two clauses, either in a paratactic or a hypotactic relation. These are authentic samples of text, except where otherwise indicated, but it is easy to find more difficult samples. (28), analyzed in Fig. 9.11, contains two hypotactic clauses, one dependent on the other. We thus have a clause complex of the pattern α, β, γ.

   (28) Phenoxy compounds can also be sprayed over a newly planted field to kill young weed seedlings as their shoots appear.

|||Phenoxy compounds can also be sprayed over a newly planted field ||	
α	
to kill young weed seedlings ||	as their shoots appear.|||
β	γ

Fig. 9.11

Example (29), from a description of pest control in Africa, involves a combination of paratactic and hypotactic relations.

(29) At first the scheme was threatened by considerable tsetse reincursion, but this has now been remedied, mainly by using insecticide sprays within the consolidation barrier, clearing more bush and hunting game which had now re-entered the cleared land.

This clause complex falls initially into two paratactically related chunks linked by *but*. We label these 1 and 2. Clause 1 is a simple clause, but 2 contains a hypotactic expansion of the dominant clause. We therefore label the dominant clause α, and since it is already 2, it is labelled 2α. The rest of the sentence, being in a hypotactic relation to 2α, is labelled 2β. This in turn consists of three (non-finite) clauses in a paratactic relation to each other; we number them 1, 2, 3, but as they are all part of 2β, they are respectively 2β1, 2β2 and 2β3. There is also an embedded clause, which does not affect the clause complex relations. This analysis can be summed up as in Fig. 9.12.

|||At first the scheme was threatened by considerable tsetse reincursion, ||		
1		
but this has now been remedied ||	mainly by using insecticide sprays	
2α	2β1	
within the consolidation barrier ||	clearing more bush, ||	and hunting
	2β2	
game [[which had now re-entered the cleared land]]. |||		
2β3		

Fig. 9.12

Sometimes, as in (30), we find clause complexes within embedded clauses.

(30) His thesis is that the actual outbreak of war is almost inevitable, provided certain broad sociopolitical, economic and technical patterns are present.

This sentence realizes a relational process in the form *X is Y*. So one line is a simple S, F, C structure. However, the Complement is realized by an embedding in the form of a hypotactic clause complex. This is illustrated in Fig. 9.13, which also includes SFPCA labels. The second line in Fig. 9.13 gives the SFPCA labels for the embedded clauses, the third line gives the clause labels and the fourth line the SFPCA labels for the clause as a whole. The items *that* and *provided*, being binders, have no SFPCA function. (Although *provided* is historically a verb participle, in this context we regard it as a binder introducing a clause of condition.) It is clear that the conditional clause applies to the first *embedded* clause and not to the first clause in the sentence, and so it belongs inside the brackets.

His thesis	is	[[||| that	the actual outbreak of war	is	almost inevitable, ||
		[[	S	F	C
			α in embedded clause		
S	F			C	

provided	certain broad sociopolitical, economic and technical patterns		are	present. |||]]
	S		F	C
	β in embedded clause			
	C *superordinate clause continued*			

Fig. 9.13

Summary

In this chapter, we have focused on various methods of combining clauses together in English by means of the clause complex. Clause complexes may involve *expansion* or *projection;* in this chapter we have considered only expansion.

Clause complex relationships are of two kinds: (i) paratactic, that is equal in status; and (ii) hypotactic, that is involving a dependency relation. Paratactic relations are labelled according to the sequence in which the clauses occur: 1, 2, etc. Hypotactic relations are labelled according to their hierarchical relationship of dependency, regardless of the order in which they occur. Greek alphabetic symbols (α, β, γ, δ, ε) are conventionally used to show 'descending' dependency. Thus β is dependent on α; γ on β; δ on γ; and so on. A clause which has another depending on it is called the dominant clause; a clause which depends on another is called the dependent clause.

Dependent clauses are not embedded. Dependent clauses differ crucially from embedded (i.e. rankshifted) clauses because in a clause complex the clauses are not 'demoted' to function at some lower rank.

Non-defining relative clauses are one kind of dependent expansion. A non-defining relative may have as its antecedent a nominal group or an entire clause or clause complex. Non-defining relatives are distinct from defining relatives, which are embedded.

In many texts, there is a complex interplay of conjunction (parataxis), dependency (hypotaxis), and embedding (rankshift). Any instance of one of these phenomena may occur inside another instance of the same phenomenon or inside an instance of one of the others.

Further study

We analyzed *provided* in (30) above as a binder similar to *if*. However, even if we see it as a Predicator with the rest of the clause as Complement, this would not affect the status of the clause as a dependent clause of condition. Bloor T. (1998) looks at varied realizations of conditionals and tentatively points to some overlaps with modality and extended hypotheticals.

Alternative approach to 'dependent' clauses

A possible alternative analysis to Halliday's treatment of hypotactic expansions as dependent clauses is to analyze them as embedded clauses functioning as Adjunct. This view is taken by Fawcett, among others (for example, Fawcett, 1974, 2000a). In this model, example (2), from the opening of this chapter, would be analyzed as a single clause with embedding rather than as a clause complex with an α, β relation. In principle, for Fawcett, *as it advances at a slower pace into the desert* is an Adjunct, though it is also a clause with its own structure; Fawcett's terminology would express this slightly differently. See also Downing and Locke (2002), who present both analyses but express a strong preference for the dependent clause analysis (as in IFG and this volume).

Exercises

Exercise 9.1

The following examples are all paratactic clause complexes, consisting of two or more clauses. Indicate each clause boundary with a double vertical line, and number the clauses.

1. The guarantee does not cover normal wear and tear, misuse or accidental damage and is conditional upon respect for the care instructions.
2. Loewi got out of bed, went to his lab, and did the experiment.

3. Remove the starter shield and disconnect the starter electrical leads.
4. He thumped the table, spilled his tea, and actually seemed to be, for a moment, steaming.
5. It's used as a last resort, but don't be frightened.

Exercise 9.2

Each of the following is a hypotactic clause complex containing one dominant and one dependent clause. Label the clauses α or β.

1. Before one can love another, one has to love oneself enough.
2. Opera works best when it refuses to be embarrassed about its artifice.
3. Though today there are no more than 400 of these magnificent trees, the cedars of Lebanon were once famous all over the ancient world.
4. Send your creditors a financial statement, showing your income and outgoings.
5. Your doctor may wish to change your dose to allow for any reduced kidney function.
6. If you are not sure about this, check with your doctor.
7. She seems almost arrogant, challenging the viewer to a fight.
8. We'll provide a free replacement car while yours is being repaired at one of our depots.

Exercise 9.3

(a) Identify the following clause complexes as paratactic or hypotactic.
(b) Indicate clause boundaries and label the paratactic clauses 1, 2, etc. and the hypotactic clauses α, β, etc.

1. You'll be treated fairly and you won't end up in jail.
2. Subsequently released, he fled to England.
3. The singers were in costume, but the stage was bare.
4. Any words can be used if they provide a space for the music.
5. When he approached Florence, seemingly stable governments crumbled overnight.

Exercise 9.4

The following sentence contains a clause complex and an embedded clause, both of these embedded within another clause. Indicate the structure using [[ ]] around the embedded clauses and ‖ between the two clauses in the complex.

The good news is that there are several steps you can take to protect your-self and your family on holiday.

Exercise 9.5

For text 9D below:
(a) mark the clause complex boundaries as |||; clause boundaries as ||; and embedded clauses as [[. . .]]. Between two clause complexes, only one clause complex boundary symbol is needed.
(b) label clauses for paratactic and hypotactic relations: 1, 2, etc; α, β; β1, etc.

> King Hu's fourth film, *A Touch of Zen,* which was made in 1968 but only released in its present form in 1975, is a remarkable and assured reflec-tion on the mesh of historic forces that define Chinese culture. Set in the Ming dynasty, a favourite period for Hu and one marked by corruption and the development of a particularly lethal secret police force, the film centres on the strange encounter between a local artist and the mysteri-ous woman who takes up residence in a nearby abandoned fortress.

Text 9D

Exercise 9.6

For Text 9E below indicate boundaries and label the clauses as in Exercise 9.4. Indicate rankshifted clauses with double square brackets.

> The more scientific systems of 'New World' commercial pastoralists keep the animals scattered, so ensuring more uniform grazing and reducing the danger of producing bare patches completely devoid of vegetation. A country with much experience of semi-arid livestock farming is Australia, where wide areas of grazing land do not receive more than 250 mm of rainfall a year. It has been found that cattle with-stand such arid conditions better than sheep. Interior Australia is still a land of pioneer settlement, and as the better-watered areas become fully settled and developed, land-hungry farmers will inevitably be forced into the so-called 'desert' country. Hitherto the carrying capacity of the outback has remained rather low, averaging 1–4 animals per square kilometre [. . .]

Text 9E (Lowry, *World Population and Food Supply*[2], p. 60).

Exercise 9.7

Analyze the following examples, indicating embedding and dependency as above but adding SFPCA labels.

1. Japan has its great cities, and it has evolved its own elaborate systems to control urban congestion.
2. Shimura is superb in the central role, and not the least of Kurosawa's achievements is his triumphant avoidance of happy-ending uplift.
3. Yuko sings quietly to herself as she watches the water.
4. One of the few films that never fails is this one, which is a Japanese classic.
5. Saddled with a slavish, boring laundry job, Kikuchi barely leaves his apartment.

Notes

1. Moorehead, Alan 1969 (originally published 1962): *The Blue Nile*. London: Hamish Hamilton.
2. Lowry, J.H. 1970: *World Population and Food Supply*. London: Edward Arnold.

10

Clause complexes: projection

10.1   *Projection*

In Chapter 6, we looked at verbal processes in terms of the experiential meta-function, identifying the functions Sayer, Quoted, Reported, Receiver, Verbiage and Target. In this chapter, continuing the issues raised in Chapter 9, we look at the same kind of utterance from a different point of view, namely, its logical organization: the paratactic and hypotactic combination of projecting and projected clauses.

10.2   *Paratactic projection*

As we have seen, when we are dealing with direct speech, where the actual words – or what purport to be the actual words – of a speaker are presented verbatim, there is usually a clause conveying something like 'X says' and a clause or a number of clauses that represent the words spoken (not necessarily in that order). In looking at the clause in experiential terms, we may label these as Sayer and Quoted, respectively. Considered in terms of dependency, the relation between these clauses can be described as paratactic. The notation for this, then, is 1 and 2, just as it is for paratactically linked expansions; see (1).

(1) ||| He said, || 'I saw it on TV.'|||
        1   2

If the order of Sayer and Quoted is reversed, of course, it is still the first clause that is numbered 1 and the second that is numbered 2; see (2).

(2) ||| 'I saw it on TV,' || he said. |||
        1   2

Representations of thought may take exactly the same form as direct speech and in such cases are analyzed in the same way.

(3) ||| I thought, || 'This is the end of the road for me.' |||
        1   2

In Text 6A, at the start of Chapter 6, there are a number of instances of quoting; these are mostly elliptical structures simulating spontaneous speech. We list them here, numbered for convenience.

(4) 'This all?' I asked Thaler.
(5) 'Nick said there were fifty of you.'
(6) 'Fifty of us to stand off that crummy force!' he sneered.
(7) A uniformed copper held the back gate open, muttering nervously: 'Hurry it up, boys, please.'
(8) 'See you later,' the gambler whispered.

All these except (5) are paratactic. In (7) the clause that contains Sayer and the quoting verb comes before the clause that realizes the Quoted function, and in (4), (6) and (8) it is the other way round. Labelling these is very straightforward, then. No matter what the function, the clause that comes first is numbered 1 and the clause that comes second is 2. Example (7) is a little more complicated than the others, and we shall return to it shortly. So the analysis of the remaining clauses is as in Fig. 10.1.

||| 'This all?' || ||| 'Fifty of us to stand off that crummy force,'|| ||| 'See you later,'	I asked Thaler. ||| he sneered. ||| the gambler whispered. |||
1	2

Fig. 10.1

In novels, memoirs, biographies and other written narrative texts, direct speech (Quoted) is sometimes presented without the Sayer function being made explicit, as we see in (9).

(9) He lowered his voice. 'That is the price you must pay.'

Clearly, the identity of Sayer here is deducible from the co-text. The author of this narrative has chosen to present the information about Sayer and manner of saying in a separate sentence. Therefore, since the Quoted is presented as an isolated clause, this is not an example of a clause complex. An approximate paraphrase is (9a), which *is* a clause complex.

(9a) In a lower voice, he said, 'That is the price you must pay.'

Example (5) is a more awkward case: it is a Quoted without a Sayer, but it is complicated by the fact that the quotation is itself made up of a clause complex in the form of a projection containing both Sayer and Reported functions. This will be discussed later.

Sometimes the clause that contains the Sayer interrupts the clause that realizes the Quoted as in (10) and (11).

(10) 'War,' he says, 'is the father of all and the king of all.'
(11) 'Apparently,' wrote Trembley to Réaumur, 'these gentlemen have some cherished system [. . .]'

The clause *he says* interrupts the Quoted (*War is the father of all and the king of all*), but, because the Quoted starts first, it is numbered 1, and *he says* is numbered 2. Similarly, in (11) the number 1 clause (*Apparently these gentlemen have some cherished system*) is interrupted by the number 2 clause *wrote Trembley to Réaumur*.

To indicate that the number 1 clause is discontinuous, interrupted by, rather than followed by, number 2, we use the notation: 1 << 2 >> ; that is, instead of two vertical lines ‖ at the clause boundary, we use double angle brackets. Clause 1 continues after the second double angle bracket. Thus the analysis in terms of clause complex structure is as in Fig. 10.2.

‖‖ 'War,'	<< he says, >>	'is the father of all and the king of all.' ‖‖
1	2	*1 continued*

‖‖ 'Apparently,'	<<wrote Trembley to Réaumur,>>	'these gentlemen have some cherished system.' ‖‖
1	2	*1 continued*

Fig. 10.2

The inversion of the reporting verb and Subject/Sayer illustrated in the first example (*wrote Trembley*) is largely restricted to formal, planned texts, usually published writing. Note that inversion cannot readily take place (in a declarative clause) where the quoting expression precedes the entire Quoted; we would not normally write:

Wrote Trembley to Réaumur, 'Apparently these gentlemen [. . .]'

The practice is not unprecedented, however. Poe wrote: '*Quoth the raven: "Nevermore!"*'; and *Time* magazine used to indulge in similar structures. In modern English, as we have said earlier, inversion of Subject/Sayer and quoting verb is a stylistic option more likely to occur with a nominal group with noun as Head than with a personal pronoun such as *he* or *she*. In (10) *says he* would be virtually ruled out in most varieties of modern English except for humorous effect.

10.3 *Hypotactic projection*

In Chapter 6, we discussed reported/indirect speech (including thought and writing) in terms of the functions Sayer and Reported. Looked at from the perspective of the clause complex, these differ from direct speech structures in that the relationship between the two key clauses is hypotactic, that is, there is a relation of dependency. The clause containing the Sayer and the reporting verb is the dominant clause and the Reported element is the dependent clause. Thus, (12) breaks down into two clauses: the dominant clause *he says* and the dependent clause *that the general ignorance on this subject is disgraceful*.

(12) He says that the general ignorance on this subject is disgraceful.

Thus, using dependency notation, we could represent the analysis of this clause complex as follows:

||| He says, || that the general ignorance on this subject is disgraceful. |||
      α   β

When we were discussing the direct speech examples above, we postponed discussion of (5), repeated here.

(5) 'Nick said there were fifty of you.'

This appears in quotation marks as Quoted, but it is not an example of a paratactic clause complex, because there is no clause explicitly giving the Sayer and verbal process verb of the Quoted. However, the Quoted element itself is a clause complex, a hypotactic one analyzed as follows:

||| Nick said || there were fifty of you. |||
      α   β

Like speech, thought projection can have direct (paratactic) or reported (hypotactic) form.

(13) Haeckel thought that the *Origin* had one grave defect.

Example (13) similarly breaks down into two clauses: *Haeckel thought*, which is the dominant clause, and *that the Origin had one grave defect*, which is the dependent clause, hence the labelling given below.

||| Haeckel thought || that the *Origin* had one grave defect. |||
      α   β

In reported speech (including thought and writing) the projected element, the speech (or thought or writing), is grammatically integrated with the reporting clause (such as *he says*) with the result that the choice of tense pronouns, and other deictic elements such as adverbs of time and place, in the reported clause may be influenced by the general orientation of the reporting clause. This does not happen with direct speech. If Haeckel's thought were to be expressed as direct speech, the verb could be in the present tense, as in the adapted version (13a).

(13a) ||| Haeckel thought, || 'The *Origin* has one grave defect.' |||
                1   2

Conversely, the direct speech of (11) might be expressed in reported speech as (11a), where both tense and determiner are realigned to the fact that, from the point of view of the reporter, the situation described is in the past and the gentlemen are, as it were, further away.

(11) 'Apparently,' wrote Trembley to Réaumur, 'these gentlemen have some cherished system [. . .]'

(11a) Trembley informed Réaumur that those gentlemen apparently had some cherished system.

In (14), the verb in the dependent clause has to be in the present tense to express this particular proposition because the projecting verb is also in the present: *he says* rather than *he said*. If the author had written *he said*, there would have been the option of a present tense verb (14a) or past tense verb (14b) in the reported clause. The reason for this choice being open is that the statement is a general truth, which can be seen in relation either to the time when it was spoken (past) or, since it is still applicable, to the time at which it is reported (present).

(14) He says that the general ignorance on this subject is disgraceful.

(14a) He said that the general ignorance on this subject is disgraceful.

(14b) He said that the general ignorance on this subject was disgraceful.

Reported speech does not always represent what was actually said in this precise one-to-one manner. Unlike direct speech, reported speech does not purport to be a precise reproduction of the words used. It may be only an approximation to what was actually said, but the point is that it is encoded as if it corresponded in the way we have outlined. Example (14) would be an acceptable account of an utterance like (14c).

(14c) The general ignorance about this is a disgrace.

The most frequent signal of a hypotactic projection (that is, a dependent reported speech clause) is the presence of the word *that*. However, *that* realizes several functions. To put it another way, there is more than one *that* in English. In Chapter 8 we discussed *that* as a relative pronoun, an alternative to *who* or *which*. *That* can also be a determiner, the singular form of *those*; hence *those gentlemen*: *that gentleman*. The word *that* which introduces a dependent projecting clause is yet another *that*, and belongs to a different word class, namely the class of binding conjunctions (or binders). This is arguably the same *that* that we find introducing embedded clauses after nominals (for example, *the argument that heat is transferred*), although a dependent clause is not, of course, the same as an embedded clause.

That differs from the other binding conjunctions (*although*, *since*, *because*, *when*, and so on) in at least one way. It is an exception to the rule that binders are not normally omitted from finite dependent clauses. It is often optional, and so we frequently hear or read sentences like (15) and (16).

(15) She said she hadn't known anything about my being called to Personville by her employer.
(16) He didn't know his father was in it as deep as anybody else.

Where the projection is a reported interrogative, with a verb such as *ask*, *enquire* or *wonder*, the binding conjunction is likely to be *if* or *whether*; or some other wh-word may be involved: *who, which, where, how, why* or *what*. These items, unlike *that*, cannot be omitted. To wonder if or whether something is the case is to ask oneself a question. For example, (17), using *if*, is a projection of an either-or question (17a); and (18) is a projection of a wh-question involving *why*, (18a).

(17)   I wondered if he meant pick him up or pick him off.
(17a) Does he mean pick him up or pick him off?
(18)   May I ask why I am being questioned in this manner?
(18a) Why am I being questioned in this manner?

Notice that the inversion of Subject and Finite which characteristically occurs in direct questions does not occur in the reported (indirect) version. In fact, (18) has a direct question with an indirect question dependent on it. There is Subject-Finite inversion in the first: *May I*, but not in the second: *I am*.

Mental processes involving verbs like *believe, hope, pretend, wish*, and *wonder* can project; and so can verbal processes involving verbs like *argue, claim, declare, explain, insist, promise, vow*.

10.4   *Non-finite projections*

Like expansion clauses (see Chapter 9), projection clauses may be finite or non-finite. Reported commands and requests are particularly strong candidates for realization as non-finite dependent clauses, and so are promises, as in (19) and (20).

(19) Ron told you to check the regulations.
(20) I promised to do that.

The verb *ask* can be used to project not only questions but also requests. Of course, one politeness strategy for eliciting what Halliday calls 'goods and services' is to use the interrogative so that instead of using the imperative, as in Example (21), we may prefer the less threatening (21a).

(21)   Give me some water.
(21a) Will you give me some water?

Hence, it is not surprising that we frequently find reported requests projected by *ask*.

(22) She asked me to give her some water.

Again, the hypotactic projection is not necessarily a one-to-one transposition of the actual wording of the original. Example (22) could be a report of (21) or (21a) or a number of other wordings. In structures of this kind *ask* is almost synonymous with *request*. Although finite clauses with *that* can express such projected requests, as in (23), they are limited to certain lexical reporting verbs.

(23) She requested that I should give her some water.

Note also that not all requesting verbs permit infinitive clause projection; for example, *insist* does not appear with an infinitive projection; *demand* can do so only when the subject of the infinitive is the same as the subject of *demand*. Thus, we have *He demanded to be released* but not **He demanded me to release him.*

These non-finite projections are analyzed along the same lines as hypotactic projected finite clauses, so the reporting clause (containing the Sayer) is dominant and the reported clause is dependent. The analysis is represented in Fig. 10.3.

||| Ron told you ||	to check the regulations. |||
||| I promised ||	to do that. |||
||| She asked me ||	to give her some water. |||
α	β

Fig. 10.3

10.5 *Grammatical metaphor: embedding versus dependency*

When we introduced the notion of grammatical metaphor in Chapter 6, we mentioned that one of the most widespread manifestations of this difficult aspect of the grammar involves nominalization, whereby a process more congruently expressed as a verb is instead expressed as a noun. Thus, a process in which someone destroys a picture becomes, as it were, a 'thing': *the destruction of the picture*. This is particularly common in the case of mental and verbal projections. As pointed out earlier, what happens is that the nominalization of the process makes it available to realize the functions that are open to any nominal group: Subject, Complement, Theme, Given, and so on, providing another powerful resource for textual development.

We have seen that when a verbal process is realized as a verb, the projection may take the form of a dependent clause functioning as Reported, as in (5) above (see Fig. 10.4).

||| Nick said ||	there were fifty of you. |||
α	β

Fig. 10.4

Exploiting the resource of grammatical metaphor, this can be nominalized as (5a).

(5a) Nick's statement that there were fifty of you

As we have seen, (5) is a clause complex. (5a), on the other hand, is a nominal group. It could show up as a Subject (*Nick's statement that there were fifty of you* was a lie) or as a Complement (No one believed *Nick's statement that there were fifty of you*) or in any other function available to a nominal group. The nominalized process *statement* is the Head of the group and the projection is an embedded clause postmodifying the Head (Fig. 10.5).

Nick's	statement	[[that there were fifty of you]]
Modifier	**Head**	**Modifier**
Nominal group		

Fig. 10.5

Most projecting verbs have noun counterparts. Figure 10.6 offers a small sample. The set of verbs in the left-hand columns is parallelled by the set of nouns in the right-hand columns. However, there are some spaces where no counterpart exists. There is no obvious reason why these particular words are lacking, but it is a widely acknowledged fact that all languages have lexical gaps. In (5a), since there is no direct nominal counterpart of the verb *say*, we resorted to another noun of saying, namely *statement*. Instead of *statement*, we might have selected *assertion, claim, declaration* or one of a number of other nouns to express the process of saying.

Though fairly long, Fig. 10.6 is by no means a complete list of relevant items. The gaps in the noun columns could be filled with gerunds (*saying, swearing, imagining*) but these exist for all lexical verbs and are not straightforward lexical nouns like the words given in Fig. 10.6. Obviously, there is a nominal equivalent of the verb *imagine* in the form *imagination*, but this does not occur with embedded *that*-clauses as the other nouns in the list do.

All the verbs and nouns in Fig. 10.6 can occur with projection clauses introduced by the word *that*. Some of them can also occur with to-infinitive clauses. There is a grammatical difference between the projections with verbs and with nouns, however, in that the clauses projected by the verbs are dependent clauses, whereas those which occur with the nouns are embedded; that is,

Verbal		Mental	
verb	**noun**	**verb**	**noun**
assert	assertion	assume	assumption
claim	claim	believe	belief
confess	confession	conceive	conception
declare	declaration	conclude	conclusion
deny	denial	desire	desire
—	—	hypothesize	hypothesis
insist	insistence	imagine	—
proclaim	proclamation	speculate	speculation
promise	promise	suppose	supposition
say	—	theorize	theory
state	statement	think	thought
swear	—	—	view
tell	(tale?)	wish	wish
vow	vow		

Fig. 10.6

the nominal projections take the form of rankshifted clauses occurring as Postmodifiers of the Head nouns in question. Examples follow.

(24) Servetus had thrown off the idea that the blood is circulated through the lungs.
(25) He demonstrated his argument that there are three innate emotions.
(26) Du Bois-Reymond himself drew the conclusion that there was no real difference between organic and inorganic nature.

Using a projecting verb instead of a noun, we can construct a marginally more congruent counterpart for (26) in (26a).

(26a) Du Bois-Reymond himself concluded that there was no real difference between organic and inorganic nature.

The crucial difference between (26) and (26a) is that, whereas (26) contains a noun *conclusion* with a projection as Postmodifier, (26a) contains a verb *conclude* with a projection as a dependent clause. The diagrammatic analysis in Fig. 10.7 highlights the difference, namely that the *that*-clause in one is a rankshifted clause embedded as part of a nominal group, and the *that*-clause in the other is a dependent clause.

Note that the grammatically metaphorical (nominalized) form *conclusion* typically co-occurs with the verb *draw,* whereas *decision* typically goes with *make,* but both can show up with *reach* or *come to*. Another curious formal difference between projections as dependent clauses and projections as embedded clauses is that the word *that* is normally optional in the former and normally necessary in the latter.

Du Bois-Reymond himself	drew	the conclusion	[[that	there	was	no real difference.]]
				S	F	C
S	F/P	C				

||| Du Bois-Reymond himself	concluded ||	that	there	was	no real difference. |||
S	F/P	S	F	C	
α β					

Fig. 10.7

10.6   *Even more complicated complexes*

Most of the examples considered so far have involved only two clauses, either paratactically or hypotactically related. However, clause complexes can be much more complicated, and we find all kinds of permutations: dependent clauses within dependent clauses, hypotactic within paratactic, or vice versa. Earlier in this chapter we promised to return to (7), repeated here.

(7)   A uniformed copper held the back gate open, muttering nervously: 'Hurry it up, boys, please.'

In this clause complex, we have a paratactic projection as part of a dependent expansion clause. The second half of the clause complex:

   muttering nervously: 'Hurry it up, boys, please.'

is in a hypotactic (expansion) relationship with the first clause:

   A uniformed copper held the back gate open.

We therefore label the first clause α and the rest β. The β part, however, consists of two clauses in a paratactic relation, and so we label these two clauses 1 and 2. Since 1 and 2 together make up the dependent β to the dominant α of the first clause, we call them β1 and β2. This information can be expressed as in Fig. 10.8.

|||A uniformed copper held the back gate open, ||	muttering nervously: ||	'Hurry it up, boys, please.' |||
α	β1	β2

Fig. 10.8

A further example of a paratactic complex forming the dependent clause within a hypotactic complex is (27), but this time only projections are involved, analyzed in Fig. 10.9.

(27)   Wallace thought that perhaps the earth's orbit had formerly been less eccentric, and that this might have made a difference.

||| Wallace thought ||	that perhaps the earth's orbit had formerly been less eccentric, ||
α	β1

and that this might have made a difference.|||
β2

Fig. 10.9

Sometimes we find a hypotactic complex (α, β) inside a paratactic complex (1, 2), as in (28); the projection here also includes an embedded clause, which has no status in the clause complex, of course, since it is rankshifted to be part of a nominal group.

(28) ||| He said, || 'I think || it's time [[I went back to the factory.']] |||
        1   2α   2β

Sometimes there is an even more complicated dependency relationship in a clause complex. In (29), we have a two-part paratactic complex (1, 2), where the second part consists of three clauses in a hypotactic sequence (α, β, γ).

(29) ||| Nixon said, || 'Krogh told me || he didn't believe || I ordered the break-in.' |||
       1   2α   2β   2γ

In (29), *I ordered the break-in* is dependent on *he didn't believe*, which in turn is dependent on *Krogh told me*; hence the labels α, β, γ. All of this, however, is in a paratactic relation to *Nixon said*; hence the labels 1 and 2.

Example (30) has a paratactic clause complex within a hypotactic clause complex.

(30) ||| She reported || Starr saying to her, || 'It will never work.' |||
       α   β1   β2

In (31), we have a clause complex within an embedded clause. *To maintain that everything could be demonstrated* is an instance of extraposition with *it* functioning as a dummy Subject. *To maintain* is a non-finite verbal Process projecting the final clause *that everything could be demonstrated*. Thus, we have a dependent projection within an embedded clause, as indicated in the analysis below.

(31) It was of the essence of his system, ethically as well as metaphysically,
    [[||| to maintain || that everything could be demonstrated. |||]]
    [[α   β   ]]

Authentic texts sometimes throw up examples of much greater complexity, a sample of which is to be found in (32).

(32) A second approach is to assume that in some fashion the cells 'know' where they are situated within a developing organism and behave accordingly.

The dependency relationships are entirely within the embedded clause complex, which is the Complement, and so the totality is in a sense a free-standing clause with the structure S, F, C.

The complexity arises within the embedding and so does not impinge on the structure of the whole, but the embedding can be analyzed in its own right as a clause complex, each clause in the complex being analyzable in its turn in terms of SFPCA.

To break this down, let us look at the complex in subsections, as in Fig. 10.10. When we put all these labels together and add SFPCA labels, we come up with Fig. 10.11. Within the embedded clause, the dependency relations are as follows: *to assume*, although non-finite, is the projecting clause (the dominant or α-clause), and all that follows it is the hypotactic projection from that α-clause. Thus, all the rest is labelled β (that is the first symbol in the string on the third and seventh lines of Fig. 10.11). However, the β section is a paratactic complex; it has two parts linked by *and*; hence we add the labels 1 and 2. The first member of this paratactic pair is itself a hypotactic projection complex consisting of a projecting, dominant clause (*in some fashion the cells 'know'*) and a projected, dependent clause (*where they are situated within a developing organism*), so we label these respectively α and β, the third symbol in the string.

to assume ||	that in some fashion the cells 'know' where they are situated within a developing organism and behave accordingly
α	β

(that) in some fashion the cells 'know' where they are situated within the developing organism ||	and behave accordingly
1	2

the cells 'know' ||	where they are situated within a developing organism
α	β

Fig. 10.10

A second approach		is	[[||| to assume ||	that	in some fashion	the cells	'know' ||
			P		A	S	F/P
			α		β1α		
S		F	C				

where	they	are	situated	within a developing organism ||	and	behave	accordingly. |||]]
A	S	F	P	A		F/P	A
β1β					β2		
C *continued*							

Fig. 10.11

10.7   *Ambiguous structures*

A potential for ambiguity arises when it is not clear whether a structure is an expansion or a projection, as in the invented example (33).

(33) He promised to placate the generals.

Where this string of words could be roughly paraphrased as (33a), the clause *to placate the generals* is an expansion. Where it can be roughly paraphrased as (33b), it is a projection. In speech, the two different readings of (33) are distinguished by different intonation. The labelling of the clauses as α, β is not affected by this distinction between expansion and projection, of course, since both involve dependency.

(33a) He made a promise in order to placate the generals.
(33b) He made a promise that he would placate the generals.

Example (33c) has only one possible reading; it must be an expansion and not a projection.

(33c) To placate the generals, he promised.

Sometimes, as in the grammatical metaphor (34), something similar happens when the clause follows projecting nouns.

(34) He made a promise to placate the generals.

There is potential confusion here between a to-infinitive clause (i) as a dependent expansion clause and (ii) as an embedded clause, Postmodifier of a Head, in a nominalized projection. In the first reading, *to placate the generals* means *in order to placate the generals*; in the second, *to placate the generals* is what he promised, paraphrasable as *that he would placate the generals*.

Summary

In this chapter we complete our treatment of paratactic and hypotactic clause complexes by considering projection.

Paratactic projection clauses are typically 'direct speech' (including verbatim speech, thought or writing). Projecting and projected clauses may occur in any order, or projecting clauses may interrupt projected clauses. Paratactic clauses are labelled 1, 2, and so on, in sequential order of occurrence, regardless of whether the projecting clause or the projected clause comes first.

Hypotactic projection clauses are typically 'reported speech' (or reported thought or reported writing). Hypotactically related clauses are labelled α, β, and so on to indicate grammatical dependency, regardless of the order in which the clauses occur. However, in hypotactic projections, projecting (dominant) clauses typically precede projected (dependent) clauses.

Hypotactic projections may be realized by finite clauses or non-finite clauses. The latter often occur as indirect questions and commands when the projecting process is realized by verbs such as *tell, order, ask, wonder* (though these verbs can also occur with finite projection clauses). When the projecting process is realized as a noun (for example, *statement, assertion, insistence*), the clause that realizes the projection is embedded as Postmodifier of that noun; that is, as a rankshifted clause within the nominal group. This means that it does not count as a clause in a clause complex.

At the end of the chapter, some more complicated examples and potential ambiguities are presented.

Further study

Clause complex versus group complex

IFG, Chapter 8 discusses group and phrase complexes in detail, including the type of structures in (35), (36) and (37), which are analyzed not as clause complexes but as verbal group complexes. (See also Further study section of Chapter 7 in this book.)

(35) The police cars started to arrive.
(36) Stop thinking about it.
(37) We'll have to organize ourselves.

On this analysis, two (or more) verbal groups are combined to make up a hypotactic group complex within a single clause.

Structures with verbs like *want* followed by a to-infinitive are on the boundary between hypotactic clause complexes and verbal group complexes.

Verbs such as *want, wish, expect, hope* obviously resemble those in (35) and (37) in their potential for combining with to-infinitives, but they also resemble mental process projecting verbs such as *think* and *believe*. When they combine with *that*-clauses (as *wish, expect,* and *hope* readily do), we do have clear cases of hypotactic projection with the *that*-clause as a dependent, as in (38).

(38) I hope that he can build one of these.

However, when they combine with to-infinitive structures, as in (39) and (40), the analysis is more debatable.

(39) I hope/want to build one of these.
(40) I want him to build one of these.

Section 8.8 of IFG points out that these structures might be analyzed as either (i) verbal group complexes in a single clause or as (ii) hypotactic projections in two clauses. The authors express some preference for treating instances like (39) as (i) and instances like (40) as (ii), but concede that the decision is not at all clear-cut. On the two-clause analysis (40) would be analyzed as in Fig. 10.12.

||| I want ||	him to build one of these. |||
α	β

Fig. 10.12

One drawback of this analysis is that the pronoun in the second clause must be construed as the Subject, yet it is clearly in the objective form. Since the clause is moodless, maybe there is no Subject, but if it is not the Subject, what is the function of *him*?

There are implications for experiential analysis in these alternative approaches (see Chapter 6). If we treat *I want to build one of these* as two clauses, we analyze it as a mental process with *I* as Senser and the infinitive clause as Phenomenon. If it is a single clause, it is a material process with *I* as Actor (since the key verb – the Event – is *build*). Similarly, if we treat (40) as two clauses, then we analyze the clause complex as a mental process with *I* as Senser and the infinitival clause as Phenomenon. But if we treat it as a single clause with a verbal complex, we analyze it as a material process with *I* realizing Initiator and *you* realizing Actor.

The Cardiff school (Fawcett, Tucker, *et al.*) do not accept the need for the category of hypotactic verbal group complexes. In fact, they do not use the concept of the verbal group at all, treating each element that Halliday would handle as an element of the group as a direct element of the clause (Fawcett 2000b, 2000c and Chapter 4 of Fawcett, in press). But they also reject the hypotactic clause analysis for projections and expansions ('dependent clause' in our terminology), treating them as embedded clauses.

Exercises

Exercise 10.1

Identify the italicized dependent clauses in the following as expansions or projections.

1. Lindgren had told him on the phone *that the man had been scalped.*
2. Driesch conceded *that the environment exerted some effect on development.*
3. Remove the steering wheel *as described in Chapter 9.*
4. They write *to remake the world.*

5. So the official spokesman always keeps his comments as vague and uncontroversial as possible *when the journalists' questions touch on more sensitive issues.*
6. Bonaparte seems to have hoped almost to the end *that Josephine would come with him.*
7. By what mechanism could he have hoped, even in principle, *to predict the future with certainty on the basis of knowledge of the present?*
8. Vito Volterra was an outstanding Italian mathematician of the first part of this century, *whose work strongly influenced the development of modern calculus.*

Exercise 10.2

Say whether the italicized clauses below are embedded or dependent. Ignore any further embeddings within the italicized section.

1. The government's efforts *to destroy Zapatismo* were futile.
2. Francisco Madero believed, however, *that Díaz could only be removed by force.*
3. Emiliano received the information *that General Huerta had crossed into Morelos.*
4. Zapata decided *that it was time for him to escape from Mexico City.*
5. He held the belief *that the land rightly belonged to those who tilled it.*
6. Carranza ordered Obregon *to advance upon Mexico City as fast as possible.*
7. Inform him *that his rebellious attitude is disturbing my government.*
8. He did not like *what he saw.*
9. In short, the hypothesis is *that every time series of price change data has Bachelier's independence, stationarity and normality properties.*
10. The stationarity hypothesis says *that regardless of when we start taking observations, i.e., the initial time t*, the time series of price changes obeys the same probability law.*

Exercise 10.3

Indicate clause boundaries and label hypotactic complexes as α, β, and paratactic complexes as 1, 2.

1. We want to remind residents that a little care can save an awful lot of heartache.
2. 'Maybe it won't get here at all,' said the waitress.
3. He promised he'd come by.

4. He concedes the effect was a touch farcical.
5. I said, 'She *may* see him.'
6. He replied: 'I am not concerned with the intention of the law.'
7. 'Can we take some pictures?' asked the man from *Labour News*.
8. I asked him whether he had ever felt threatened.

Exercise 10.4

Label the following examples in the same way as the previous exercise. These are more challenging. Indicate embedded clauses with double square brackets.

1. 'It looks like a film shoot,' said the woman, pointing at the floodlights in the charred field.
2. I think Martinssen went out to get something to eat.
3. 'But you said you'd have a real holiday,' said Paul, 'and now you work.'
4. If he didn't, his colleagues would think he was arrogant.
5. Weir said, 'Get out before another one blows.'
6. David Rigg explains: 'As you poise your pen over the piece of paper, you think of your girlfriend's number.'
7. 'There's one thing that's odd,' said Högland.
8. It wasn't natural to think that someone would intentionally have torn off his hair.
9. Bachelier thought it was reasonable to assume that the Central Limit Theorem of probability theory would apply to these price fluctuations.
10. Geldof just says that when he sees something he thinks could be changed he considers it his duty to do anything in his power to flag it up.

Exercise 10.5

Analyze the following clause complex (α, β, etc; 1, 2, etc.) and add SFPCA labels.

Seated in Sawiyeto's second house, we were asked if we wanted coffee and we accepted.

Exercise 10.6

Consider the dialogue in Text 10A.

> 'You mean you're going to tell me you knew me when you braced me yesterday?' I asked. 'And you're going to tell me Bush hadn't told you to bet on him? And you didn't until afterwards? And you knew about his record because you used to be a bull? And you thought if you could get me to put it to him you could clean up a little dough playing him?'

Text 10A   (Hammett, *Red Harvest*,[1] p. 85). Note: obsolete American slang: *brace* – face up to; *bull* – policeman; *dough* – money.

(a) What impression do you think the narrator (the I-character) is trying to give?
(b) How does he achieve this?
(c) What is striking about the clauses in the first paragraph?
(d) How many clauses are there in the first sentence: 'You mean … asked?'
(e) What is the clause relation of *you knew me* to *you're going to tell me*?
(f) What is the clause relation of *when you braced me yesterday* to *you knew me*?
(g) Indicate clause boundaries and label the clauses in the clause complex: *And you're going to tell me Bush hadn't told you to bet on him?*

Exercise 10.7

(a) Give a nominalized (grammatical metaphor) equivalent of the following verbal projection clause complexes.
(b) Double-bracket embedded clauses [[ ]], and analyze the structures as Modifiers and Head.

   1. We assume that x equals y.
   2. He insists that he is innocent.
   3. She concluded that he was lying.

Exercise 10.8

(a) Suggest a more congruent version of the following nominalizations.
(b) Indicate clause boundaries in your version and label for dependency (α, β).

   1. … her son's promise to burn the sofa …
   2. … Ernst Meyer's remark that advances in biology involve conceptual shifts …

Note

1. Hammett, Dashiel 1975: (originally published by Cassell & Co. 1950): *Red Harvest*. London: Pan Books.

11

Applications of functional analysis

11.1 *Explanations and theories*

Perhaps the main message of this book is that language is worth studying for its own sake. In the same way that scientists have sought for many hundreds of years to understand the nature of the universe, the secret of living things and the functions of the human body, grammarians and other linguists have struggled to understand more about how human language is structured and to explain how communication takes place. Some people, however, not only find this objective daunting but they fear that the analysis of language, even a functional analysis, may subtract from the richness and beauty of language.

The American philosopher Daniel C. Dennett (1991, p. 454) writes about explanations in the following way:

> When we learn that the only difference between gold and silver is the number of subatomic particles in their atoms, we may feel cheated or angry – those physicists have explained something away: the goldness is gone from the gold; they've left out the very silveriness of silver that we appreciate. And when they explain the way reflection and absorption of electromagnetic radiation accounts for colors and color vision, they seem to neglect the very thing that matters most. But of course there has to be some 'leaving out' – otherwise we wouldn't have begun to explain. Leaving out something is not a feature of failed explanations, but of successful explanations.

In the previous chapters of this book, we have introduced methods of analysis that can be used to give insight into how the English language is structured. Each method of analysis can be seen as a hypothesis about *part of* the structure of English. We can see, for example, that the analysis of clause as exchange (by splitting it into its SFPCA components) is making the claim that clauses are constructed of up to five kinds of constituents, each having its own distinct characteristics. Similarly, the analysis of clause as message (into Theme-Rheme and Given-New) makes the claim that information is structured by the ordering of two sets of parallel elements selected on the basis of the speaker's and hearer's shared understanding and on the textual constraints that govern the speaker's choice of starting point for the clause. These hypotheses, along with all the other claims about language summarized in this book, make up together a linguistic theory, a theory that incorporates the idea mentioned in Chapter 1 of this book that a language is a set of systems.

In this chapter we address some major questions. How can we test the truth of individual hypotheses and the validity of the theory? What use is the theory to the non-linguist who may nevertheless have an interest in language and the use of language: the teacher, the writer, the politician, the translator, the literary critic, the therapist, and so on? If a functional theory of language has any validity, it should, we believe, render insights into the way language works in social interaction.

Halliday (1994, p. xxix) described a theory as 'a means of action'. By this he means that we should be able to use a theory, and the hypotheses related to it, as the basis for a very wide range of tasks, not only our grand aim of understanding the nature and functions of language, but also more practical tasks like helping people to learn foreign languages, improving our writing skills, or training interpreters. Halliday, in fact, lists 21 distinct applications of functional linguistics and concedes that there are more.

11.2   *Writing in science and technology*

One area of interest for applied linguists is the way in which scientific and technical ideas are expressed in English. Many people, both native speakers and non-native speakers, find the language of scientific thought extremely difficult to access, and some educators believe that the language of science acts as a barrier to learning in the field, discouraging some children from achieving success in science. There are also many adults, with no technical training or background, working in business, journalism or the arts, who have, in recent years, needed to learn computational techniques and have had to struggle with instruction manuals that they found difficult to understand. Internationally, scientists whose first language is not English often need to read textbooks or research articles published in English, and many wish to publish in English themselves. Such practical problems of teaching and learning in relation to science have led to a number of investigations into the nature of scientific writing.

Halliday and Martin (1993) address the problem from two points of view: the identification of the particular characteristics of scientific prose and the issues involved in educating children to use and understand language appropriate to specific contexts. In both these tasks, they use aspects of functional grammar to analyze and describe the language and to explain how it developed (from an historical perspective) in the way that it did.

Among the specific grammatical features of scientific writing discussed by Halliday and Martin is grammatical metaphor (see our Section 6.8) and in particular the nominalization of processes, and we discuss this further here as an example of the type of application that has proved enlightening.

Nominalization allows a process, more obviously realized as a verb, to be realized as a noun and hence to become a participant in a further process. Many anaphoric nouns (see Chapter 5) are of this type. Some examples can be seen in Fig. 11.1.

Verb	Noun
suggest	suggestion
indicate	indication
describe	description
compare	comparison
apply	application

Fig. 11.1   Nominalized processes

If we use a verb to express a process in a declarative clause, it is necessary to give the verb a Subject, and in the case of some verbs, like *describe,* for example, a Complement as well. This entails expressing the participants in the process. However, if we nominalize the process, we can exclude the participants relating to that process, as we can see from the following invented examples, numbered (1) and (2).

(1)   Moorehead described the journeys of Bruce.
(2)   The description is incomplete.

With the use of the verb in (1), it was necessary to include a reference to the person who wrote the description (Moorehead in this case) and also a reference to *what* he described (the journeys of Bruce), whereas in (2), where the process is nominalized, neither of these participants is required. It follows that where authors are not concerned with assigning responsibility for actions or events but are more interested in what is going on, they may well prefer to use a grammatical metaphor.

The explanation of the term *pollination* in (3) comes from an agricultural textbook by Akinsanmi.

(3)   Pollination is the physical transfer of pollen grains from the anther to the stigma. There are two types of pollination: self-pollination and cross-pollination. Self-pollination takes place when the pollen grains are transferred from the anther to the stigma of a flower on the same plane. Cross-pollination occurs when the pollen grains are transferred from the anther of a flower of one plant to the stigma of a flower of a different plant of the same species.

Here the Agent of the process of pollination is not mentioned as a participant in the process. The text refers to the *physical transfer of pollen grains* but does not explain how this transfer takes place or what causes it. The writer in the passage above presents the transfer as an abstract process in such a way as to cover all cases. A few sentences further on in the same text, however, we find (4), a clause where the writer of the text chooses to introduce, as New information, precise details about the animate and inanimate things which undertake the work of pollination.

(4) The common agents of pollination are insects, birds, wind and animals, especially man.

The writer makes the assumption that the reader 'understands' that there must be agents of pollination and so feels able to put *the common agents of pollination* in Theme position. He can then present his New information (*are insects, birds, wind and animals*) in Rheme position.

The tendency to use nominal groups has a number of major effects on scientific text. First, it is a means whereby all reference to people can be omitted, and scientific knowledge can be presented as though it has some external objective reality quite apart from the people who are engaged in observing or researching it. This facilitates the expression of general 'truths' and 'claims' about the nature of the world. Second, it gives the writer a wide choice of elements for Theme position in the clause. Not only can a process easily become the starting point in the clause (which can be useful for textual cohesion as we saw in Chapter 5), but it allows agents – or even further processes – to be left to the end of the clause (in Rheme position) where they carry more communicative dynamism. Third, as discussed in Section 6.8, it allows the process to become the Head of a nominal group and, so available for modification, or Classifier in a nominal group. Examples can be seen in Fig. 11.2.

Nominal as Head	Nominal as Classifier
oil gallery *lubrication*	*lubrication* process
muscular *contraction*	*contraction* rate
root *penetration*	weld *penetration zone*
sheet metal *fabrication*	*fabrication* engineering
technical *information*	*information* technology

Fig. 11.2   Nominalized processes in nominal groups

Furthermore, the nominalization of processes enables the writer to concisely display relationships (like *cause, result, reason, comparison* and *dependency*) between processes, as in the following examples, the first of which is quoted by Halliday (Halliday and Martin, 1993, p. 87).

(5) The rate of crack growth *depends on* the chemical environment.
(6) Evaporation *causes* cooling.
(7) The multiplication of fractions *is easier than* addition or subtraction.

Halliday (Halliday and Martin, 1993, pp. 86–93) refers to verbs like *cause, depend on, result in*, as expressing 'internal relations' between different parts of the clause. 'Cooling', in (6), is an example of the gerund form of a process and is representative of an alternative form of nominalization in English.

Nominalization and other grammatical characteristics of scientific texts are discussed by Martin (Halliday and Martin, 1993), who shows, in some detail, both how important they are for the expression of scientific knowledge and also how schoolchildren need to be oriented into the use of appropriate scientific language at an early age. In a perceptive critique of misguided syllabus documents for primary education (in an Australian context but equally applicable in many countries), Martin (Halliday and Martin, 1993, p. 172) makes the following observations (slightly abridged here):

> People sometimes complain that science uses too much technical language which they refer to pejoratively as 'jargon'. They complain because the jargon excludes: it makes science hard to understand. This is a problem. Jargon is often used where it is not needed. . . . However, the simple fact is that no scientist could do his or her job without technical discourse. Not only is it compact and therefore efficient, but most importantly it codes a different perspective on reality, a perspective accumulated over centuries of scientific enquiry. It constructs the world in a different way. Science could not be science without deploying technical discourse as a fundamental tool. It is thus very worrying when syllabus documents discourage teachers from using technical language with students, especially in the early years.

Support for Martin's position can be found in Lassen (2003) who worked on accessibility and acceptability in technical manuals. She was interested in finding out about the different attitudes of expert and non-expert readers to specialist texts, and her empirical research found that the readers for whom the texts were designed preferred the texts that used grammatical metaphor and had no problems with comprehension.

Martin does not, of course, deny that it is perfectly possible to have popularizations of science designed to explain scientific research to non-scientists. School textbooks (which are a main concern of Martin's discussion) are a type of popularization of scientific information, but efficient textbooks gradually introduce the important technical language for expressing scientific concepts and functions (like *classification, definition, analysis*, and *explanation*) so that the student is oriented into scientific discourse and empowered to take on roles in scientific communities (see also Martin, 1989).

On the issue of accessibility to knowledge, there have been a number of studies of the differences between the discourse of research articles published in specialist journals and the discourse of popular versions directed at non-scientists, written for popular books, newspapers or magazines.

Using the tools of thematic analysis and the description of processes, mood and modality, Francis and Kramer-Dahl (1991) contrast the writing of two neuroscientists, one (Kertesz) who writes in the traditional 'dry and factual' style of a professional case report and one (Sacks) who consciously breaks away from the 'objective', restrained style and replaces it with an apparently more subjective, popular and less 'scientific' style, closer to narrative and biography. Starting from the three metafunctions, ideational, interpersonal and textual, Francis and Kramer-Dahl are able to show how Sacks incorporates science into his storytelling and how he is making a serious attempt to 'bridge the gap between distant and near experience, between scientific and everyday knowledge and between specialized and everyday audiences'. This is not, however, to say that popular versions could replace scientific 'expert to expert' discourse.

Nwogu and Bloor (1991, pp. 369–84) show how the patterns of thematic progression (explained in Chapter 5) differ in two types of medical text. Although the constant Theme pattern and the linear Theme pattern occur frequently in both types, journalists who write popular versions of medical reports seem to prefer the linear Theme pattern. In contrast, in professional versions, the scientists prefer the constant Theme pattern. A further distinction is that Themes in popular versions are normally realized by names of scientists acting as agents in the clause rather than by nominal processes, which are more often found in serious research articles. They comment as follows:

> It is a truism of register analysis that scientific prose is by convention impersonal, and the received rationale for this is that it is the 'science' that matters rather than the individuals who engage in it. To a large extent this is the correct explanation. Although no one who has experience of the academic world can believe that individual scientists genuinely wish to play down their own role in the enterprise, they do wish to give the impression of doing so, thereby conforming to the expectations of the scientific peer group.

The study of thematic progression in texts has also been used to compare the work of native speakers writing in English with that of non-native speakers (sometimes known as 'contrastive rhetoric'). Ventola and Mauranen are separately and jointly responsible for a number of studies of this type and jointly edited a collection of articles on academic writing in 1996. From research into ways in which Finnish scientists write in English, Ventola and Mauranen (1991) analyzed patterns of thematic progression and found that the native speaker texts showed more variation in thematic patterns than the Finnish writers' texts. The Finnish writers used, almost exclusively, either a linear Theme or a constant Theme pattern whereas the native speakers used all available patterns. The study also found that Finnish writers, on the whole, used less lexical cohesion between Themes, fewer cohesive conjunctions and overused a very limited number of 'favourite' connectors, such as *however*, *thus*, *therefore*, and *also*. A useful summary of similar work including references to that of other authors, can be found in Mauranen's chapter in Hewings (2001).

A rather different application of functional grammar to academic writing has concerned the use of different verbal processes in research articles. So-called *reporting verbs* commonly function as sources of projection, as in the following examples.

> Keyseling *pointed out* that . . .
> McGin *explains that* . . .
> Nagel *claims* that . . .

These are generally known as *reporting verbs* since they are used to introduce the ideas and views of cited authors whose work is being reported. Their use in research articles has attracted some attention, usually with the objective of preparing teaching materials for overseas learners of English for academic purposes.

Using a functional model, Thompson and Ye Yiyun (1991) investigate the reporting verbs used in the introductions to one hundred research articles from a variety of fields. They propose a three-part classification of reporting verbs as follows.

> *Textual.* Verbs referring to processes in which the verbal expression is an obligatory component. For example: *state, write, challenge, point out, deny.*
> *Mental.* Verbs referring primarily to mental processes. For example: *believe, think, consider, prefer.*
> *Research.* Verbs referring primarily to the mental or physical processes that are part of research work. For example: *measure, calculate, quantify, obtain, find.*

They also consider the stance (or attitude) of the author being cited to the reported information and the stance of the writer as revealed in the reporting verbs chosen.

Thomas and Hawes (1994) followed up this study with a detailed analysis of the reporting verbs in medical journal articles and identified the patterns of choice available in terms of a network. They name their major categories: (1) real-world activity verbs, such as *observe, find* and *categorize*; (2) cognition verbs, such as *think, believe* and *consider*; and (3) discourse activity verbs, such as *state, suggest*, and *report*.

More recently, a variety of books and research articles have been published concerning the language of specific scientific disciplines and specific types of interaction, including work on computer science (Bloor M., 1996 and 1998), cancer research articles (Gledhill 2000), as well as a number of studies comparing discipline-specific texts (for example, Bloor M., 1999 and 2004). The collection edited by Martin and Veel (1998) brings together key articles on aspects of scientific and technological discourse, including work on popular science writing, writing in industry and science fiction texts. Such work can be enlightening not only to those concerned with bringing scientific developments to a wider readership but also to teachers who wish to support novice writers in scientific fields.

11.3   *Valued texts*

The question of how to speak or write more effectively is one that has been of interest to educators and critics for hundreds of years. Most teachers and literary critics have something to say on the subject, and innumerable books and leaflets have been written setting out advice on public speaking and on how to write everything from school essays to business letters. Although classical rhetoric considered the relationship between language and communicative effects in some detail, most educational approaches in recent times (at least for English) have focused on matters such as preparation and planning and how to approach the topic without overt discussion of language. For public speaking and lecturing, we find advice on tone of voice and volume, and for writing, on correct layout and the mechanics of spelling and punctuation, but lexicogrammar is largely neglected, except for pointing out common stylistic 'errors' or infelicities.

Most people would agree that language users differ in their ability to communicate effectively. There is an intuitive concept of 'valued text', which is to say instances of speaking or writing that are considered 'better' in some ways than others. Yet it is very difficult sometimes to explain precisely why one speaker or writer seems better than another. We tend to use vague descriptive terms such as 'clearer', 'more interesting', 'easier to understand', but novices often find that advice given in such terms is not of much practical use. The teacher puts 'write more clearly' or 'confusing' at the end of a student's essay, but the student is none the wiser about *how* to write more clearly, and the teacher might also be hard put to specify the differences between the clear writer's text and the poor writer's text.

In recent research in applied linguistics, some of the techniques of functional grammar are being used to discover the precise features of valued texts, and there is clearly a lot of scope for further work in this area, not only for educational purposes but also for business, journalism, politics and other fields where effective communication is important. Recently, for example, interest has been expressed in the discourse of public administration and calls have been made for application of strong analytic methods to this area. Iedema (2003) has already made a relevant contribution in this area.

Methods of linguistic analysis give us the tools for investigating the characteristics of valued text, and a number of research studies have identified measurable characteristics of such texts. The outcomes can be used to evaluate the relative success of written and formal spoken language, and to make useful comparisons between texts. We illustrate this type of study with typical examples.

Berry (1989) uses the analysis of Theme to investigate children's ability to write appropriately in the specific genre of a guidebook for tourists. The task of writing a town guide was set as a writing competition for schoolchildren. Some children clearly captured a recognizably adult style for a tourist guide (*Grantham is 108 miles north of London*), especially in their selection of third person topical Themes, whereas others used a less appropriate style with first and second person pronoun Themes, such as *I think Grantham is a nice place to visit.* Berry shows how the more successful writers were able to control their thematic choices more consistently than the less successful writers.

McCarthy and Carter (1994) show how an advertisement for time-share holidays utilizes contrastive thematic structure within the same text. The persuasive section of the text is written in an interactional, informal style, with the use of personal pronouns (*we* and *you*) in Theme position (*You could be enjoying a five star holiday*; *All we ask is that you spend two hours of your time attending a Barratt sales presentation*). The 'small print' section of the text, where the restrictions and regulations are listed, displays a more formal style with a different selection of Themes (*To qualify you must be over 21*; *Present owners are not eligible*; *All flight arrangements are made by ...*). McCarthy and Carter claim that the latter type of writing can 'distance the reader from the text' and discourage 'any sustained reading of this section', which may be to the advantage of the advertiser. Such work is, of course, of interest to copywriters, but studies like these also provide a strong argument for raising the linguistic awareness of consumers, since readers who are aware of linguistic tricks are better equipped to evaluate persuasive texts.

There is a popular view that short sentences and simple clauses are easier to understand than clause complexes or clauses with multiple embedding. Comparative research can be used as a way to test this hypothesis. Anderson and Davison (1988) considered a wide body of research in this area and concluded that complex clause structures can actually facilitate text comprehensibility because clause relationships are more clearly indicated. Turning to spoken English, Tyler (1994) studied the effect of hypotactic and paratactic structures on the comprehensibility of lectures. Previous research had shown that native speakers of English used more hypotactic structures than paratactic structures in planned spoken discourse (see Chapters 9 and 10 for an explanation of these structures). Tyler found that there was little evidence for the popular view that less complex structures are easier to understand. One analysis found that a lecturer who used a high frequency of hypotactic structures and embedded relatives was rated by students as easier to understand than another who used far simpler structures.

We agree with Tyler that a quantitative analysis (such as counting sentence length, lexical density, or number of clauses per sentence) is only part of the story. Since hypotaxis can signal the speaker's intended logical and prominence relations, it can work as a comprehension aid. To discover why complex structures are sometimes easier to understand, we need to consider their functions within the text, or possibly within whole context of use.

It is clear that there are significant grammatical features of valued texts that can be learned by speakers or writers who wish to improve their communication skills. Work of this type supports the view that simplistic linguistic analysis, based only on grammatical infelicities, such as so-called 'error analysis', is little help in the evaluation of the success of communicative acts. For such purposes we need a rich linguistic system, such as that provided by a functional lexicogrammar, in order to identify what is successful within its own communicative context.

11.4   *Language development and language teaching*

Children's acquisition of language and their early language development are of interest to educators, psychologists, the medical profession and parents. SFL has been used as an analytic tool in both of these applications following Halliday's (1975) original study of a child's acquisition of English as a mother tongue using a functional model. Halliday (2003b) is a selection of Halliday's extensive work on child language.

A major contributor to this application as well as to language in education is Painter, who in a detailed study (1984 and 1989) of acquisition processes and achievements made more explicit the criteria for recognizing the intended functions of the child's speech, something which Halliday had not dealt with in any detail. More recently, Painter (1999) has recorded and analyzed the way a pre-school child uses language as a learning tool and the ways in which the child constructs meaning. This is particularly interesting in that it shows how and when a child begins to talk about abstract entities and develops reasoning skills, using the grammar needed to express conditions, cause and effect, and so on.

Of relevance to those working with children of school age is the work of Christie, who has looked at both natural language development and language in education as, for example, in Christie (2002). As well as having been one of the earliest series editors for books relating language education and SFL theory (for Oxford University Press), she has published influential articles on language in teacher development, the school language curriculum, and language use across disciplines. Writing from a social constructionist position, she has interesting things to say about the ways in which content and language are linked, supporting the views of Martin in Section 11.2 above. She also worked with Martin on social processes in the workplace and school (see Christie and Martin, 1997). Her work also includes a book (2002) on discourse in the classroom and edited collections on literacy and other issues in language education: Christie (1999) and Christie and Mission (1998).

Martin (1989) considers factual writing by both children and adults within an SFL framework and draws comparisons between them. The book is revealing about the state of language education at the time and Martin made a strong case for the importance of a sound approach to the teaching of writing by linguistically informed teachers. It was also ground-breaking in its focus on the importance of lexical and grammatical metaphor as a means of establishing 'objectivity' in expository writing and of the need for children to be exposed to such stylistic devices. In a small but related application of grammatical analysis, Martin (in Halliday and Martin, 1993: pp. 211–13) uses Theme analysis to show the differences between the writing of an eight-year-old and the more sophisticated writing style of a 16-year-old on the same topic. The older writer used much lengthier themes (for example, *the atmosphere at the dawn service*) than the younger writer, who favoured Themes like *I*, *some* and *there*.

Applied linguists such as Carter and McCarthy, have been strong advocates for linguistics in teacher education. They argue that teachers not only need to pass on language skills to their students, they also need to understand the processes of language development that their students undergo and the uses (and varieties) of language in the society at large. Working within a largely SFL tradition, with a clear focus on discourse, they advocate teaching 'language awareness' in schools so that children grow up with a better understanding of how language is used to construct social practices (including political and institutional structures, the media, advertising, and so on). These different applications within an educational context are illustrated in works such as McCarthy (1991), McCarthy and Carter (1994), Carter and McRae (1996) and Carter (1997). The last mentioned investigates the uses of words such as 'proper' and 'standard' in relation to language in an educational setting, an issue not unrelated to the topic of how society values language use. He presents the case for the teaching of grammar through the analysis and investigation of real language use (spoken and written), rather than as an isolated and abstract study of individual sentence structure, so that the learner can appreciate the role of grammar in the creation of meaning. He proposes four tenets which modern language study should follow, each of which has a firm basis in SFL theory (1997, pp. 14–17). These hold that the study of the English language in school

- should be rooted in texts and contexts;
- must be principled and systematic;
- should be intimately connected with a study of social and cultural change;
- must recognize that the study of literature is central.

With respect to the final point, the writers make it clear that they include in the term 'literature' not only 'highly valued canonical texts' but also texts from a wide range of cultural contexts.

Further evidence of the importance SFL can have for language education can be seen in the work of Butt *et al.* (2000), an introductory course on SFL, which includes advice for teachers. Like Carter (1997), they advocate a text-based approach to language education which is firmly based in the context of language use. However, they differ from Carter in recommending the teaching of a standard *metalanguage* for talking about language both for teachers and students in school. This view has been widely encouraged in Australia with some success. Carter concedes that his grammatical focus 'may be seen by some linguists to be insufficiently formalized'. He favours a gentler approach, where grammar and discourse terms are introduced to teachers, going along 'with the not inconsiderable – though generally unformalized – knowledge that teachers already possess' (1997, p. 44).

Lock (1996), in his introductory book on functional English grammar for teachers, supports the view that there is a place in school for 'grammar as a resource for making and exchanging meanings in context'. He writes: 'Grammar teaching is now very much much on its way back into favour. However, it is important that there should not be a return to some of the practices of the past.' He argues that a systemic functional approach can be used to facilitate communication in all its modes.

Halliday himself has been personally involved in applying his insights to teaching ever since the early days of Systemic Functional Linguistics when he was a co-author with McIntosh and Strevens of the influential work *The Linguistic Sciences and Language Teaching*, first published in 1964. This work provided guidance for a whole generation of teachers, textbook writers and teacher trainers on the phonology and intonation of English, syllabus design and language for specific purposes.

Over the years, probably the most widespread Hallidayan influence on language teaching has been the work on cohesion. Nowadays work on cohesion is often related to specific genres, but from the date of the publication (1976) of *Cohesion in English* by Halliday and Hasan, it attracted the attention of teachers of English as a foreign language, who realized that here was an aspect of English that had been seriously neglected. A glance at textbooks written before that time reveals that most cohesive devices were not taught at all in any systematic way, and certain aspects of the grammar, particularly the nature of ellipsis and substitution in English, had previously been misrepresented in pedagogic grammars. Nowadays, all general course books and most reading and writing courses incorporate work designed to help learners grasp the cohesive devices of written English. Nuttall (1985), in her important book for teachers on the development of reading skills, emphasized the importance of readers' mastery of cohesive devices. She commented:

> Pronoun reference, elliptical sentences and so on are often so straightforward that their potential difficulty is overlooked, and it is only when he [*sic*] encounters problems that the student will think them worth attending to. The problems that arise concern the signification of sentences: the reader who does not know what a pronoun refers to, or who cannot supply the full version of an elliptical sentence, will not be able to establish its signification.

It is only recently, however, that teachers and course designers have become aware of other linguistic aspects of textual coherence, such as thematic patterns. Similarly, very little of the work on evaluative functions of language use, such as those available from the astute use of modal and comment adjuncts (see Section 3.4.3 and below) has yet found its way into the language classroom. There is also scope for the application of work on appraisal (see, for example Christie and Martin, 1997, and an introduction to appraisal theory by White (2003)).

In one study, Bloor and Bloor (1992) identified three types of stylistic infelicity in written academic texts caused by unusual use of the Theme–Rheme and Given–New dimension of the grammar. They found that inexperienced writers do not always have sufficient command of the grammatical devices that can be used to control the position of Given and New information in the clause. Since there can be no recourse to intonation and stress in written English, they suggest that more attention needs to be given in teaching to this aspect of the grammar. A sophisticated writer in an academic context needs a good control of the grammar of thematic equatives, predicated theme, and the various exponents of textual theme (see Chapters 5 and 6) as well as an understanding of the distribution of Given and New information. This control is, of course, often intuitive, but there is no doubt that some writers, particularly those working in a foreign language, can be helped to improve their style by teachers who can raise their awareness of such issues.

In other respects, functional grammar has been particularly useful in the development of course design in English for Specific Purposes (ESP) and English for Academic Purposes. Munby's work (1978) on the design of communicative syllabuses, which calls for close attention to appropriate language use in course design for adult learners, is based on the assumption that 'language varies as its function varies; it differs in different situations' (Halliday *et al.*, 1964).

In fact, much of the descriptive research using a Hallidayan model has been driven by the needs of language course designers who have found that not enough was known about typical linguistic behaviour in specific social contexts. Some of this work is reported by Dudley-Evans and St John (1998), who stress the importance of the relationship of grammar to discourse domains for teachers of ESP. Teachers need to appreciate the features of the genres that their students need to master so that they are able to convey to learners how a particular text performs the function for which it was intended.

In a particularly useful piece of genre analysis, Ventola (1983; 1987) investigated the structure and language of goal-directed verbal exchanges in a shop, a post office and a travel agency. Similarly, Swales (1984; 1990; and elsewhere) is influenced by functional models in his development of *genre analysis* as an aid to the teaching of language skills for specific communicative events, spoken and written. He develops a methodology for analyzing rhetorical *moves* in written texts (specifically the introductions to research articles) and identifying the significant linguistic expressions related to each move.

A major interest of genre analysts has continued to be writing in an academic context, particularly research articles published in academic journals. Such work has involved the use of both lexical and grammatical analysis, and a particularly interesting and fruitful line of enquiry has been concerned with features of modality. Stubbs (1986), while providing a fascinating overview of work on modality at the time of writing, made a strong case for continued analytical field work into the use of modal forms and 'vague language'. Since his paper was published, more work has been done on vague language and the use of hedging in academic journal articles (see, for example, Pindi and Bloor, 1987, and Channell, 1994, and, in particular, the work of Myers discussed below.)

Surprisingly, when researchers writing in English make knowledge claims based on their research evidence, they rarely make bald confident statements, but they usually modify their propositions by the use of modal verbs such as *may*, modal adjuncts such as *possibly* or lexical items that decrease the force of a proposition such as *indicate* or *appear*. Thus, we find, for instance, *This would appear to be in conflict with . . .* rather than *This is in conflict with . . .* and *These results may have relevance to . . .* rather than *These results have relevance to . . .* and (in an example from Myers' 1989 data) *These results suggest that U1 RNP is essential for the splicing of mRNA precursors . . .* rather than *These results show that. . . .*

Myers (1990; and elsewhere) has argued that hedging of this type in scientific articles does not, as some have argued, indicate a lack of commitment to the proposition on behalf of the writer(s) – indeed, it is clear in most cases that the writers are fully committed to the value of their claims – but rather that hedging is used to mitigate what might otherwise be considered a face-threatening activity, something that could cause offence to fellow researchers, after the earlier work of Brown and Levinson (1987) on politeness in spoken English. Myers sums up his own view in the following (suitably hedged) claim: 'The hedging of claims is so common that a sentence that looks like a claim but has no hedging is probably not a statement of new knowledge.'

Myers' work on hedging in scientific articles was followed up with work on economics articles (Dudley-Evans, 1993; Bloor and Bloor, 1993) where a

rather more complex picture emerges. Hedging is equally common in economics, particularly hedging of major claims on theoretical issues in economics, but a variety of types of claim can be observed, some of which are not
hedged. It has also been noted that hedging of claims may be more common
in English than in some other languages (Bloor and Bloor, 1991), which has
implications both for translation of research articles and for writers whose
first language is not English but who are seeking to publish in English language journals.

Hyland (1994; 1998) not only provides a useful overview of many
studies of hedging not discussed here but also surveys the teaching of such
aspects of modality in textbooks on English for academic purposes. He
finds that this area of the language is widely neglected even in the teaching
of writing with only a patchy coverage of a limited range of items. Hyland
supports Dudley-Evans' view that: 'Materials writers need detailed analyses
of the rhetorical and linguistic organization of the tasks (that need to be
taught) if they are not to be over-reliant on their own intuition.' Hyland
(2000) looks in more detail at authorial stance and other social interaction
in academic writing.

It is precisely because of such detailed analysis that genre and register
studies have proved useful in many educational projects in schools and
universities around the world.

11.5   *Language and literature: stylistic analysis*

The discussion of valued texts (Section 11.3) leads, almost inevitably, to the
thought of great works of literature since these are the texts most highly valued in literate societies. In non-literate societies, spoken rhetoric and story
telling are equally highly valued and speakers are honoured for their contributions. Of course, we are not suggesting here that scientific, academic,
media texts and so on should be *less* valued in their own contexts than literature (see Kress, 1998).

Literature has traditionally been the province of literary critics and the academic discipline of literary study, but, after the innovative work of I.A.
Richards, 1929, an increased interest was shown in the language of literature
and this led to what came to be known as *stylistics*, which used linguistic techniques to support the investigation of literary texts.

Of historical interest is Leech's *A Linguistic Guide to English Poetry*,
which was published in 1969, but, by the 1970s, a range of what Quirk in his
Preface to Leech and Short (1981) referred to as 'the new stylistics' was being
produced, much of it firmly grounded in SFG. *Style in Fiction* Leech and
Short (1981, p. 382) was a key work in establishing the type of analysis that
could prove insightful to our understanding of literature. They credit

Halliday, the Prague School and Chomsky (Chapter 12) as influences on their linguistic thinking although even for a careful reader it is difficult to find much of Chomsky in the book. They take on board the metafunctional theory of Halliday (Chapter 1) and see language within literature as contextually governed.

Overall, published work in stylistics varies in the attention given to the role of different metafunctions in literary text as well as to the degree in which the analysis is quantitative or qualitative. Some analysis focuses more on the ideational, some on the interpersonal and some on the textual.

Halliday's key work of 1971, which looked in some detail at Golding's novel *The Inheritors*, compares the language at different stages of the novel, largely in the variable use of linguistic patterns. Each of the three sections of the novel is written in a different style, each with a preferred set of grammatical patterns, such as nominal group modification and transitivity options. The language is shown to reflect the behaviour and social interaction of the characters and communities represented. Thus, the first style, supposedly used by a character from pre-history with a limited construct of the world around him, has very few instances of human Actors. Humans more often appear as 'affected' participants in mental processes. In addition, in this section of the book, Golding uses an 'excessive' number of circumstantial elements, mostly concerning objects in the natural environment ('in the bushes', 'under water', etc.). Consequently, there is no cause–effect relationship expressed in this part of the book. Halliday contrasts this style with those used in the other two sections, making the point that the frequency of linguistic forms establishes a 'norm' within a particular text, or part of a text, which may differ from the rest of the literary work and may not represent the linguistic norms of the language as a whole.

General, broad spectrum work on language in literature can be found in Cummings and Simons (1983) and Birch and O'Toole (1988). In addition, Cummings has used SFL in studies of Old English clause structure. Toolan (1998; 1992) is noted for his detailed investigation of narrative, drawing on rhetorical models and theories of plot structure as well as on more detailed functional analysis. Elsewhere, he has used linguistics as a tool in the sensitive analysis of short stories and poetry.

Much work in stylistics, and especially Halliday's own work on 'norms' metioned above, is of direct relevance to the current interest in *domain models,* that is to say variants of the general model of the language (Halliday and Matthiessen, 1999, pp. 320–3). A domain model would operate only in a specific context, specifying 'which of the semantic systems in the overall model are activated in a particular contextual field'. Such a model could allow for a narrow or wider band of domains. 'Narrow' domains might be *recipes* or *Shakespeare's sonnets*; wider domains incorporating these might be *instruction manuals* or *Elizabethan poetry.*

11.6   *Language and power*

Since language is a human social phenomenon, it develops and changes as people use it for social purposes. Much of our understanding of reality (our models of the world and the way in which we represent the world) is dependent on language. Usually we take this for granted and imagine that we can talk and write about the world in a completely objective way, using language as a tool that is separate from our experience, but, if we stand back, and look at the language that we use or the language that is used around us, we can see how the words and grammar picture reality in certain ways that at the same time reflect our attitudes and influence our future perception of the world. Halliday (1990) illustrates this with the way in which modern societies use the word *grow* with favourable connotations even when writing about activities that may not be good for the planet in any real long-term ways. Starting from the association of *growth* with such ideas as the *growing child* or the *growth of food and plants*, we now talk about *economic growth*, *industrial growth*, *growth in air transport*, and so on, and, regardless of reality, the idea that 'growth is good' permeates the language. He quotes from the *Sydney Morning Herald*, 12 March 1990, to the effect that the annual market forecast of an airplane manufacturing company 'says airline traffic to, from and within the Pacific area *will lead the growth* with rates unmatched anywhere else in the world' and adds that 'the rationale for *a more optimistic outlook* includes prolonged air travel expansion *driven by continued growth* in discretionary incomes' (our italics). This relates to a very common, but questionable, idea of Western culture that 'more is better' and 'bigger is better' discussed by Lakoff and Johnson (1980).

The example of *growth* is a good illustration of how a particular ideology can become set into the form of the language (in this case the lexical item 'grow') and where what might appear to be a standard – even objective – form is in fact coloured by a stock of opinions and attitudes.

A similar case, this time involving the grammatical use of possessive pronouns, concerns the use of the word *my* or *our* in conjunction with nominals representing things that, in fact, cannot be owned in any real sense, as for example in well-attested examples like *our language, my country, my home town, my wife/husband*. It seems likely that the use of possessives in this way can colour people's attitudes to the world and, as well as encouraging traditional loyalty and care, can also encourage possessiveness, nationalism and other negative emotions. If we think of a national group, for example, as belonging to 'us', we may seek to exclude others from having any right to live in that community. This is the type of situation that can lead to so-called 'ethnic cleansing', where people from one community, who may not actually be the sole owners of the land they live on, assert a privileged position with respect to land or property and force other people (the 'not-us') to leave on pain of death. In this way, political or national power can be reflected in the language and the language in turn can reinforce such power. Similarly, if we talk about the language we learn as infants as 'our' mother tongue or 'our' language, we are encouraged towards an affinity to that language which may discourage us from a desire to engage in interaction in other languages (which may be seen as 'belonging' to foreigners). It seems that some Central African languages, used in regions where most people tend to be multilingual, moving from one small language group to another, do not have the linguistic possibility of using possessive adjectives with the word *language* or of using a possessive pronoun to stand in place of the word *language*. Although speakers can talk about the language of such and such a village or such and such a region, the language is considered to be available to those who use it whether they are native speakers or not, and the notion that a language can be the 'property' of any group is considered nonsense.

Andersen (1988), who used linguistic approaches to look at political issues and at power and success in the academic world, believed that, although our experiences are largely shaped by the discourses of the societies in which we grow up, we can use our consciousness to re-articulate our experience. He wrote:

> Language can help us to become aware of the unconscious pressures that operate on the ways we think and behave. These pressures are not all related to deep and distant experiences lost in our infancies, but also to immediate social expectations that we should act out certain roles, behave and talk in certain ways. We can become more aware of these pressures and so make ourselves less liable to be influenced by them.

The exertion of power by individuals with certain social roles in particular social situations is often revealed in the form of the language, as is the corollary, lack of power. This has been studied, for example, in the context of the traditional classroom, where teachers, who have responsibility for both discipline and learning, dominate the interaction. Reynolds (1990) provides examples from classroom discourse which show how the teacher controls turns at speaking: (a) by naming the pupil they want to speak; (b) by preventing certain pupils from answering questions (calling on 'someone else'); (c) by taking turns themselves by interrupting a pupil's turn; and (d) by control of the topic. He points out that there are cases in his data where pupils challenge the teacher's power by commenting or initiating questions, and he shows how the teacher adapts his language, by making it more forceful, to re-assert control.

Fairclough (1989) comments on the range of linguistic features that he has noted in his investigations into the exercise of power relations in discourse, and adds that he hopes his readers who do not have a background in language analysis will appreciate how a close analysis of texts can help us to an understanding of power relations and ideological processes in discourse. In a recent article (1999), he explains that his objective is to show 'how a systematic and detailed textual analysis can add to a variety of current approaches to discourse analysis'.

In the earlier work, while stressing that *description* is only one stage in critical discourse analysis (the others are *interpretation* and *explanation*), Fairclough specifies the type of linguistic analysis that is appropriate for critical investigations into language use and suggests ten questions concerning vocabulary, grammar and textual features that we can ask about the features of a text. The questions concern the choice of words, grammatical form and text structure in terms of their experiential values (*how is the speaker/writer's experience of the world represented?*), relational values (*how are social relationships between interactants expressed?*) and expressive values (*how are the speaker/writer's attitudes to the topic expressed and social identities revealed?*). As lack of space here prevents a more detailed consideration, we list Fairclough's grammar questions, somewhat abridged, below:

1. What experiential values do grammatical features have?
   What types of *process* and *participant* dominate?
   Is agency unclear?
   Are processes what they seem?
   Are *nominalizations* used?
2. What relational values do grammatical features have?
   What *modes* (*declarative, interrogative, imperative*) are used?
   Are there important features of *relational modality*?
   Are the pronouns *we* and *you* used, and if so, how?
3. What expressive values do grammatical features have?
   Are there important features of *expressive modality*?
4. How are clauses linked together?
   What logical connectors are used?
   Are complex sentences characterized by *co-ordination* or *subordination*?

None of these questions will seem strange to readers of this book, who, if they have worked through Chapters 1 to 10, will now have a command of the skills necessary for this type of applied analysis. Of course, discovering what is in a text is insufficient in itself. The analyst must also be aware of alternative semantic or grammatical choices that a writer could have made in the context of the text.

11.7   *On applications and SFL theory*

In this chapter we have introduced some examples of where SFL has been used in the analysis of actual social events. This sample is inevitably highly selective and reflects our personal experience and interests. We could have considered applications in translation studies, medical discourse, psychology, corpus linguistics, the formulation of computational language modelling and text generation, and no doubt other areas.

It is clear, however, even to the critical observer, that SFL theory has proved productive as a tool for analyzing language in context and as a means of approaching real problems in human communication and social control. But what does this tell us about the answer to the other questions posed in the first section of this chapter concerning the truth of the hypotheses and the validity of the grammar as a whole?

The fact that a grammar or a linguistic theory can lead to insights about the use of language in social contexts does not mean, in itself, that it captures the whole truth about language. A theory must be internally consistent, sufficiently complex to handle all the phenomena, and, some would say, have the potential to provide an algorithm for the generation of language or even of discourse. No theory of grammar has yet achieved anything approaching these three goals. There is much still to be discovered about language. SFG, however, since it is a grammar that incorporates strong hypotheses about the linguistic nature of textuality as well as a means of analyzing processes and their participants, is already a useful tool for social action. It is only through such action that the theory can be developed.

As a direct result of the uses to which it has been applied, the theory of SFL has been improved, extended and polished. 'Ideally,' wrote Martin (1989) 'practice gives rise to new theory, which in turn enables new practice.' This precept is a useful one for those who are engaged in any branch of applied linguistics. If we understand the theory we are using, our applications will be more soundly based and we will be able to contribute the findings from our individual projects to the general body of theoretical knowledge. In short, SFL is an on-going research project to which every practitioner can contribute.

Summary

In this chapter we have looked at just a few of the ways in which the functional analysis of English has been used to help us understand human communication in social contexts. This type of applied research can, we have claimed, help us to use language more effectively, to develop language teaching syllabuses, to resist linguistic pressures and to recognize when people are using language to exploit or oppress others. The fact that functional linguistics has proved to be an effective tool for practical analysis in such a wide variety of research can act to some extent as a justification for the model. This chapter began with a discussion of justification of linguistic theory and the nature of applications and continued with a survey of just a few of the applications of functional grammar that have proved productive: understanding the language of science and technology, investigating the features of valued texts – including works of literature, and studies of the grammatical variation between professional and popular versions. The chapter also discussed applications of functional analysis to the teaching of English, and studies of child language acquisition and development. Finally, it looked at some of the work on language and power relations in social settings and the relationship of theory to practice.

Further study

A vibrant area of interest for applied SFL is the study of what is now referred to variously as *appraisal, stance* and *evaluation*. This work investigates the linguistic means by which a text carries the attitude of the speaker or writer or (in fiction) of characters in the text. Work in this area has provided insights into all the areas of application discussed so far in this chapter. The work on reporting verbs in academic writing (see Section 11.2 above) overlaps with this area of interest. Hunston and Thompson (2000) is a collection of key articles on this topic, which deals in the main with theoretical and linguistic issues although it does include some examples of application. White (2003) explains the general principles of appraisal and, in another application (2004), he presents a close study of stance in newspaper reports, focusing on the implicit evaluation in lexical choices which act as 'attitudinal triggers'.

Like the work of Fairclough discussed above, much of the current work on discourse analysis is conducted within the general framework of functional approaches to language study as is work on language in advertising and the media. This includes work on newspapers, television and radio discourse (for example, Bell and Garrett, 1998), and overlaps into studies of political discourse and gender. Issues of language and power often arise in this work. Useful introductory collections include Johnson and Meinhof (1997), and Jaworski and Coupland (1999).

A collection of work by Halliday on the language of science (2004a) is essential reading for those interested in this area of application. Halliday's and Martin's work, however, deals mainly with general characteristics of scientific language and discourse rather than specific genres or domains within science, which is of particular interest to ESP teachers. For example, domain-related studies are often published in the journal *English for Specific Purposes* and in specific collections (see, for example Bloor, M., 1998, on innovative language in a Computer Science department). For further interesting work, not precisely within a Hallidayan framework but with many identifiable links, you cannot do better than to read *Writing Biology*, the work by Myers (1990). This discusses the construction of scientific knowledge through writing. This book also contains an interesting discussion of the relationship between science and ideology, relating to the role of language in power structures.

For those interested in the language of poetry, the work of Gregory (1974; 1978; 1995) is well worth seeking out. In fact, many functional linguists have engaged in some poetic analysis. Some references can be found in Butler (1985; 2003b, pp. 443–9). Ghadessy (1995) includes articles on poetry, as well as a variety of other genres, where linguists have used the analysis of thematic structure.

The study of how language varies depending upon who is using it and for what purposes it is being used is the basis for 'forensic linguistics'. This uses descriptive linguistic techniques to discover features in recorded or written texts. These features can often be used to help identify a speaker or author. Criminal cases where such work has been of use are reported in the journal *Forensic Linguistics*. See also Caldas-Coulthard and Coulthard (1996, pp. 166–79). A broad collection of work on forensic linguistics and language in the legal processes, from the police emergency room to the appeals court, can be found in Cotterill (2004). Language and power in the courtroom is the subject of Cotterill (2003), an in-depth study of language in a long criminal trial. A different type of application to the law can be found in Terauchi (2001), which is concerned with the teaching of legal English to Japanese speakers and focuses mainly on the specialized use of English lexis in the legal context.

The relationship of language to social issues and processes has long been of primary concern to Halliday (see Halliday, 1978; 1993) and also to Kress, who uses a Hallidayan framework for, among other things, showing how newly formed social groups develop new classification systems through language (for example Kress, 1989; Kress and Hodge, 1979).

Two important applications of SFL which we have not examined in this chapter are (i) the use of SFL in corpus linguistics (but see Chapter 12) and (ii) SFL as a tool for producing computer-generated text. Useful introductions to these applications can be found in Butler (2003b, pp. 430–43). For readings on two approaches to the computational modelling of text see Matthiessien and Bateman (1991) and Fawcett *et al.* (1993). For work on corpus linguistics (with a mainly SFL base) applied to English language teaching, see Ghadessy *et al.* (2001) and for a corpus-based study of related genres in tourist information see Castello (2002). For a broad coverage of a variety of applications of SFL, see the collection by Coffin, Hewings and O'Halloran (2004), which includes a number of articles on corpus linguistics. Halliday (2004b) is a collection of his work on computational and corpus studies.

12

Historical perspectives

12.1 *Origins*

> We ignore the achievements of our predecessors not only to our individual detriment but
> greatly to the peril of our collective scientific enterprise.
> (Charles Hockett, cited by Robert de Beaugrande, *Linguistic Theory*, 1991)

Given enough background knowledge and determination, we can trace most
ideas back to earlier ones, or can at least see that they have their origins in
some notion that was present in earlier work. This volume is primarily concerned with one particular approach to the study of language, Systemic
Functional Linguistics. In many respects this is unique, but it has its origins in
the work of earlier scholars. It is informative to consider what these are, and
it may also be of interest to see how SFL differs from some other approaches.

12.2 *Before the twentieth century*

There is a long history of ideas about language. Perhaps it might be more
accurate to say that there are numerous histories, with various traditions in
different cultures (Western, Middle Eastern and Far Eastern) and different
preoccupations and purposes. These histories are complex and not always distinct from each other.

The main line of Western thought about grammar can be traced back to the
Ancient Greeks from about the fourth century BC, a tradition which arguably
reached its peak with the grammar of Dionysius Thrax in about 100 BC,
though it has continued up to the present with modifications – first by the
Romans, adapting Greek models to Latin, later by others. Although modern
grammars may differ from traditional grammar in very significant ways, they
all owe something to this tradition. Among the many valuable concepts that
we inherit from the ancients are the word classes (or parts of speech); and also
the notion of *active* and *passive voice*; *tense*; *subject* and *object*; *gender, person, number* and *subject–verb agreement*, to name but a few.

The Western classical tradition, however, has been greatly affected at various times in history by contact with other traditions, notably those of the Arab world and of India. With the exception of Hebrew, investigated primarily in connection with Biblical studies, non-European languages were relatively neglected in the West for centuries, but in the Middle Ages Arab culture and scholarship had spread widely and were well established in Spain as well as the Middle East and North Africa so that Islamic philosophy and linguistic studies made a major contribution to medieval thought. The complexity of the relationship can be seen in the fact that the Arab grammarians had themselves long been aware of Classical Greek ideas. Similarly, Jewish scholars working with Hebrew had a symbiotic relationship of ideas with Arab and European grammarians.

The influence of Indian scholarship was at least as important. At the end of the eighteenth century, largely as an indirect result of British imperialism, there was an expansion of European interest in Asian languages. Beginning with the work of a British colonial officer, Sir William Jones, startlingly new information about the relationship of many Indian and European languages became available; in addition, an impressive long-standing Indian tradition of linguistic analysis, more sophisticated in many respects than the classical European tradition, was revealed to European scholars, and some were quick to profit from it. Much Hindu scholarship had conservative religious motivations and focused on the sacred texts. The best-known exponent of the Indian tradition is Panini, a grammarian of Sanskrit, who wrote between the fourth and seventh centuries BC.

For over a hundred years after Jones, linguistic research was dominated by a concern with tracing the historical connections between languages, particularly those in the Indo-European family, and accounting for the changes that languages undergo as time passes. Research into regional dialects played a part in this, as it does today.

Meanwhile, traditional grammar dominated the education system. A quaint, beautifully illustrated booklet for children called *The Infant's Grammar or a Picnic Party of the Parts of Speech* (Harris, 1824, republished 1977) introduces (in verse) the parts of speech personified as people attending a party. A sample fragment gives the tone.

And these actors the VERBS, when they'd room to DISPLAY
Both WRESTLED, and TUMBLED and GAMBOLLED away.

The value of this as an educational tool is open to doubt, but its very existence, clearly targeted at young children, says something about the status of grammatical studies in the early nineteenth century. Although modern linguistics differs significantly from traditional approaches, the insights of earlier times underpin much modern thought, including Halliday's, and provide a core of terms and concepts, which is crucial to the grammatical analysis of most modern schools of linguistics. In the words of J.R. Firth (1957, p. 216):

> The great languages of the older civilizations were well served by grammarians whose eminence has not been levelled or overlaid by the thousands of grammars of modern languages [. . .]. What modern linguist would wish to find serious fault with the grammatical outlines of Panini for Sanskrit, of Dionysius for Greek, of Donatus and Priscian for Latin, or of Sibawayhi and Al Khalil for Arabic?

There may be a suggestion in Firth's words that, good as they were for their original purpose, traditional grammars are inadequate for the task of describing other languages, and this has been a widespread view among linguists. Nevertheless, it would be wrong to suggest that the centuries of applying traditional grammar to languages other than Sanskrit, Classical Greek, Latin and Classical Arabic were wasted effort. It would also be wrong to think that there is one monolithic traditional grammar, unchanged since ancient times. In fact, there has been debate and reformulation of ideas about grammar throughout history. However, there is enough common ground to justify this broad label, and outside the linguistic community, some form of traditional grammar is still the most widely known.

12.3   *De Saussure*

Discussion of the development of modern linguistics often starts with the Swiss scholar, Ferdinand de Saussure (1857–1913), whose *Course in General Linguistics* was put together by his students and colleagues and published in 1916, three years after his death. De Saussure (translated by Baskin, 1959) set out what he considered to be the principles of a science of linguistics, and many of these remain central to modern approaches. Though few, if any, linguists accept all his views, they at least take account of them and usually have recourse to some of his terminology. Although his fame in his lifetime rested on his historical comparative work, including his doctoral thesis completed at the unusually early age of 21, one of de Saussure's contributions was the redirection of linguistic studies away from historical concerns to the 'synchronic' analysis of contemporary language. Others had already suggested a need for less historically oriented studies, but his comments distinguishing linguistic descriptions as either diachronic (through historical time) or synchronic (at a particular point in time) provide a historical marker for this shift of emphasis. Not all linguists accept this dichotomy, and Halliday has expressed reservations about it.

De Saussure argued that a language in general could never be fully explained, but that it can be perceived on the one hand as *langue*, which is the collectively inherited set of *signs*, the language system; and, on the other, as *parole*, which can be roughly glossed as the individual's use of the system. (For de Saussure a *sign* is a combination of a concept and its representation.) He argued that *langue*, and not *parole*, is the proper object of linguistic enquiry. Half a century later Chomsky took a similar line in his positing of *competence* and *performance* (or later *I-language* and *E-language*). In answer to a direct question on this point, Halliday (1978, p. 51) rejects the need for the dichotomy, citing his mentor, Firth; but he adds that whether you need to make such suppositions depends to some extent on why you are looking at the language. Halliday does not find it useful for his purposes.

Another key contribution to linguistic thinking, and one that plays a significant part in Systemic Functional Grammar is the Saussurian distinction between *syntagmatic* and *paradigmatic* dimensions. De Saussure observed that linguistic items are significant only in relation to other linguistic items in the system. Using a spatial metaphor, he says that language is systematically organized along two axes: horizontal and vertical.

The horizontal (*syntagmatic*) axis is typified by the fact that, in any utterance, words follow each other in prescribed sequences; in the sequence *if I rewrite this chapter*, each word has a syntagmatic relation to every other word: *if+I+rewrite+this+chapter*. In compound words such as *rewrite*, the two morphemes (*re-* and *write*) relate syntagmatically. We could say that *re-* is significant in English because (among many other things) it combines with *write*; that the significance of the word *this* is in part its potential for co-occurring with *chapter*, and so on. Also syntagmatic are phenomena such as Subject-Finite agreement and word order. Likewise, sounds relate to each other sequentially: for example, /i/ and /f/ combine syntagmatically to make up /if/.

However, items are significant also because they relate on the *paradigmatic* axis to other items. Part of the significance of *write* is that it contrasts with *read*. When we say *write*, we choose not to say *read*. The same can be said of *write* with regard to *inscribe*, or *scribble*, or for that matter any other verb. The relation is a paradigmatic one in that the items are in a sense alternatives within sets. The relation between *write*, *writes*, *wrote*, *written* and *writing* is thus also paradigmatic, as is the relation between *written*, *bitten*, *spoken*, *taken* and *broken*. In the sound system, the paradigmatic significance of the phoneme /i/ is that it is not /o/ or some other sound; so /i/ and /o/ are paradigmatically related, and, by extension, /if/ has a paradigmatic relation to /of/.

Moreover the /i/ and /f/ in /if/ exemplify both paradigmatic and syntagmatic relations, since /i/ relates syntagmatically with /f/ because they combine in a sequence, and /i/ also relates paradigmatically with /f/ by virtue of being a distinct sound in the English sound system. Syntagmatic relations, then, realize the items' potential for combination in a string; paradigmatic relations are the alternations between items. In Systemic Functional Grammar, syntagmatic and paradigmatic relations are sometimes discussed as *chain* and *choice*, but the terms syntagmatic and paradigmatic are more usual in recent publications; a *system* is a set of paradigmatic choices; a *structure* is a syntagmatic phenomenon, a chain of elements, in which each element is the result of some paradigmatic choice.

De Saussure saw linguistics as merely part of a larger discipline, at that time non-existent, which he called *semiology*, 'a science that studies the life of signs within society' (1959, p. 16). In addition to linguistics, he mentions such systems of signs as 'writing, the alphabet of deaf mutes, symbolic rites, polite formulas, military signals, etc.' (1959, p. 16). In the second half of the twentieth century, de Saussure's thinking was perhaps as noticeable in the field of semiotics as in linguistics itself. European philosophers and semioticians such as Roland Barthes and Umberto Eco, whose essays included studies of such social phenomena as wrestling, striptease and blue jeans, might be regarded as de Saussure's intellectual grandchildren, but the influence on linguistics has also been profound, especially in Europe. One collection of Halliday's work is entitled *Language as Social Semiotic*, and the introduction begins with a detailed reference to de Saussure, albeit to distance Halliday somewhat from his views. Incidentally, SFL linguists have recently made considerable headway into the semiotics of visual imagery and graphics; for example, Kress and van Leeuwen (1996; 1998).

12.4   *Linguistics in America*

The foundations of American linguistics were laid by the German émigré Franz Boas (1858–1942), an anthropologist, and Edward Sapir (1884–1939), who was also born in Germany. Under Boas' influence, Sapir turned away from orthodox European historical linguistic studies (philology) to examine the languages of Native Americans (or North American Indians, as they were then called). The work of Boas and Sapir led to new ways of describing the grammatical structure of languages, rejecting the classical model which had evolved from Ancient Greek grammar.

Sapir (1921, p. 8) gave a definition of language that clearly places him in an empiricist tradition that sees language as a social – and arbitrary – communication system:

> Language is a purely human and non-instinctive method of communicating ideas, emotions, and desires by means of voluntarily produced symbols.

This statement occurs as part of the introduction to Sapir's classic work, *Language* (1921), a chapter subtitled 'Language Defined'. In this, Sapir (1921, p. 4) contrasts language with the human capacity for walking, which is 'an inherent biological function of man'.

Not so language. It is, of course, true that in a certain sense the individual is pre-destined to talk, but that is due entirely to the circumstance that he is born not merely in nature, but in the lap of a society that is certain, reasonably certain, to lead him to its traditions.

Probably the most prestigious figure in the first half of twentieth-century American linguistics, however, was Leonard Bloomfield (1887–1949), who also began as a philologist and had studied in Germany. Bloomfield estab-lished the basis for structural analysis which dominated American linguistic scholarship for nearly thirty years. He set out to make linguistics an autonomous subject and a scientific one, and the type of analysis which he developed, usually called American Structuralism, had a major effect on lan-guage teaching in providing the linguistic basis for pattern practice drills and other aspects of the so-called 'audio-lingual approach', dominant in the 1950s and 1960s and still in use today in many classrooms. Bloomfieldian linguis-tics was strong in the areas of phonology (pronunciation) and morphology (word-formation) and made some inroads into syntax (sentence structure) but it had little to say about semantics (meaning). Many modern linguists see this last point as its major weakness, together with Bloomfield's espousal of behaviourist psychology, which argued that language is merely a set of acquired habits.

The dominance of Bloomfieldian linguistics lasted in America until the late 1950s, when it was side-lined by Noam Chomsky. Chomsky (born 1928) was himself a product of American Structuralist training, and his linguistics reflects that fact, not least in its relative downgrading of meaning, but it also represents a significant departure from Bloomfield's (or Sapir's) approaches, especially in its psychological and philosophical orientation. In the first fif-teen years or so of Chomsky's reign, his most significant contributions seemed to be in two technical notions in the field of syntax: (i) deep and sur-face structure; and (ii) the mechanism of the transformation (which gave rise to the name Transformational Grammar). Both these apparently central notions gradually faded from view as the case for them became less tenable under the pressure of further research, and they now appear vestigially, if at all. Chomsky's overwhelming dominance in America and beyond was well established by the mid-1960s and his approach still remains highly influen-tial, perhaps partly because of his unrelated but significant left-wing political writings.

It is interesting to compare Chomsky with Halliday: they are linguists of the same generation but Chomsky's linguistics position is in many ways the antithesis of Halliday's.

One of Chomsky's preoccupations is with the universals of language; hence the model's later preferred name of Universal Grammar. Unlike Halliday, and most of the people mentioned above, Chomsky has no interest

in the social aspect of language, but views language as essentially a biologically determined phenomenon: something with which we are endowed by
our genetic structure as humans. Comments by Chomsky about the nature of
human language contrast markedly with the quotations from Sapir (above).
Halliday's views are closer to Sapir's on this score since, for both, language
is primarily a social phenomenon.

Furthermore, Chomsky has a view of language comparable to de
Saussure's dichotomy of *langue* and *parole*, regarding actual manifestations
of language as E-language (external), which is only a very rough, 'degener-
ate' representation of I-language (internal) (e.g. Chomsky, 1993). Originally,
he discussed this aspect of the theory using the terms *performance* and *competence*. For Chomsky, the goal of linguistics is to explain the human grammatical faculty by focusing on I-language. As we have seen, Halliday rejects
such dualistic claims. In his comment on de Saussure's langue and parole, he
concedes that some degree of abstraction is necessary but says that it should
be kept to a minimum.

Chomsky's concept of I-language leads to a process of *idealization*, discussing abstract forms rather than authentic samples of language in use. The
linguistic data which Chomskyans examine are not texts, or even fragmentary
utterances actually produced in communication, but examples thought up by
the linguist to check the plausibility of the grammar that is proposed.
Chomsky is interested in models of mental grammars; Halliday is interested
in languages and communication.

Functionalist views are incompatible with Chomsky's views on other
issues, too, notably the Chomskyan claim that the grammatical structure of a
sentence (its syntax) is autonomous with regard to meaning (semantics): that
is to say that the rules of syntactic structure operate without reference to
semantics. For Chomsky semantics merely interprets the syntactic structures.
For Halliday, meaning is at the heart of everything in language. Chomsky is a
formalist, and Halliday is a functionalist.

Yet another contrast lies in the self-imposed criteria for the grammar.
Chomsky pursues a policy of 'parsimony' (also known as 'economy' or 'simplicity'), attempting to limit the grammar to the smallest possible set of principles and parameters. His claim is that this will explain how children are able
to master the apparently insuperable task of mentally developing a grammar.
He assumes that the optimal grammar must be a short one; hence one of the
many labels assigned to his approach over the years was the Minimalist
Programme. Halliday and his followers, working from different assumptions
about the object of investigation and the nature of language acquisition, are
happier with a rich multistratal account of language or what they call an
'extravagant' grammar.

The American linguists labelled as generative functionalists (Ellen Prince
and others), although they have some functional concerns such as authentic

data and interaction of discourse and grammar, are in some ways closer to Chomsky's formalism than to SFL, accepting some of the fundamental principles of formalist approaches such as the autonomy of the grammar and innateness of the language faculty. Nevertheless, Prince has produced interesting work in pragmatic situation-based discourse analysis. The West Coast functionalists such as Talmy Givón have more in common with SFL and are discussed below.

In fact, the category 'American' as applied to linguists is largely unhelpful since it does not reflect any theoretical homogeneity. There are important American contributors to SFL working in the USA: Peter Fries (mentioned elsewhere) and Jay Lemke, for example. Limitations of space preclude discussion of major modern American scholars whose interests are more akin to Halliday's than some we have considered: Bolinger, Chafe, Grimes, Hymes, Lamb, Longacre and Pike spring to mind, and, less obviously, Labov and Lakoff. But one American demands his own short section here. His name is Benjamin Lee Whorf.

12.5 *Whorf*

Whorf (1897–1941) was a fire-insurance inspector, a graduate in chemical engineering and an amateur linguist, who contributed what has since become one of the most disputed theories of the language field: the Whorfian Hypothesis. Sapir's name is often linked with that of Whorf to give the alternative name: the Sapir–Whorf Hypothesis.

To simplify, Whorf places great emphasis on the role of language in culture by arguing that a society's perception of reality is determined by the language of that society. Thus, a person who speaks a language will experience a different world from a person who speaks a fundamentally different type of language. Whorf based his opinion on his extensive knowledge of the Native American language, Hopi, which, he claimed, interprets – or creates – the world in a different way from the languages which he called collectively 'Standard Average European' (SAE). Popular examples of this phenomenon are: (i) the large range of expressions for different kinds of snow in Inuit ('Eskimo') languages, where SAE has very few (*snow, sleet, slush*); and (ii) the way different languages split up the colour spectrum at different points, so that the speakers of one language may describe two objects as, say, *red* and *orange* (English) where those who speak another will describe them with the same term, say, *kai* (Amharic) – or, even within SAE languages, English describes two objects as *brown* and French distinguishes the same objects as *brun* and *marron*. In the scales of Whorf's hypothesis, however, these are lightweight, trivial examples. (The claims about words for snow are also frequently disputed.)

According to Whorf, the Hopi's perception of time (among other things) is fundamentally different from that of the speaker of SAE because the Hopi language and SAE languages have fundamentally different ways of dealing with time. Indeed, Whorf goes so far as to claim that the Hopi language has:

> no words, grammatical forms, constructions or expressions that refer directly to what we call 'time', or to past, present, or future, or to enduring or lasting, or to motion as kinematic rather than dynamic [. . .] Hence the Hopi language contains no reference to time, either explicit or implicit.
>
> (1956, pp. 57–8; originally written about 1936)

Thus, Whorf argues, there is no reason to suppose that the Hopi has any conception of time as flowing from past through present into future or of time as separable from a static space, perceptions which Europeans and Euro-Americans (speakers of SAE) often take to be universal, even indisputable, facts of physical reality.

This does not mean, however, that the Hopi has a defective or less subtle perception of the world than the SAE speaker:

> The Hopi language is capable of accounting for, and describing correctly, in a pragmatic or operational sense, all observable phenomena of the universe.
>
> (Whorf, 1956, p. 58)

Where SAE languages separate phenomena in terms of time (expressed linguistically as tense and aspect), Hopi 'gets along perfectly without tenses for its verbs' (1956, p. 64). However, Hopi makes distinctions on such bases as objective reality versus subjective experience (though the terms *subjective* and *objective* are themselves SAE concepts and may not be perceived in the same way by the Hopi).

What one culture may perceive as a *thing* another may perceive as an *event* (Whorf, 1956, p. 63):

> Hopi with its preference for verbs, as contrasted with our own liking for nouns, perpetually turns our propositions about things into propositions about events.

This has an obvious bearing on Halliday's notion of grammatical metaphor.

Furthermore, far from suggesting that SAE languages or world-view are superior, Whorf says that Hopi does things with grammar that SAE languages simply do not deal with. For example:

> The Hopi realize and even express *in their grammar* that the things told in myths and stories do not have the same kind of validity as things of the present day, the things of practical concern.
>
> (Whorf, 1956, p. 64; our italics)

The opinion that European and Euro-American thinking may not have a monopoly of truth with regard to the physical nature of the world, or that so-called 'primitive' societies may have some insights that are lacking in more 'civilized' societies, has acquired considerable popular currency in recent years, but at the time of Whorf's writing (mostly in the 1930s), it was a startling idea to many Americans and Europeans (notwithstanding the 'noble savage' concepts of the Romantic movement, more than a century earlier). The relativistic approach to the nature of the world, the debate about whether there is an objective reality independent of our perceptions, is a hardy perennial in philosophy, as is the debate about the extent to which we are products of society or of nature, but Whorf's work puts these ideas in a new light.

There are, of course, heated disputes about the validity of the Sapir–Whorf hypothesis (other people's label; not theirs). Sapir's mentor, Boas himself, had expressed views diametrically opposed to it:

> It does not seem likely, therefore, that there is any direct relation between the culture of a tribe and the language they speak, except in so far as the form of the language will be moulded by the state of the culture, but not in so far as a certain state of culture is conditioned by morphological traits of the language.
>
> (Boas, 1964; originally written 1911)

Debates also take place about what Whorf actually meant, and whether Sapir agreed with Whorf, and so on, but we shall not pursue this further here. Of the earlier American linguists mentioned here, Whorf is the one who is closest to the thinking of Michael Halliday although Halliday (1973, p. 106) denies an extreme Whorfian position while explaining that 'Whorf himself was never extreme.'

Modern preoccupations with the centrality of metaphor in language (Lakoff and Johnson, 1980; Lakoff, 1987) directly relate to the Whorfian hypothesis, and thus can also be linked to the *grammatical metaphor* concept.

12.6   *The Prague School*

In the 1920s a group of linguists, mainly Czech and Russian, and centred on Prague and Vienna, formed the Linguistic Circle of Prague and published a series of scholarly papers. Some of their thinking can be attributed to Saussurean principles. Major members included the Russians Trubetskoy and Jakobson and the Czech Mathesius. With World War II, the circle broke up and some members were obliged to leave for other countries, but the tradition has survived and still flourishes in the Czech and Slovak republics and elsewhere in Europe. This approach is known as Prague School Linguistics and has more recently been associated with such figures as the late Jan Firbas at Masaryk University and František Daneš at Prague.

The prestige of the Prague School has perhaps been most identified with their insights into phonology, but, for the purposes of this volume, that is not their most interesting contribution. Unlike some of the Americans discussed here, the Prague linguists were not content simply to describe grammatical structures but were interested in finding functional explanations for them. The example of Theme and Rheme as conceived by the Prague School may suffice for our purposes here (see Chapters 4 and 5). Like the Prague School's grammar, Halliday's has also come to be called Functional Grammar, and like theirs, it places considerable emphasis on the investigation of thematic organization, though, as we have seen in this volume, unlike Prague linguists, Halliday usefully separates the concept of Theme/Rheme from the related concept of Given/New.

Prague School linguists were greatly influenced by the German psychologist Bühler ('arguably the greatest psycholinguist and psychologically oriented language theorist of the first half of the twentieth century', according to Innis, 1987, p. 125). Bühler's model of three functions of language (*expressive*, *conative*, and *referential*) can be seen as a forerunner of Halliday's three metafunctions: interpersonal, textual and ideational, which differ significantly from Bühler's, but are probably in part inspired by them. Halliday gives a concise explanation of the similarities and differences (Halliday, 1978, p. 48).

12.7   *Malinowski and Firth*

When influences on Halliday are discussed, the two names most frequently cited are Firth and Malinowski.

Bronislaw Malinowski was a Polish (later British) anthropologist, an innovator in descriptive ethnography, whose professional career was mainly in Britain. Later described as 'one of the giants among the founding fathers' of anthropology (Sampson, 1987), he was a colleague of J.R. Firth at London University, where he was Professor of Anthropology from 1927. Malinowski's best-known work was carried out in the Trobriand Islands in the South Pacific, now part of Papua New Guinea, where he spent years living with the village community. This was fairly unprecedented though it later became the norm for such research. Malinowski argued that language was primarily a tool for getting things done. He based this view partly on his observations of the Trobriand islanders' fishing expeditions where verbal exchanges were a central part of doing the work. At first, he thought that this 'doing' aspect of language was largely restricted to what he then called 'primitive' languages, but later he sensibly dropped the notion of 'primitive language' and extended this functional view to all forms of language, including Western academic discourse.

Malinowski coined the term *context of situation*, a notion which was to play a large part in Firth's thinking and, later, in Halliday's. The claim made here was that, in order to understand an utterance, we need to know not only the literal meanings of the words, in the form of their approximate equivalents in another language, for example, but also all the complex of social detail in which the utterance occurs. The same is true for any cultural artefact. Indeed, meaning in language is its meaning in the events where it is used, taking into account all the relevant factors: the people engaged in the discourse, the social context in which they are functioning, the broader presuppositions of the society, the nature of the task in hand, and so on.

J.R. Firth became the first person to hold a chair of general linguistics in a British university when he was appointed professor at the School of Oriental and African Studies, London University, in 1944. Firth had studied Oriental, especially Indian, languages. (Halliday, too, specialized in Oriental languages early in his career: in his case, Chinese.) Firth had been Professor of English at the University of the Punjab before returning to teach phonetics at University College London in 1928. He did not publish a great deal, and his influence has been felt mainly through the work of his successors, Halliday most notably. Perhaps it is in the field of phonetics and phonology that Firth's direct contribution to current practice is most apparent, particularly in work on *prosody* (intonation, tempo and stress), which can be found in the publications of Halliday and others such as Brazil *et al.* (1980), Davies (1994) and Tench (1996).

One very important concept of Firth's that has played a large part in the work of Halliday is the *system*, a paradigmatic set of choices (see earlier chapters). Firth argues that the grammar of a language is polysystemic, a system of systems. Halliday (1972) defines a system as follows:

> We define a system as a set of options together with an entry condition, such that if the entry condition is satisfied one option from the set must be selected.

In SFL, Firth's somewhat sketchy suggestions about system have been developed with greater rigour into elaborate networks representing the choices available to users of the language.

Where Firth differed most significantly from de Saussure was in his refusal to accept that the proper topic of investigation for a linguist was *la langue*, the system of language signs divorced from actual use – or even to accept that this was a realistic construct. In 1950, he endorsed a criticism that de Saussure's approach was 'static mechanical structuralism'. He added:

> For my own part and for a number of my colleagues, I venture to think linguistics is a group of related techniques for the handling of language events [. . .] In the most general terms, we study language as part of the social process.
>
> (Firth, 1957, p. 181; originally written 1950)

As already indicated, this characteristic contrast of approach is even more marked between Halliday (or Firth) and Chomsky, for de Saussure did at least regard language as a social phenomenon, whereas Chomsky entirely excludes social factors from his analysis, focusing exclusively on individual mental processes, which he perceives as being biologically determined.

Like Malinowski, Firth stressed the role of the individual as a member of society; hence the important interaction between *nature* and *nurture:*

> You weave *nurture* into *nature*, and you do this with the most powerful magic – speech. In order to live, the young human has to be progressively incorporated into a social organization, and the main condition of the incorporation is sharing the local magic – that is, the language.
>
> (Firth, 1957, p. 185)

In works such as *Explorations in the Functions of Language* (1973), *Learning How to Mean* (1975), and *The Language of Early Childhood* (2004a), Halliday takes such general observations as a starting point for an extensive theory of child language development.

12.8   *Corpus linguistics*

Advances in computer technology have facilitated great progress in *corpus linguistics*, which involves the computational analysis of vast collections of textual data. Halliday was closely involved in the Cobuild project and has used it explicitly in his own research (for example, Halliday and James, 1993; Halliday, 2004b). Many, probably most, systemic functionalists are strongly committed to corpus-based work, not least because it can support the notion of markedness, which is based on the relative frequency of forms.

A forceful advocate for corpora is John Sinclair, who established the Cobuild corpus at Birmingham University. Sinclair is a former colleague of Halliday's. With Malcolm Coulthard, he developed the seminal discourse analysis model on Hallidayan principles ('All the terms used – structure, system, rank, level, delicacy, realization, marked, unmarked – are Halliday's', Sinclair and Coulthard, 1975, p. 24). The Cobuild project produced, among other publications, a major dictionary and spin-offs as well as the Cobuild Grammar and a pedagogic student's grammar (Willis, 1991). The main grammar research project carried out by Gill Francis, Susan Hunston and Elizabeth Manning built on Halliday's model though it has much in common with the work of the British structuralist and editor of the *Oxford Advanced Learner's Dictionary*, A.S. Hornby (Cobuild Grammar Patterns Series 1996 onwards). Other works using this Birmingham corpus include Hunston and Francis (2000) on grammatical patterns and Hunston and Thompson (eds) (2000), a collection of papers on *evaluation*, a cover term for authorial *stance, modality, affect* and what James Martin, Peter White and others call '*appraisal*'. Cotterill (2003) uses Cobuild, alongside other tools, to closely examine power relations in the language of legal trials, specifically the controversial O.J. Simpson trial in America.

Corpus linguistics is not a model of language like Halliday's, Bloomfield's or Chomsky's, but rather a tool for analysis. It has the ability to provide powerful challenges to common assumptions about linguistic phenomena, enabling the analyst to discuss such issues as frequency of occurrence and patterns of collocation (i.e., co-occurrence) of items whose relationship is not transparent to intuition.

More recently, corpus research has looked into the textual phenomenon of *colligation* (a term coined by Firth), which is the frequency of occurrence of grammatical patterns with given lexical items. This is a current interest of the SFL-oriented discourse analyst, Michael Hoey (see Hoey, in press).

Nor is corpus linguistics an entirely modern development. More traditional grammarians such as the great Danish scholar Otto Jespersen (1860–1943) used literary sources to produce descriptive grammars. Jespersen's massive work *A Modern English Grammar on Historical Principles* (1909–1949) is still a valuable source of information about English usage. The American structuralists also advocated the use of corpora, and C.C. Fries (eminent father of the Systemic Functional linguist Peter Fries) recorded telephone conversations as a basis for his iconoclastic model of English grammar (Fries, 1952). In fact, Chomsky's refusal to use a corpus might be viewed as an eccentric departure from normal practice in twentieth-century linguistics. The computer has revolutionized corpus studies, first, in terms of the sheer quantity of material that can be stored and, second, in the techniques for analysis.

One of the best-known products of computer-stored corpus work is the descriptive reference grammar of Quirk and colleagues (Quirk *et al.*, 1972; Quirk *et al.*, 1985) and its various spin-offs. In terms of the grammatical model, this is eclectic. It is easy to identify Hallidayan characteristics but there are other influences, too. The Quirk description is the outcome of a major research project, the Survey of English Usage, which set up the London–Lund corpus. A later corpus-based reference grammar is Biber *et al.* (1999), which takes into account variations in grammar across different domains.

Other notable corpora are the Brown University corpus of American English, the oldest of this type and scale, and the Lancaster–Oslo–Bergen (LOB) corpus of British English established by Geoffrey Leech and Jan Svartvik. Corpora of various sizes and significance continue to be established.

Much corpus work operates on a large scale without any concern for differing domains and registers. But there has recently been an increase in the use of 'small corpora', more selective samples of the language (e.g. from a specific genre), which permit different kinds of investigation. See, for example, Ghadessy *et al.* (2001) and also Gledhill (2000), who analyzes a small corpus of cancer research articles, as we mentioned earlier. O'Halloran and Coffin *et al.* (2004) and Koller and Mauntner (2004) demonstrate the contributions that corpus linguistics can make to critical discourse analysis (see Chapter 11).

As far as grammar is concerned, it seems so far that, besides providing a major tool for implementing and testing existing grammatical models, corpus linguistics throws up interesting facts about the language rather than suggesting major theoretical shifts in areas such as grammatical categories. One claim of profound theoretical significance, however, is Sinclair's argument that linguistic choices are much more tightly constrained (by lexical considerations) than had previously been suggested. This field has made great strides in recent years and continues to do so.

12.9   *Some functional alternatives*

In the past few decades there has been a proliferation of models of grammar, a few of which we will briefly mention here.

Talmy Givón is the best known of a small number of American linguists loosely grouped as West Coast Functionalists. Sandra A. Thompson and P.J. Hopper work within a similar cognitive framework, also arguing that grammar emerges from discourse requirements. We say 'loosely grouped' because as Givón himself says:

> We have refrained from anointing – or even electing – leaders. We have refused the label of 'Theory', 'Grammar', 'school'.
>
> (Givón 1995, p. 22)

Most of Givón's titles include the word *functional,* and he is clearly a functionalist, seeing language as being primarily about communication and stressing the importance of textual considerations. Unlike formalists such as Chomsky, Givón starts from the assumption that language is essentially communicative and his focus is on discourse and pragmatics. However, he is also very concerned with the neurological aspect and places considerable emphasis on the individual cognitive dimension. West Coast Functionalists resemble SF linguists in rejecting discrete grammatical categories, preferring the notion of prototypes, where an item may be a more or less central example of a category (compare Halliday's idea of clines); Givón suggests that we need to balance flexibility with rigidity (1995, p. 13), which few functionalists would dispute. Also their views on language acquisition are close to Halliday's.

Another grammar which calls itself Functional Grammar (FG), was originated by Simon Dik (1978) and seems to have a following mainly among linguists in Belgium and the Netherlands. It shares many of the concerns of Halliday's linguistics and claims to be more 'explicit':

FG shares with other functionally oriented models all the major theoretical assumptions of the functional paradigm; chief among them is the priority of the communicative over the cognitive function of language, with the accompanying socio-cultural as opposed to psychological bias.

(Siewierska, 1991, p. 3)

One striking difference between Dik's and most other functionalist approaches is that Dik's grammar restricts itself to the sentence and tends to work with idealized data rather than authentic text. It is also heavily influenced by predicate logic, which plays no part in SFL.

We hesitate to place the work of Fawcett, Tucker, Tench, Huang and colleagues in this section since theirs is not merely a related approach but an actual variant of SFL – in a frequently heard analogy, a 'dialect' of SFL. However, for want of a better location, we include it here although references to their work have been made at other points. The version of SFL developed by this group (and others) is often referred to (e.g. by Butler, 2003a, 2003b) as the Cardiff Grammar. Their work is notable for its extreme rigour and its serious commitment to linguistic argumentation, decisions usually being carefully and explicitly justified.

Fawcett spells out the differences between the mainstream model associated with Halliday and the Cardiff version of SFG very clearly in Fawcett (2000a; 2000b; 2000c). The approach remains Systemic Functional and many differences are differences of detail, albeit often very significant detail, but some are more sweeping, for example, the rejection of the rank scale and of the notion of hypotactic dependency as distinct from embedding, and hence the Cardiff rejection of hypotactic clause and group complexes; this last was touched on in Chapter 9, Further study. What we have described (in Chapter 9, in line with IFG) as a dependent hypotactic expansion is analyzed in the Cardiff model as an Adjunct that is 'filled' by an embedded clause. (See also Banks, 2003b.) Further, a projected clause (see our Chapter 10) is, in Cardiff terms, an embedded clause that 'fills' Complement and Phenomenon. Further innovations are the *quality group* (see our Chapter 3, Further study) and *quantity group*, which can fill both an Adjunct like *very much* in *I like it very much* and also a Premodifier like *tall* in *a tall tree*, which departs significantly from any IFG-influenced analysis. Fawcett (personal communication) also argues that, in the Cardiff Grammar, grammatical metaphor becomes an unnecessary concept.

A broader but less tangible difference is that, in Cardiff Grammar, parsimony seems to be more of an issue than it is for Halliday and his colleagues. (See the discussion of Chomsky above.)

12.10   *Systemic functional 'grammars'*

Throughout this volume we have used the term *grammar* mostly in an abstract sense to refer to the principles on which language, or more particularly a specific language, is organized. Or we have used it to refer to a model, or account, of this, as in 'traditional grammar'. In this section we use it in a sense that is perhaps more frequent outside academic circles, namely for a book describing the grammar of a language. In this context, we can mention in passing the reference grammars of Jespersen or of Quirk *et al.*, the latter showing many features found in Halliday's work but not committed to this or any other orientation.

In addition to the various editions of IFG, there are numerous expositions of Hallidayan grammar as applied to English. We have already mentioned Berry's classic (1975; 1977) two-volume *Introduction to Systemic Linguistics,* which is a straightforwardly expository book without exercises. An early one was Scott *et al.* (1968), *English Grammar,* the work of a group of scholars at the University of Auckland. Four years later Sinclair's *A Course in Spoken English: Grammar* was published (Sinclair, 1972), and 1980 saw the publication of David Young's *The Structure of English Clauses.* A very comprehensive SFL reference grammar is Downing and Locke (1992; 2002), *A University Course in English Grammar.*

Most of these works combine the task of description (as in Jespersen or Quirk *et al.*) with an explanation of the model and exercises in its application. Thus, they combine the features of a reference grammar with the expository qualities of a book such as IFG (Halliday, 1985, 1994; Halliday and Matthiessen, 2004) or, to take a less exalted example, the present volume. Also, Downing and Locke present their volume as a pedagogic grammar for non-native speakers. It is impossible to list all the introductory SFG texts now available, but they include Eggins (1994), Butt *et al.* (1994, 2000) and Morley (2000). Martin *et al.* (1997) has been referred to at various points: a valuable aid especially for analysts faced with difficult choices. Thompson (1996, 2004) is a book with similar aims to our own, though with some differences of emphasis.

There are some differences of terminological and conceptual detail among some of these books and the IFG model (though less profound than those between IFG and the Cardiff approach). In the case of the earlier ones this is partly because the model has evolved since they were published, and in some it is presumably as a principled decision. However, the variations are relatively small, and, it is to be expected – and desired – that there will be some differences of opinion even in the best run schools of linguistics. As Halliday and Fawcett jointly remark:

> We present our proposals for modelling language to our fellow explorers, orally or in writing, in a discourse in which evidence and counter-evidence is offered and

ideas are exchanged, adopted, adapted and occasionally rejected – and there is no reason why this discussion should not be friendly.

(Halliday and Fawcett 1987, p. 20)

Summary

This chapter is a very brief survey of the linguistics background to SFL. Inevitably, we have left a lot out and sacrificed depth, but rather than trying to give a full picture we merely raise a few of the basic issues and demonstrate some affinities and contrasts.

The relation of de Saussure to Halliday is somewhat ambivalent, and, of major modern schools of thought, both Bloomfield and Chomsky are strikingly different from Halliday in their goals and methods. A significant influence on the Hallidayan approach to language study was Whorf, who believed that the language of a community has a causal relation to the way in which that community perceives reality. Another important source is the Prague School's 'functional' account of language, particularly the concept of Theme and Rheme, considerably modified in SFL work. More direct input is provided by Firth and Malinowski with their emphasis on the importance of context of situation and language as action. Halliday's model of linguistics, at least at the outset, has been seen as essentially a detailed and rigorous development of Firth's less well-worked-out proposals, but it has far excelled Firth's work.

Computer-based corpus linguistics is perceived as fully compatible with Halliday's grammar, or even integral to it, enhancing and reinforcing it rather than challenging it.

Alternative functional approaches include, among others, those of Givón and Dik. The Cardiff model makes some significant departures from mainstream SFL, while maintaining considerable solidarity. We conclude with a brief mention of grammar books which develop or present the Halliday model.

Further study

Robins (1967) gives a chronologically organized summary of the history of Western linguistics from the ancient Greeks to the twentieth century. Readers with a good knowledge of French would do well to consult de Saussure in the original 1916 version as edited by Bally and Sechehaye in collaboration with Reidlinger. Probably the best-known English translation is by Wade Baskin (de Saussure, 1959), and compared with most later linguistics publications, it is not difficult to read.

Also quite intellectually accessible is Bloomfield's substantial volume *Language* (1934), a fairly detailed but lucid account of the American structuralist view of language and linguistics. Sapir's *Language* (1921) is also very readable. A selection of Whorf's original work was published in a volume edited and introduced by Carroll (Whorf, 1956).

Radford (1997) is a student textbook introducing Chomsky's 'minimalist' approach. There are numerous other introductory texts such as Ouhalla (1999).

A collection of Firth's papers was made in 1957. These are mostly on phonology and phonetics, and the chapters most relevant to the present book are Chapter 15 and Chapter 16. See also Firth (1964). Gunther Kress's (1976) introduction to his selection of Halliday's papers has a penetrating discussion of the roles of Firth and Malinowski and also Whorf in the development of Halliday's thinking. The first chapter of Butler's scholarly critique of systemic linguistics (1985) also gives a very succinct account of Firth in relation to Halliday.

For an extensive language account of the Prague School terminology and concepts, see Duskova (2003). The relationship between the linguistic theory of the Prague School and that of Halliday is explained in Davidse (1987).

De Beaugrande (1991) gives a valuable breakdown of the theories of de Saussure, Sapir, Bloomfield, Firth, Chomsky, and a few others not mentioned in this chapter. Hudson (1992), a former systemicist, gives an enlightening overview of ten contemporary theories of syntax, including Halliday's and his own more formalist model, which is called Word Grammar.

In *Computational and Quantitative Studies* (2004b), Halliday collects his publications in computational corpus linguistics over the past fifty years. Sinclair (1991) is an excellent short introduction to this field. See also the edited collection by Sinclair *et al.* (1993). Stubbs (1996) is a standard work on the topic with a strong Hallidayan orientation. Coffin, Hewings and O'Halloran (2004), mentioned in Chapter 11, is a useful collection of articles on applications of SFG and corpus analysis.

The classic introduction to SFL by Margaret Berry (1975), one of the earliest workers in SFL, includes a section which answers the question 'In what ways is systemic linguistics different from other schools of linguistics?' Among other things, Berry gives a clear explanation of networks as perceived at the time. For a highly advanced treatment of systems and networks, see Halliday (1973), Halliday and Matthiessen (1999) and various publications by Robin Fawcett (for example, Fawcett, 1987; and Fawcett, forthcoming). A more introductory treatment can be found in Eggins (1994). Fawcett (2000a) includes in the first part of the book a study of Halliday's syntactic theory from the early days when it was known as Scale and Category Grammar to the second edition of IFG; in the second part, he explains the 'Cardiff' alternatives. Butler (1985) offers a critique of SFL theory, including networks. Butler (2003a, 2003b) gives a detailed and evaluative account of three theories, which he classes as structural-functional: SFL, Dik's Functional Grammar and Role and Reference Grammar, with references to some other approaches. This is an invaluable reference work for advanced students and practitioners of this type of linguistics.

Answer key

Chapter 1

Exercise 1.1

There are, of course, many possible ways of wording this request. Here are three attempts:

Interrogative: Would you turn on the radio, please?
Imperative: Please turn on the radio.
Declarative: I'd like to listen to the news.

Exercise 1.2

(a) Once more, there is a wide variety of possible answers. Here are some of them:

1. You ought not to smoke.
2. I don't think we are allowed to smoke in here, are we?
3. Why on earth are you smoking?
4. Stop smoking for goodness sake!
5. Put that filthy cigarette out.
6. Be an angel will you and stop smoking?
7. I'd be very grateful if you'd put your cigarette out.

(b) Which form would be best for which person depends to some extent on your relationship with them. From the list given above, one could choose (1) if speaking to a child (2) if speaking to a boss or other senior person, (3) or (4) to a close friend or family member (7) to a new friend. (5) could be used in English only to someone with whom you are very close indeed as it suggests either anger or an attempt to make a joke.

Exercise 1.3

1. A question on the form of application for a British driving licence.
2. From the method section of a recipe for brandy snaps from Robin McDouall's *Cookery Book for the Greedy*, Penguin, 1955.

3. The caption under an illustration in an undergraduate engineering textbook.
4. From the directions on a packet of Scholl (UK) felt callous pads for the treatment of sore feet.
5. A mathematics exercise from a school textbook, *A First Course in Modern Mathematics*, Volume 1, by Marie Anderson, Heinemann Educational Books (Metric Edition), 1973.

Exercise 1.4

Some possible answers:
(a) The text begins with a welcome and words of encouragement to visit the city. It then describes a sample tour, presenting information about the four stages of the tour in chronological order. The first stage simply begins '*One tour* ...', the subsequent stages are signalled with the words: *next, then, final.*
(b) Some indicators of attitude are the adjectives *magnificent, unique, vibrant,* and the noun *charm.* Note that generally the writer appraises the tour positively from the beginning by implying that 'sights', 'fun' and 'adventure' are desirable.
(c) There is no direct reference to the writer. Readers are referred to directly only twice: *your* and *you.*

Chapter 2

Exercise 2.1

(a) 1 and 2 (Head nouns in italics).
[1] *Water.* [2] Small *plants.* [3] a motor car *tyre.* [4] *a tyre* [5] it [6] a *plant* short of water on a hot day. [7] Most of the *water* taken up by a plant. [8] A maize *plant.* [9] the *stomata.* [10] water *vapour.* [11] *Transpiration.*
(b) *Transpiration*: noun; *actually*: adverb; *helps*: verb; *to draw*: verb; *water*: noun; *up*: preposition; *the*: determiner (or definite article); *plant*: noun; *in*: preposition; *a*: determiner (or indefinite article); *way*: noun; *similar*: adjective; *to*: preposition; *sucking*: verb (or, arguably, noun); *liquid*: noun; *up*: preposition; *a*: determiner (or indefinite article); *straw*: noun.
(c) *constantly*: adverbial; *cell processes*: nominal; *just as*: conjunction; *wilts*: verbal; *evaporation from the leaves*: nominal; *about two litres*: nominal; *is lost*: verbal; *very rapidly*: adverbial.

Exercise 2.2

1. (a) *had quoted*: active. (b) *had*: finite operator; *quoted*: lexical. (c) *Robins, Stevenson*: proper nouns; *passage*: common noun; *from Stevenson*: prepositional phrase; *from*: preposition; *Stevenson*: nominal group.

2. (a) *was willing to use*: active. (b) *was*: finite operator; *willing*: lexical; *to use*: lexical. (c) *government*: common noun; *strategy*: common noun.

3. (a) *must have smiled*: active. (b) *must*: modal operator; *have*: non-finite auxiliary; *smiled*: lexical. (c) *Johnson*: proper noun.

4. (a) *were wiretapped*: passive. (b) *were*: finite operator; *wiretapped*: lexical. (c) *people*: common noun; *the FBI*: proper noun. (d) *by the FBI*: *by* preposition; *the FBI*: nominal group.

5. (a) *must be mentioned*: passive. (b) *must*: modal operator; *be*: non-finite auxiliary; *mentioned*: lexical. (c) *ingredient*: common noun.

6. (a) *worked*: active. (b) *worked*: lexical. (a) *had been brought*: passive. (b) *had*: finite operator; *been*: non-finite auxiliary; *brought*: lexical. (c) *He, who*: pronouns; *Bronstein, Kaplan*: proper nouns. (d) *with Bronstein*: *with*: preposition; *Bronstein*: nominal group; *into the firm*: *into*: preposition; *the firm*: nominal group; *by Kaplan*: *by*: preposition; *Kaplan*: nominal group.

7. (a) *did . . . know*: active. (b) *did*: finite operator; *know*: lexical. (c) *we, it*: pronouns; *time*: common noun. (d) *at that time*: *at*: preposition; *that time*: nominal group.

8. (a) *must have looked*: active. (b) *must*: modal operator; *have*: non-finite auxiliary; *looked*: lexical. (c) *her*: pronoun. *future, relations, moment*: common nouns. (d) *in corporate public relations*: *in*: preposition; *corporate public relations*: nominal group. *at that moment*: *at*: preposition; *that moment*: nominal group.

Exercise 2.3

This is an open question, but plausible answers might include the following considerations. Such expressions do not play an integral part in the structure of clauses; they do not interact with other word classes. Some might argue that most examples are not strictly speaking items of vocabulary or grammatical items at all but rather represent emotive noises. Items like *Help!* seem to be included on dubious grounds since *help* occurs in other contexts as a verb and a noun, and there seems to be some confusion here between grammatical word classes and utterance classifications such as exclamations. *Rubbish* is a noun. The fact that it is regularly uttered as an exclamation does not make it something other than a noun. The same might be said of *Help!* though it is a moot point whether it is a noun or a verb in exclamations. However, some categorial term seems to be needed for items like *Ouch!*, and *interjection* is as good as any other, but perhaps this is not a category on a par with nouns, verbs, or even conjunctions and prepositions.

Exercise 2.4

Open question. Examples follow:

as Modifier: the supply of food would increase *six* times; most experts agree that a daily intake of about *3,000* calories is adequate; each person needing *70* grams per day; for the *fourth* time.

as Head: less than *2* per square kilometre; it is hoped to increase Australia's present population of *11.5 million* to *20 million*; *thousands* have to be recruited; we are always *second*.

Exercise 2.5

This is an open question about personal pronouns, raising points about prescriptivism and individual/dialectal, conscious and unconscious variation in usage.

Many speakers of English sometimes use 'subject pronouns' (e.g., *I, he*) in non-Subject functions while many sometimes use 'object pronouns' (e.g., *me, him*) in Subject functions. The (a) versions in 1 and 2 show the 'subject-pronoun' preference, and the (b) examples offer the corrected version. Some people condemn the usage exemplified in the (a) version, but it is widespread. It seems to occur when the pronoun in question is postmodified as in (1) and (4) or when it is linked with another noun or pronoun as in (2) and (3). 'Subject-pronoun' preference may be partly due to over-correction by people trying to avoid misplaced object-pronoun preference. Except in some regional dialects, we do not find it happening with simple pronouns: **I don't mind giving money to they* or **I like she.*

In (1) the structure is somewhat stilted and (1a) could be a result of hyper-correction. It may be influenced by *who* being Subject in its own clause (see Chapter 8). Doubtful speakers might choose to say *those who*, thereby avoiding the problem.

In (3a) an 'object-pronoun' is used in a Subject function. (3b) seems to some people to suggest insecure carefulness whereas (3a) is more dialectal and unselfconscious; or, possibly, aiming at an informal, colloquial effect. Some speakers substitute the reflexive pronoun *myself* in combinations of this kind, possibly reflecting the widespread insecurity about the appropriate form.

Example (4a) is exceptional. In John Mortimer's *The Trials of Rumpole*, *She Who Must be Obeyed* is a comic nickname Rumpole gives to his wife. Hence, the capital letters. *She Who Must be Obeyed* is treated as though it were a single noun and therefore invariable.

(5a) is recommended by a few pedants, but it is contrary to common and educated usage, which is typified by (5b). IFG (Section 5.4.4.2) states that the usage exemplified in (5a) is 'just bad grammar, in the sense that it conflicts with the general principles that apply to such a clause'.

Exercise 2.6

Honestly, usually, still, very, energetically, now, tonight, probably, outside, home, exceptionally early.

Chapter 3

Exercise 3.1

Complements and Adjuncts are subclassified in the answers, but a simple C or A will suffice.

1.

They	cannot	choose.
S	F	P

2.

The nature of the city around us	changed.
S	F/P

3.

This	required	positive effort.
S	F/P	C^{do}

4.

All over the city	the divisions	increased.
A^{cir}	S	F/P

5

The locations	filled	beyond capacity.
S	F/P	A^{cir}

6.

The Ninomaru Palace itself	is	a national treasure.
S	F	C^{int}

7.

Industrialization	brought	a flood of people	to the city.
S	F/P	C^{do}	A^{cir}

8.

Telephones	are	reserved	for trivialities.
S	F	P	A^{cir}

9.

Now	we	too	were	singing	songs	in the bath.
A^{con}	S	A^{con}	F	P	C^{do}	A^{cir}

10.

In Japan	the word 'duty'	has	special meaning.
A^{cir}	S	F	C^{do}

11.

Every appointment	must	be kept.
S	F	P

12.

He	handed	me	the document.
S	F/P	C^{io}	C^{do}

13.

The papers	declared	the strike	a failure.
S	F/P	C^{do}	C^{int}

14.

The castle	was	built	in 1603.
S	F	P	A^{cir}

15.	In its day	it	served	as a symbol of power and authority for the Tokugawa military government.
	Acir	**S**	**F/P**	**A**cir

16.	No word	may	be	<carelessly>	spoken	in front of the children.
	S	**F**	**P**	**<A**cir**>**		**A**cir

Note When one item interrupts another, as here A interrupts P, the symbol <....> encloses the interrupting element.

17.	The transoms	are	carved	from massive cypress blocks.
	S	**F**	**P**	**A**cir

18.	We	had	been protected	from criticism	for years.
	S	**F**	**P**	**A**cir	**A**cir

19.	These	have	been designated	Important Cultural Properties	by the Japanese Government.
	S	**F**	**P**	**C**int	**A**cir

20.	The disciplines	are	never	obliterated.
	S	**F**	**A**mod	**P**

Exercise 3.2

Conjunctive Adjuncts: *Since then, furthermore*.
Modal Adjuncts: *no doubt, possibly, normally*.

Exercise 3.3

The joke depends on the fact that in the hotel guest's meaning the pronoun *me* is indirect object Complement and *a taxi* is direct object Complement (paraphrase: *Call a taxi for me*); but the porter unexpectedly interprets (or pretends to interpret) *me* as direct object Complement and *a taxi* as intensive object Complement (compare: 'Call me Ishmael').

Exercise 3.4

This is entirely open-ended so we cannot offer an answer.

Chapter 4

Exercise 4.1

(a) The Given and New distribution in Text 4I is unmarked, with the Given information first in each clause. Two clauses consist of just New elements: *came to
Britain in 1960* and *has been translated into thirteen languages*. The Given
elements are: *Kazuo Ishiguro* or *Kazuo Ishiguro was born*; *He*; *His first novel, A
Pale View of Hills*; *His second novel, An Artist of the Floating World*; *it*.
(b) An open-ended question. One possible answer might be:

Kazuo Ishiguro, novelist, born Japan 1954, educated in Britain and lives in
London; awarded Winifred Holtby Prize for *A Pale View of Hills* and the
Whitbread Prize for *An Artist of the Floating World* (1986).

Unless you have used full clauses, the only Given is likely to be *Kazuo Ishiguro*.

Exercise 4.2

Given: *The best way to avoid developing skin cancer*
The title *Sun safety tips* is presented as Given in the context of the article, but, of
course, it might appear as New to some readers when taken out of context.
New: The rest of the text is New.

Exercise 4.3

(a) The marked Themes in Text 3A are:
The night before Easter Sunday, 1920
When he awoke again about six
The next night, at three a.m.
Seventeen years before
(b) The marked Themes tell us the *time* of the event reported in the Rheme; three are
circumstantial Adjuncts and one (*When he awoke again about six*) is a temporal
clause. They help the reader organize the order of the reported events. This type
of Theme is common in stories and the use of it here gives a narrative effect. You
may also have noticed the example of multiple Theme:
for instance: textual Theme
the vagus nerves: topical Theme

Chapter 5

Exercise 5.1

(a) The Themes are: *Once upon a time* (marked topical Theme); *The youngest; she; her elder sisters; they; they* (all unmarked topical Theme).
(b) The two nominal groups without nouns as Head are *the youngest* and *the prettiest*. They are both examples of elliptical nominal groups. The Head nouns (*daughter* in each case) have been omitted but can clearly be replaced from the context. They are cohesive with *daughters* in the first Rheme.
(c) *She* forms a tie with *the youngest* (*daughter*) and *the prettiest* (*daughter*). Both uses of *they* form ties with *her elder sisters*.
(d) Two possibilities are:
   beautiful – prettiest – quite attractive (i.e. linked by reference to physical attraction)
   good – kind – greedy – selfish (i.e. linked by reference to attributes of character).
However, you may have chosen to place *good* and *kind* in the first group, putting together all the characteristics with favourable connotations. That grouping may better represent the ideology of traditional fairy tales, from which this example is taken.

Exercise 5.2

The Theme and Rheme of the first clause refer essentially to the same concepts: *the two basic periods* and *the year and the day*, the latter being an example of a split Rheme. The Theme of the second clause, *These*, refers to both the Theme and the Rheme of the first clause. So we have either (or both!) constant and linear progression. The third clause has the Theme *the year*, which progresses linearly from the Rheme of Clause 1 and the final clause has the Theme *The day* which also progresses linearly from the split Rheme in Clause 1. The clause beginning *the earth* is embedded (see Chapter 8) so we do not analyze its internal structure for Theme and Rheme.

Exercise 5.3

1. Clausal substitution.
   So, in the second sentence, stands in place of '(if) *the contract is severable*'.
2. Nominal ellipsis.
   Fifteen people were killed; five [E: people] are missing.
3. There are two parts to this answer.
   (a) There are two examples of substitution:
      One stands in place of *path* in the phrases *the short one* and *the long one*.
   (b) There is one example of ellipsis:
      Both [E: *paths*] in my judgement are satisfactory.

4. This one is slightly tricky. There is a clear case of nominal ellipsis in the second sentence:
    The car radio said more (E) was forecast.
    We cannot be clear whether the speaker meant *more rain* or *more sleet*.
    The first seems more likely, but this is an example of slightly confused reference, which sometimes occurs in real speech and writing. It may lead to breakdown in communication or the potential ambiguity may be resolved by the context.

Exercise 5.4

The doctor intends *one* as a substitute for *toe*. The man interprets *one* as a substitute for *crab*. Since the role of the doctor is to cure the human body, he is much more likely to express an interest in a toe than in a crab. Hence, the man's response is unexpected.

Exercise 5.5

This is an open-ended question so there are many possible answers. But have you considered the following in each text?

context – cohesive ties – lexical chains – thematic progression

If you found this exercise difficult, remember that sometimes models of grammar are difficult to apply. Maybe you need to find out more details of the model by more advanced reading.

Chapter 6

Exercise 6.1

1.

Neurotoxins	will kill	the insects.
Actor	**Process: material**	**Goal**

2.

You	can write	him	a note.
Actor	**Process: material**	**Beneficiary**	**Goal.**

3.

Sufficient water	should be added.
Goal	**Process: material**

4.

Standing crops	can be trampled	by wild animals.
Goal	**Process: material**	**Actor**

5.	Dylan	sang*	a few of his classic numbers.	
	Actor	**Process: material**	**Scope (or Range)**	

6.	They	might swim	the pack-horses	across the river.
	Initiator	**Process: material**	**Actor**	**Circumstance**

7.	Someone	had found	the fugitives	a suitable hiding-place.
	Actor	**Process: material**	**Beneficiary**	**Goal**

8.	The prisoners	were given	small concessions.
	Beneficiary	**Process: material**	**Goal**

Note: Some people analyze 'sing' as behavioural.

Exercise 6.2

1.	He	saw	the whole room.	
	Senser	**Process: mental**	**Phenomenon**	

2.	Perceptual relationships	were seen	correctly.
	Phenomenon	**Process: mental**	**Circumstance**

3.	I	loved	her	in the springtime.
	Senser	**Process: mental**	**Phenomenon**	**Circumstance**

4.	They	were <also> noticed	by the researcher.
	Phenomenon	**Process: mental <Circumstance>**	**Senser**

5.	Must <we> envisage	the question	in a purely intellectual sense?
	Process: mental <Senser>	**Phenomenon**	**Circumstance**

6.	Considerable discomfort	may be experienced.
	Phenomenon	**Process: mental**

7.	Does <this explanation> convince	anyone?
	Process: mental <Phenomenon>	**Senser**

8.	The next report	fascinated	all of us.
	Phenomenon	**Process: mental**	**Senser**

Exercise 6.3

1. Material. *The transoms*: Goal.
2. Mental. *The patient*: Senser.
3. Material. *Hormones*: Goal.
4. Relational. *Mary*: Carrier.
5. Material. *The castle*: Goal.
6. Relational. *This*: Carrier.
7. Mental. *I*: Senser.
8. Material. *Chemicals*: Goal.
9. Mental. *He*: Senser.
10. Relational. *He*: Carrier.
11. Material. *Herbivores*: Actor.
12. Mental. *People*: Senser.
13. Mental. *Such a man*: Senser.
14. Relational. *One of the witnesses before the committee*: Identified.
15. Mental. *I*: Phenomenon.
16. Relational. *Hunt*: Carrier.
17. Material. *They*: Goal.
18. Mental. *Not a sound*: Phenomenon.
19. Relational. *The only important risk*: Identified.
20. Mental. *I*: Senser.

Exercise 6.4

(a)

1.

He	asked	me	if the money was traceable.
Sayer	**Process: verbal**	**Receiver**	**Reported**

2.

Dean	said,	"That's the good news."
Sayer	**Process: verbal**	**Quoted**

3.

Then	he	said,	"Can we meet again soon?"
	Sayer	**Process: verbal**	**Quoted**

4.

Someone	suggested	we should do it differently.
Sayer	**Process: verbal**	**Reported**

5.

The informants	told	the police	everything.
Sayer	**Process: verbal**	**Receiver**	**Verbiage**

(b)

He	asked	me,	'Is the money traceable?'
Sayer	**Process: verbal**	**Receiver**	**Quoted**

Various alternative answers include (omitting the Receiver): He said, 'Is the money traceable?' It is also possible to start with the Quoted: 'Is the money traceable?' he asked/said.

(c)

Dean	said	(that) that was the good news.
Sayer	**Process: verbal**	**Reported**

Note: Other 'saying' verbs are possible, of course, including: *declared, stated, commented, conceded, pointed out, observed,* and many more. Adding a Receiver, we could have said, for example, *Dean told us that that was the good news.*

Exercise 6.5

    1. little understanding of acoustics.
    2. beige curtains.
    4. no ventilation.
    5. many traitors.

The item *there* in the existential processes is a dummy Subject. In 3 and 6 it is an adverb of place (Circumstance). 3 is Process: mental and 6 is Process: material.

Exercise 6.6

This is another joke based on ambiguity. Comedian B is asking about the dog's ability to smell things. In the intended meaning (the most obvious meaning) of his question, the process is mental and *he* (that is, the dog) is Senser. Comedian A, ignoring the relevance of the question, surprisingly interprets it as an entirely new topic concerning the odour carried by the dog. In this reading of the question, the process is relational and *he* (the dog) is Carrier. Comedian A treats the verb *smell* as a copular verb.

Comedian B's intended meaning

How	does <he> smell?
Circumstance	**Process: mental <Senser>**

Comedian A's interpretation

How	does <he > smell?
Attribute	**Process: relational <Carrier>**

Comedian A's answer (without ellipsis)

He	smells	terrible.
Carrier	**Process: relational**	**Attribute**

Exercise 6.7

This is a relatively open-ended question. The following are merely suggestions.

1. She announced that her husband's spirit had contacted her.
2. Someone (?) decided years ago that no patent for such a device would be considered.
3. Someone (?) may/might/could publish a similar book.
4. One can understand why crystals interest us./Crystals interest us and we/one can understand why they do so.
5. A keel boat will lean much more easily because/as/since she has no hard bilge and so does not resist.
6. The *I-Ching* succeeds/People like the *I-Ching* because it flatters and does not threaten them.
7. Someone (?) has/People have searched for the elusive substance and while doing so he/she/they/someone else (?) has/have discovered several processes of merit.
8. Soil which crumbles easily is more stable.

Exercise 6.8

(a) Debatable, but we consider (2) to be more congruent because the process of 'melting' is realized by the verb.
(b) In fact, (1) is the original. *Melting point* and *boiling point* are grammatical metaphors.

Exercise 6.9

Our answer is that at first sight this is a relational process (possession).
  Subject/Carrier: *India.*
  More congruently: *Many such dams exist in India.*
  Process: existential. Subject/Existent: *many such dams.*
  In this version, *in India* is Circumstance (location).

Chapter 7

Exercise 7.1

1. This can be interpreted as *He loved the teacher of Japanese* (Classifier) or *He loved the teacher who was Japanese* (Epithet).
2. This is ambiguous because *Swiss German* can be the name of a variety of the German language, i.e. the German traditionally spoken in Switzerland. So it could mean (a) *Ingrid is Swiss and teaches German*; or (b) *Ingrid teaches Swiss German.* In (a) *Swiss* is Epithet and *German* is Classifier; in (b) *Swiss German* is

Classifier. (However, in (b) if we break down *Swiss German*, *Swiss* has an internal classifying function in relation to *German*.) A third interpretation seems less plausible: (c) that Ingrid is a teacher (of unspecified subjects) who is a German-speaking Swiss. If this is a possible reading, *Swiss German* is Epithet.

3. *working*: Classifier: i.e. *The road was blocked by working-class men* VERSUS *working*: Epithet, i.e. *The road was blocked by men who were* (*in the process of*) *working*.

Exercise 7.2

1.

The	three	red	wires
Deictic	Numerative	Epithet	Thing

one	terminal
Numerative	Thing

2.

Car	factories
Classifier	Thing

millions of	cheap	vehicles
Numerative	Epithet	Thing

3.

Domestic	manufacture	of goods
Classifier	Thing	Qualifier

several	significant	changes
Numerative	Epithet	Thing

4.

Rapid	extensive	technical	development
Epithet	Epithet	Classifier	Thing

older	concerns
Epithet	Thing

5.

The	disastrous	slump
Deictic	Epithet	Thing

three	unforeseen	factors
Numerative	Epithet	Thing

6.

much	economic	dislocation
Numerative	Classifier	Thing

7.

The	available	financial	statistics
Deictic	Epithet	Classifier	Thing

the	many	optimistic	claims	made
Deictic	Numerative	Epithet	Thing	Qualifier

8.

The	first	dam	on the Indus
Deictic	Numerative	Thing	Qualifier

the	Indus
Deictic	Thing

9.

This	vast	forested	river	basin
Deictic	Epithet	Epithet	Classifier	Thing

10.

A	broken	brake	cable
Deictic	Epithet	Classifier	Thing

Exercise 7.3

1. Adjunct. 2. Postmodifier. 3. Adjunct. 4. Adjunct. 5. Postmodifier.
6. Postmodifier. 7. Postmodifier. 8. Adjunct. 9. Postmodifier. 10. Adjunct.

Exercise 7.4

1. *no past and no future*: nominal group complex.
2. *utterly and completely*: adverbial group complex.
3. *low pay or poor working conditions*: nominal group complex.
4. *low carbohydrate diets and low protein diets*: nominal group complex.
5. *criticize nor condone*: verbal group complex.
6. *Chinese New Year, a major festival*: nominal group complex.
7. *above and below*: prepositional group complex.
8. *on the payment of debts and as gifts to relatives*: prepositional phrase complex.
9. *seemed to shrink and grow*: verbal group complex.
10. *here and now*: adverbial group complex.

Exercise 7.5

All except (a) are open questions and the answers given here are only suggestions.
(a) Replacement windows; patio doors; timber; softwood; hardwood; aluminium; plastic; unplasticized polyvinyl chloride; uPVC.
(b) In *timber (softwood or hardwood)* the linked nominal groups in brackets form a complex; they expand on the meaning of *timber* by specifying that it can be of either type; timber must be either softwood or hardwood. In *plastic (unplasticized polyvinyl chloride – uPVC)* the bracketed pair of nominal groups similarly expand on the meaning of *plastic* by specifying the type of plastic in question. *Plastic* is a superordinate, general term and *unplasticized polyvinyl chloride* is both a specialized (as used by specialists in the field) and more specific term (a hyponym of *plastic*).
(c) The Subject function is realized by a paratactic nominal group complex *replacement windows and patio doors*. The Complement is realized by a paratactic nominal group complex *timber (softwood or hardwood), aluminium or plastic (unplasticized polyvinyl chloride – uPVC)*. This is a particularly complicated group complex because it contains complexes within it. That is to say it is possible to identify a hierarchy of groupings within it. *Softwood and hardwood* form a complex which immediately combines with *timber*. *uPVC* forms a complex with *unplasticized polyvinyl chloride* and together they combine with *plastic*. Together with *aluminium* (the only simple group) they all form a larger complex realizing Complement.
(d) uPVC forms a complex with *unplasticized polyvinyl chloride*. It expands on *unplasticized polyvinyl chloride* by offering an alternative (abbreviated) name. It could have been bracketed but it seems that, as the whole complex is in brackets, the author decided to use a dash to avoid confusion.

(e) *Wooden*, made-to-measure, *aluminium, uPVC.* (Italicized items introduced in the first sentence; *wooden* only obliquely.)

(f) The preceding clause suggests that *ones* is a substitution for *made-to-measure windows* rather than just *windows.*

Chapter 8

Exercise 8.1

1. of this discovery: pp
2. on re-investment: pp
3. that must be addressed: rel
4. of grain: pp
5. open: other
6. in hand: pp
7. for oil: pp
8. which is self-reliant: rel
9. available: other
10. they cannot operate in: rel

Exercise 8.2

1. where livestock grazing predominates: full.
2. linked by a network of narrow roads: reduced.
3. now destroying our highways: reduced.
4. they bring to the work: contact.
5. in which it is intended: full.

Exercise 8.3

1.

This	is	an area	[[where	livestock grazing	predominates]].
			[[A	S	F/P]]
S	F	C			

2.

Settlements	[[linked	by a network of narrow roads]]	lack	certain advantages.
	[[P	A]]		
S			F/P	C

3.

These trucks	resemble	the monsters	[[now	destroying	our highways.]]
			[[A	P	C]]
S	F/P	C			

4.

The dedication	[[they	bring	to the work]]	pays	dividends.
	[[S	F/P	A	]]	
S				F/P	C

5.

Accept	this	in the spirit	[[in which	it	is	intended]].
			[[A	S	F	P	]]
P	C	A				

Exercise 8.4

These	are	men	[[who	always	serve	the faction	[[that	is	in power]].]]
							[[S	F	C	]]
			[[S	A	F/P		C		]]
S	F					C			

Exercise 8.5

(a) 1.

It	<is	clear>	[[that	there	is	always	a difference]].
			[[	S	F	A	C	]]
S	F	C	*Subject continued*				

(a) 2.

[[That	she	had	an appointment]]	is	easily	verifiable.
[[	S	F	C	]]			
S				F	A	C

(b) 1. That there is always a difference is clear.
2. It is easily verifiable that she had an appointment.

Exercise 8.6

(a) The relative word is not omitted:

    (i) when it is the Subject of the relative clause;
    (ii) in prepositional phrase relatives, when the preposition comes at the beginning of the relative clause;
    (iii) when it is possessive *whose*;
    (iv) when it is *where*.

With regard to (i), the grammar gives us:

    This is the man [[*that* she married]]. (Relative pronoun as Complement.)

OR:

This is the man [[^ she married]].

and ALSO:

This is the man [[*that* married her]]. (Relative pronoun as Subject.)

but NOT:

*This is the man [[^ married her]].

With regard to (ii), the grammar gives us:

the road [[^ you're driving on]]
the road [[on *which* you're driving]]

but NOT:

*the road [[on ^ you're driving]].

Or, to look at it from the opposite direction, if we omit the relative pronoun when it is Complement of a preposition, the preposition has to be at the end, not the beginning, of the relative clause.

With regard to (iii) the grammar gives us:

the woman [[whose research was so influential]]

but NOT:

*the woman [[^ research was so influential]]

With regard to (iv), the grammar gives us:

the street [[where you live]]

but NOT:

*the street [[^ you live]]

Note: Here, ^ indicates an omitted relative and * indicates an ungrammatical form.
(b) *that*-relative cannot occur after a preposition. The grammar gives us:

the house which she lives in
the house in which she lives
the house that she lives in

but NOT:

*the house in that she lives.

It is possible to make a connection between the constraints on the occurrence of *that* and the omission of the relative pronoun.

Chapter 9

Exercise 9.1

1. ||| The guarantee does not cover normal wear and tear, misuse or accidental damage ||

1
   and is conditional upon respect for the care instructions.|||

2

2. ||| Loewi got out of bed, || went to his lab,|| and did the experiment.|||

1   2   3

3. ||| Remove the starter shield || and disconnect the starter electrical leads.|||

1   2

4. ||| He thumped the table, || spilled his tea, || and actually seemed to be, for a moment, steaming. |||

1   2   3

5. ||| It's used as a last resort, || but don't be frightened. |||

1   2

Exercise 9.2

1. ||| Before one can love another, || one has to love oneself enough. |||

β   α

2. ||| Opera works best || when it refuses to be embarrassed about its artifice.|||

α   β

3. ||| Though today there are no more than 400 of these magnificent trees,||

β
   the cedars of Lebanon were once famous all over the ancient world.|||

α

4. ||| Send your creditors a financial statement,|| showing your income and outgoings.|||

α   β

5. |||Your doctor may wish to change your dose || to allow for any reduced kidney function.|||

α   β

6. ||| If you are not sure about this,|| check with your doctor.|||

β   α

7. ||| She seems almost arrogant, || challenging the viewer to a fight.|||

α   β

8. ||| We'll provide a free replacement car || while yours is being repaired at one of our depots.|||

α   β

Exercise 9.3

1. Paratactic
   ||| You'll be treated fairly,|| and you won't end up in jail. |||
         1   2

2. Hypotactic
   ||| Subsequently released, || he fled to England. |||
          β   α

3. Paratactic
   ||| The singers were in costume,|| but the stage was bare. |||
          1   2

4. Hypotactic
   ||| Any words can be used|| if they provide a space for the music. |||
        α   β

5. Hypotactic
   ||| When he approached Florence,|| seemingly stable governments crumbled overnight. |||
          β   α

Exercise 9.4

The good news is   [[||| that there are several steps   [[you can take]] ||
[[α

to protect yourself and your family on holiday |||]].
β   ]]

Exercise 9.5

||| King Hu's fourth film, *A Touch of Zen,*	<< which was made in 1968 ||	but only released
α	β1	β2
in its present form in 1975, >>	is a remarkable and assured reflection on the mesh of historic	
	α continued	
forces [[that define Chinese culture]]. |||	Set in the Ming dynasty, a favourite period for Hu	
	β	
and one [[marked by corruption and the development of a particularly lethal secret police force]], ||		
the film centres on the strange encounter between a local artist and the mysterious woman		
α		
[[who takes up residence in a nearby abandoned fortress]]. |||		

Note: The non-defining relative consists of a clause nexus (a two clause-complex within a larger complex) interrupting the α clause and labelled β1 and β2. You could use three sets of angle brackets to reflect this, but it is unusual. The clause beginning *Set in the Ming dynasty* (including its long nominal group in apposition, which contains an embedded clause) is analyzed as a dependent clause. The final clause is analyzed as a defining relative, but if you thought it was a non-defining relative and hence αβ, you could be right.

Exercise 9.6

||| The more scientific systems of 'New World' commercial pastoralists keep the animals		
α		
scattered,||	so ensuring more uniform grazing ||	and reducing the danger of [[producing bare
β1		β2
patches completely devoid of vegetation.]].	||| A country with much experience of semi-arid	
	α	
livestock farming is Australia,||	where wide areas of grazing land do not receive more than	
	β	
250 mm of rainfall a year. |||	It has been found [[that cattle withstand such arid conditions better	
than sheep.]]	||| Interior Australia is still a land of pioneer settlement, ||	and as the better-
	1	
watered areas become fully settled and developed,||	land-hungry farmers will inevitably be forced	
2β	2α	
into the so-called 'desert' country. |||	Hitherto the carrying capacity of the outback has remained	
	α	
rather low.||	averaging 1–4 animals per square kilometre. |||	
	β	

Exercise 9.7

1.

||| Japan	has	its great cities ||	and	it	has	evolved
S	F	C		S	F	P
1				2α		
its own elaborate systems ||		to control	urban congestion.|||		
C		P	C			
			2β			

2.

||| Shimura	is	superb	in the central role,||	and	not the least of
S	**F**	**C**	**A**		
1					

Kurosawa's achievement	is	his triumphant avoidance of happy-ending uplift. |||
S	**F**	**C**
2		

3.

|||| Yuko	sings	quietly	to herself ||	as	she	watches	the water. |||
S	**F**	**A**	**A**		**S**	**F/P**	**C**
α				β			

4.

||| One of the few films	[[that	never	fails]]	is	this one, ||
	[[**S**	**A**	**F/P**]]		
S				**F**	**C**
α					

which	is	a Japanese classic. |||
S	**F**	**C**
β		

5.

||| Saddled	with a slavish boring laundry job, ||	Kikuchi	barely	leaves	his apartment. |||
P	**A**	**S**	**A**	**F/P**	**C**
α		β			

Chapter 10

Exercise 10.1

1. projection. 2. projection. 3. expansion. 4. expansion.
5. expansion. 6. projection. 7. projection. 8. expansion.

Exercise 10.2

1. embedded. 2. dependent. 3. embedded. 4. dependent. 5. embedded.
6. dependent. 7. dependent. 8. embedded. 9. embedded. 10. dependent.

Exercise 10.3

1. ||| We want to remind residents || that a little care can save an awful lot of heartache. |||

        α   β

2. ||| 'Maybe it won't get here at all,' || said the waitress. |||

          1   2

3. ||| He promised || he'd come by. |||

     α   β

4. ||| He concedes || the effect was a touch farcical. |||

     α   β

5. ||| I said || 'She may see him.' |||

    1   2

6. ||| He replied: || 'I am not concerned with the intention of the law.' |||

    1   2

7. ||| 'Can we take some pictures?'|| asked the man from *Labour News.* |||

        1   2

8. ||| I asked him || whether he had ever felt threatened. |||

    α   β

Exercise 10.4

1.

||| 'It looks like a film shoot,' ||	said the woman, ||	pointing at the floodlights in the charred field. |||
1	2α	2β

2.

||| I think ||	Martinssen went out||	to get something [[to eat]]. |||
α	β	γ

3.

||| 'But you said ||	you'd have a real holiday,'||	said Paul, ||	'and now you work.' |||
1α	1β	2	3

4.

||| If he didn't, ||	his colleagues would think ||	he was arrogant. |||
β	αα	αβ

5.

||| Weir said, ||	'Get out ||	before another one blows.' |||
1	2α	2β

6.

||| David Rigg explains, ||	'As you poise your pen over the piece of paper, ||
1	2β

you think of your girlfriend's number.' |||
2α

7.

||| 'There's one thing [[that's odd]],' ||	said Högland. |||
1	2

8.

||| It wasn't natural ||	[[to think ||	that someone would intentionally have torn off his hair]]. |||
	[[α	β]]

9.

||| Bachelier thought ||	it was reasonable	[[to assume ||	that the Central Limit Theorem
		[[α	β
α		β	

of probability theory would apply to these price fluctuations]]. |||
embedded β clause continued
superordinate β clause continued

10.

||| Geldof just says ||	that	<<when he sees something [[he thinks could be changed]] >>
α		ββ

he considers it his duty [[||| to do anything in his power ||	to flag it up |||]]. |||
[[α	β]]
βα	

Note. We have indicated here that the binder *that* belongs with the βα clause, hence the angle brackets but this is a refinement. You could simply place a normal clause boundary after the embedding.

Exercise 10.5

||| Seated	in Sawiyeto's second house, ||	we	were	asked ||
P	A	S	F	P
β		α1α		

if	we	wanted	coffee ||	and	we	accepted. |||
	S	F/P	C		S	F/P
α1β				α2		

Exercise 10.6

(a) Open-ended question. One answer is that he is trying to create an impression of knowing a great deal about the situation, to show that he is one step ahead of the other speaker. (Out of context, it may appear that he is expressing incredulity.)

(b) By predicting what the other character was going to say. (A more technical answer would be the same as the answer to c.)

(c) Lots of hypotactic projections; projections within projections. Lots of sentence-initial *and*.

(d) Five.

(e) Hypotactic projection.

(f) Hypotactic expansion.

(g) ||| And you're going to tell me || Bush hadn't told you || to bet on him. |||
　　　　　　　α　　　　　　　　　　　　β　　　　　　　　　　γ

Exercise 10.7

1.	our	assumption	[[that x equals y]]
	Modifier	**Head**	**Modifier**

2.	his	insistence	[[that he is innocent]]
	Modifier	**Head**	**Modifier**

3.	her	conclusion	[[that he was lying]]
	Modifier	**Head**	**Modifier**

Exercise 10.8

(Suggestions only)

1.

||| Her son promised ||	to burn the sofa|||
α	β

2.

||| Ernst Mayer remarked ||	that in order to understand biology better ||
α	ββ
scientists/people (?) must think in new ways. |||	
βα	

Glossary

Note: The capital letters used in this glossary follow the conventions of SFG.

adjective A word class. Typically realizes Modifier in a nominal group, but can also be Head of a nominal group.

Adjunct (A) A function at the rank of clause (the others being Subject, Finite, Predicator, Complement). A grammatically optional element with a wide range of positions in the clause. Subclasses: **circumstantial** (A^{cir}, telling when, where, how, who with, etc.); **conjunctive** (A^{con}, signalling how the parts of a text relate to each other); **modal** (A^{mod}, indicating the speaker/writer's degree of commitment to or viewpoint on what he/she is saying). Realized in various ways, most typically by prepositional phrase or adverbial group.

adverb A very large and diffuse word class with many subtypes. Sometimes characterized by the suffix -ly. Typically Head of an adverbial group, but some (e.g., intensifiers like *very*) can realize Modifier in (i) an adverbial group or (ii) a nominal group with adjective as Head.

adverbial group A group with adverb as Head (and as Modifiers where these are present). Typically realizes Adjunct.

anaphoric Referring back to something already mentioned in the text.

anaphoric noun (A-noun) A noun used to encapsulate the semantic content of a previous section of the text; e.g., *development, explanation, concept, ideas.* Often modified by *the, this* or *these.*

article A word class, subclass of determiner. Can be more delicately classed as **definite article** (*the*); **indefinite article** (*a/an*).

Auxiliary An experiential function in the verbal group. When there is more than one in a given verbal group, they are numbered in a labelled analysis. (See Finite and Event.)

auxiliary (verb) One of a closed set of verbs whose meaning is largely grammatical (contrast lexical verbs). Combines with lexical verb in verbal group. Sometimes used specifically to mean a non-finite auxiliary.

binding conjunction (or **binder**) A conjunction which joins two units of unequal status, where one is dependent on the other (also known as 'subordinating conjunction'); e.g., *because, until, if.*

Circumstance One of a set of three experiential functions in the clause as representation, the others being Process and Participant. Expresses the circumstances, conditions, constraints, etc., of the Process. Subtypes are: **Extent, Location, Manner, Cause, Contingency, Accompaniment, Role, Matter** and **Angle**. Normally conflates with Adjunct.

circumstantial Adjunct See Adjunct.

Classifier One of a set of experiential functions in the nominal group (the others being Deictic, Numerative, Epithet, Thing, Qualifier). Its function is to subclassify the Thing. Typically conflates with Modifier. Typically realized by a noun, participle (gerund) or adjective. Examples (in italics): *bird* cage; *mineral* deposits; *supporting* beam, *floppy* disk.

clause The highest rank in the rank scale, immediately above the rank of group. Analyzable into the following functions: Mood and Residue; SFPCA; Process, Participant, Circumstance; Theme and Rheme; Given and New. Either 'full', i.e. including Finite, or moodless, i.e. lacking a Finite.

clause complex A combination of two or more clauses by linking or binding, i.e. by parataxis or hypotaxis. Roughly corresponds to traditional 'compound sentence' and 'complex sentence'.

cline A continuum of meaning where categories have fuzzy boundaries.

closed set A set of items that cannot readily be added to (e.g., personal pronouns, auxiliary verbs).

cohesion The quality of being woven together as a text. (See textuality.) Cohesive resources are **reference, conjunction, ellipsis, substitution** and **lexis**.

colligation The statistical tendency in text for a particular grammatical pattern to co-occur with a given lexical item.

collocation The statistical tendency for a pair of lexical items to co-occur in text within some specified degree of proximity; in current corpus linguistics this is often within a distance of four or five words each way from the word being measured but can be much greater.

Complement (C) A function at the rank of clause (the others being Subject, Finite, Predicator, Adjunct). Typically follows Predicator in an unmarked declarative clause but there are many exceptions to this. Subclasses include: direct object Complement (C^{do}), indirect object Complement (C^{io}), intensive Complement (C^{int}). Typically realized by nominal group. The nominal group in a prepositional phrase is sometimes described as Complement of the prepositional group.

complementizer A label in formal linguistics for the word *that* used as a binder, e.g., in projected clauses like (*No one believes*) *that he is guilty;* and in nominalizations, e.g., (the belief) *that he is guilty.*

conflate When a single element or structure realizes two or more functions, these functions are said to conflate (or be conflated); e.g., in *The boat has left a stormy land*, the functions of Actor, Subject and Theme conflate and are realized by the nominal group *the boat*.

congruent Not grammatically metaphorical. See grammatical metaphor.

conjunction See binding conjunction and linking conjunction.

conjunctive Adjunct (A^{con}) See Adjunct.

contact clause A finite relative clause with relative pronoun omitted; e.g., in *Here is a book you will enjoy,* the contact clause is *you will enjoy.*

copular verb A grammatical verb (as opposed to a lexical verb) which indicates relation, typically relating Subject and an intensive Complement in a relational Process; e.g., *be, seem.*

declarative An option in the MOOD system, contrasting with interrogative and, indirectly, with imperative. A declarative clause is characterized by the sequence S, F. Stereotypically identified with the speech acts 'statement', 'assertion', but there is no absolute correspondence.

defining relative clause (Also **restrictive relative clause**) A rankshifted clause embedded as Postmodifier in a nominal group. Semantically restricts the scope of reference of the Head (its antecedent).

Deictic An experiential function in the nominal group, (the others being Numerative, Epithet, Classifier, Thing and Qualifier). Typically realized by a determiner, a possessive pronoun (e.g., *my*) or a possessive noun (e.g., *Michael's*) as Modifier. The 'pointing' function.

delexicalized verb A verb which has (more or less) lost the semantic force of its 'dictionary meaning'; e.g., *take* in *Take a walk* as opposed to the more lexical *take* in *Take this bag upstairs.*

dependent clause A clause which depends on another in a clause complex, the other being **dominant**. The relation between the two is hypotactic. If the dominant clause is labelled α, the dependent is β. Functions as an expansion or projection.

determiner A word class typically realizing Deictic function in the nominal group; e.g., *the, a/an*; *this, these, that, those, each, every, some, any.*

domain model An account of the lexicogrammatical and textual patterns regularly associated with a particular type of text such as weather forecast, recipe or laboratory report.

dominant clause See dependent clause.

dummy Subject Also 'empty Subject' or 'empty pronoun'. A non-referring pronoun in Subject position; e.g., *it* with postposed clause structures; also *there* in existential Process clauses: e.g., *There* are three applicants.

ellipsis Systematic omission of a word, group or clause where the meaning can be recovered from the context; a feature of cohesion.

embedded clause A clause functioning as a group or part of a group and therefore describable as rankshifted; e.g., as Postmodifier in a group or as Subject of a clause.

empty Subject see dummy Subject.

Epithet An experiential function in the nominal group (the others being Deictic, Numerative, Classifier, Thing and Qualifier). Usually conflates with Modifier but may be Head when Thing is absent. Typically realized by adjective or participle. Example (in italics): a *beautiful, old* country house.

Event The key experiential function in the verbal group, comparable to Thing in the nominal group. Related functions in the verbal group are Auxiliary and Finite.

expansion One of a pair of alternative functions of a continuing clause or dependent clause in a clause complex, the other being projection. A clause is linked or bound to another clause in order to develop it, by explanation, addition, description, etc. May also be realized as an embedded clause.

experiential see ideational metafunction.

extraposed clause See postposed clause.

finite That auxiliary verb which in principle has tense and agrees in person/number with the Subject; e.g., *has* in She *has been studying in Osaka*; the first item in a finite verbal group of more than one word; the verbal item in a mood tag. A finite verbal group is one which has tense and in principle agrees in person and number with the Subject. A finite clause is a clause which has a finite verbal group as Finite and Predicator. (See also Finite and operator.)

Finite (F) (i) A function at the rank of clause (the others being Subject, Predicator, Complement, Adjunct). Interacts with Subject in the Mood part of the clause. Precedes Predicator in an unmarked declarative clause and may be fused with Predicator in a one-word verbal group (e.g., *goes*). When not fused, it is realized by a modal operator or finite operator. (See also finite.) (ii) Also used as the label for the first experiential element of the verbal group (others being Auxiliary and Event).

fused Finite When the Finite and Predicator are combined in a single word, they are said to be fused.

genre A type of text identified by its communicative purpose and its conventional form; e.g., editorial, sermon, lecture, begging letter, recipe, sonnet.

gerund A 'verbal noun': morphologically a verb participle (*-ing* form) but functionally a noun, realizing Head of a nominal group (His *shouting* is offensive) or Classifier (a *typing* class).

Given A function in information structure, contrasting with New. Given is treated by the speaker as mutual knowledge to be taken for granted though usually stated.

grammatical metaphor A non-congruent mode of expression, e.g., a nominalized process; a modal adverb, modal adjective or modal noun (e.g., *probability*) instead of a modal operator (*may, might*).

group The rank below clause and above word in the rank scale. Logically analyzable as Head with or without Modifier(s). Groups are: nominal, verbal, adverbial, preposition(al), conjunction(al) and, in some versions of SFL, 'adjectival'.

group complex Combination of two or more groups to fulfil a single function. Either hypotactic or paratactic.

Head The dominant logical element at the rank of group, the other (dependent) being Modifier. In a nominal group, the Head is typically (not always) realized by a noun and usually conflates with the experiential function of Thing. In an adverbial group the Head is an adverb, and so on.

hypotaxis The binding of unequal elements where one is dominant and the other dependent. Symbolized as α, β, γ, δ, ε, ζ.

ideational metafunction One of the three metafunctions (the others being interpersonal and textual). Subdivides into (i) **experiential:** to do with conceptual content, the representation of 'goings-on' in the world (or elsewhere); (ii) **logical**: to do with the semantic relations between experiential elements, e.g., Head/Modifier; dominant/dependent.

IFG *Introduction to Functional Grammar* (Halliday 1985, 1994; Halliday and Matthiessen 2004. In our volume, usually 2004.) Either the book or the model of grammar presented there.

imperative Option in the MOOD system, contrasting with indicative. Characterized by absence of Subject. Stereotypically associated with the speech act *command*, but there is no one-to-one relationship.

indicative Option in the MOOD system contrasting with *imperative*. (In fuller accounts it also contrasts with subjunctive and exclamative.) More delicately classifiable as declarative or interrogative.

inflection Grammatically motivated morphological variation in a lexical item; e.g. choice between zero and */-s/* at the end of a noun to indicate singular or plural.

information structure Organization of the clause in terms of the functions Given and New. Realized by intonation.

interpersonal metafunction One of the three metafunctions (the others being ideational, textual). Concerns the interactional aspect of language, the speaker-hearer dimension: typified by vocatives, MOOD options, modality (expressions of degree of certainty, commitment, etc.).

interpersonal Theme Theme realized as an interpersonal element: e.g., vocative, modal Adjunct (e.g., *maybe*, *surely*), Finite in interrogatives. Usually combines with topical Theme in a multiple Theme.

interrogative Option in the MOOD system, contrasting with declarative, and, less directly, with imperative. A **polar interrogative** is an interrogative 'inviting' the answer *yes* or *no*; a **wh-interrogative** is more open-ended. An interrogative clause is typified by the sequence **F**, **S** (Subject-Finite inversion); exception: wh-interrogative where wh-word is Subject or part of Subject. Stereotypically identified with the speech acts 'question' and 'request', but there is no one-to-one relationship.

lexical verb A verb with 'dictionary meaning'; that is, with semantic content other than purely grammatical meaning (contrast auxiliary and copular verbs). Realizes the experiential function Event in the verbal group.

lexicogrammar A term reflecting the SFL view that grammar is inseparable from lexis.

linking conjunction (or **linker**) A conjunction which joins two units of equal status (also known as 'co-ordinating conjunction'); e.g., *and, but, or.*

logical See ideational metafunction.

marked Theme A Theme which is untypical; e.g., in a declarative clause, anything other than Subject. Markedness is graded: Subject (unmarked) – circumstantial Adjunct (marked) – Complement (more marked) – Predicator (even more marked).

metafunction One of the three superordinate functional categories which characterize meaning in language. These are: ideational, interpersonal and textual. They co-exist in all texts.

metalanguage Language used for discussing language: grammatical terms, rhetorical categories, etc. For example, most of the language in this book.

metalinguistic Pertaining to metalanguage.

modal adjectives Small set of adjectives. Examples include: *possible, probable, likely, certain.*

modal Adjunct See Adjunct and modal adverb.

modal adverbs Small set of adverbs; often realizes Head of modal Adjunct. Examples include *perhaps, possibly, maybe, certainly.* Semantically akin to modal verb, modal noun and modal adverb.

modal nouns Small set of nouns. Examples include: *probability, possibility, likelihood, certainty.*

modal verb One of a closed set of verbs, always finite but invariant in form; e.g., *may, might, can, could, shall, should, will, would, must.* Where present in a verbal group, it is the first item: the operator. Its function is to modulate or modularize the verb (i.e., say something about the degree of certainty, obligation, etc.), a function similar to that of some modal Adjuncts.

Modifier The dependent element in the logical function of the group (the other – the dominant element – being Head). Subclassifiable as Premodifier or Postmodifier, according to its position in relation to the Head.

MOOD A system offering the choices declarative, interrogative, imperative. Conventionally printed in small capitals.

Mood The part of the clause that expresses MOOD choices, made up of Subject and Finite. Conventionally printed with capital M only.

moodless clause See non-finite clause.

mood tag Also question tag. A structure consisting of a Finite (which may be positive or negative) and Subject (pronoun), attached to the end of a declarative or imperative clause, producing a kind of interrogative structure; e.g., You will be there, *won't you?* (tag in italics).

morpheme The lowest rank in the rank scale, immediately below *word*. A constituent of a word, e.g., the word *indoctrinates* consists of the morphemes: *in+doctrin+ate+s*.

morphology (i) The formal structure of a word. (ii) The study of word formation.

multiple Theme A Theme made up of two or more Themes, i.e., the topical Theme in a clause plus any textual and interpersonal Themes preceding it.

network A set of inter-related systems.

New A function in information structure, contrasting with Given. New is the information which is not treated as mutual knowledge.

nexus A single linkage in a complex (e.g., a paratactic or hypotactic pair of clauses inside a clause complex). Rarely used in this volume.

nominal group A group which can function as Subject and Complement in a clause and complement of a preposition in a prepositional phrase. Its Head is typically noun or pronoun, but also sometimes adjective, numeral, or determiner.

nominalization See grammatical metaphor.

non-defining relative clause Also 'non-restrictive relative clause'. A dependent clause expanding on (but not restricting the scope of reference of) a nominal group in the dominant clause, or expanding on the entire dominant clause. Usually signalled by commas or 'comma intonation'; e.g., *He is constantly acting, which can be a strain*.

non-finite clause Also moodless clause. A clause without a Finite (e.g. *Looking to the west*, they spied land).

non-restrictive relative clause See nondefining relative clause.

noun A word class. Functions as Head of a nominal group; sometimes also Modifier/Classifier. Subtypes include: **proper noun** (e.g., personal names: *Michael*); **common noun** (e.g., *book*); abstract noun (e.g., *beauty*; *division*); concrete noun (e.g., *book*). Nouns are also classed as **countable** (e.g., *book*) or **uncountable** (*bread*).

number (In verbs and pronouns) singular or plural.

numeral A word class which includes cardinal numbers (*three, seven*), ordinal numbers (*third, seventh*) and quantitative words like *many, several, numerous, few*.

Numerative An experiential function in the nominal group. Usually conflates with Modifier but can be Head. Typically realized by a numeral.

open set A set of lexicogrammatical items that can readily have new items added (e.g., common nouns).

operator The finite or modal word in a verbal group. Realizes the function Finite in the clause. It appears with the Subject in a mood tag.

paradigmatic relations The phenomenon of 'choice' in the linguistic system; e.g., the choice between *he/she/it* or the choice between *has gone* and *had gone*. In SFG, described in terms of systems and networks. Identified with de Saussure's two major organizing principles of language: 'paradigmatic' (or 'associative') and 'syntagmatic'.

parataxis The linking of equal elements, symbolized by **1, 2**, etc., in order of occurrence.

participant An ideational (experiential) function in the clause, typically realized by a nominal group. Certain participant roles are associated with certain Process types: e.g., Actor and Goal with material Process; Senser and Phenomenon with mental Process.

participle See present participle and past participle. See also gerund.

parts of speech A traditional term for word classes; typically: noun, verb, adverb, adjective, preposition, conjunction, pronoun, article, interjection. Some can be subclassified.

past participle A form of verb. Its most distinctive morphological marker is the suffix *-en* (e.g., *broken*), but the most common is *-d* or *-ed* (e.g., *scattered*). Combines with auxiliary *have* for present perfect and past perfect tenses and with *be* or *get* for passive voice. Frequently realizes Modifier in a nominal group.

person (in verbs and pronouns) Examples: 1st: *am, I, we;* 2nd: *you;* 3rd:*is, he, she, it.*

POLARITY A system offering the choices: positive and negative. Conventionally printed in small capitals.

Postmodifier Modifier placed after the Head which it modifies. Postmodifier conflates with Qualifier and is usually realized by a prepositional phrase, embedded clause or participle.

postposed clause Also 'extraposed clause'. An embedded clause separated from the Head which it modifies and placed at a later point in the superordinate clause; e.g., the continuation of a discontinuous Subject with dummy *it* in Subject position, as in: It is obvious *that this will happen.*

Predicator (P) A function at the rank of clause (the others being Subject, Finite, Complement, Adjunct). The 'verb' element minus Finite. Follows Finite in an unmarked declarative clause and may be fused with Finite in a one-word verbal group. Realized by lexical verbs plus non-finite auxiliaries where these are present. Finite and Predicator together are realized by a verbal group.

Premodifier Modifier preceding the Head which it modifies. In a nominal group, Premodifier may be realized by several word classes, stereotypically by determiner and adjective, but also frequently by numeral, noun, and participles or combinations of any or all of these; conflates with the experiential functions: Deictic, Numerative, Epithet and Classifier.

preposition A word class which functions as Head of a prepositional group; e.g., *in, on, over, by.*

preposition(al) group A group with preposition as Head (rarely modified). Combines with a nominal group to make a prepositional phrase.

prepositional phrase A phrase consisting of a prepositional group and a nominal group. Note: not the same thing as a prepositional group and outside the rank scale. Typically functions as Postmodifier in a group or Adjunct in a clause.

present participle A form of verb. Invariably has the morphological suffix *-ing*. Combines with auxiliary *be* for continuous (progressive) aspect. Frequently realizes Modifier function in nominal group. See gerund.

probe A test or check to confirm an analytical decision; a means of identifying a function or category; e.g., the mood-tag probe for Subject.

Process (i) The ideational (experiential) meaning of a clause: the representation of 'goings-on'. (ii) The experiential meaning associated with the Predicator (and sometimes Finite) in a clause. Type of Process determines the Participant roles available. Process types are material, mental, relational, verbal, existential and behavioural.

projection A projection expresses a representation of speech or thought rather than a direct representation of experience; the projection is direct or indirect speech (or thought), respectively paratactic and hypotactic. It may also be realized as an embedded clause in a nominalization. Contrasts with expansion.

pronoun A word class; a type of nominal. Has various sub-classes; e.g., personal pronoun: *I, you, it*, etc.; possessive pronoun: *my, mine, your*, etc.; wh-pronoun (also called relative and interrogative pronoun): *who, which, what, whose*, etc.

Qualifier An experiential function in the nominal group (the others being Deictic, Numerative, Epithet, Classifier, Thing). Conflates with Postmodifier, following Thing. Typically realized by embedded clause, prepositional phrase or participle. Examples (Qualifier in italics): the talks *proposed by the government*; the best beach *in Portugal*.

question tag See mood tag.

Range A superordinate participant function incorporating Scope (material Process); Phenomenon (mental Process); Behaviour (behavioural Process).

rank scale A hierarchy of grammatical constituents (clause, group, word, morpheme) in which each rank is made up of one or more members of the rank below.

rankshifted clause A clause functioning at a lower rank, as part of a group; e.g., embedded as postmodifier in a group or as Subject or Complement in a clause. See embedded clause.

recursion The process whereby one structure is embedded in another of the same kind; e.g., a prepositional phrase in a nominal group which is part of a prepositional phrase; a relative clause in a nominal group in another relative clause.

reduced relative clause Non-finite relative clause (i.e., moodless, lacking the functions S and F).

register Variety of a language as determined by social context; e.g., formal written academic English; casual spoken English.

relative clause See defining relative clause and non-defining relative clause.

relative pronoun Wh-pronoun or *that* realizing Theme in a relative clause.

Residue The clause minus the Mood. Includes any of P, C, A, but not S and F.

restrictive relative clause See defining relative clause.

Rheme One of a pair of textual functions of the clause, the other being Theme. Rheme is that part of the clause which is not Theme. Typically carries the New in the information structure, but there are many exceptions to this.

sentence A unit of written language, usually signalled with an initial capital and a final full stop.

SFG An initialism for Systemic Functional Grammar, the subject of this book.

SFL An initialism for Systemic Functional Linguistics, the Neo-Firthian school of linguistics developed by Michael Halliday and his followers.

SFPCA An initialism for Subject, Finite, Predicator, Complement, Adjunct. Sometimes used in this book to refer to the 'clause as exchange' in general.

Standard English A convenient shorthand term for a variety of English with no regional base. A fictional construct of dubious linguistic validity.

structural Theme A subcategory of textual Theme.

Subject (S) Function at the rank of clause (the others being Finite, Predicator, Complement, Adjunct). Interacts with Finite (F) in the Mood part of the clause; determines person and number agreement of finite verb, where such agreement is manifest. Co-refers with the pronoun in a mood tag. Typically realized by a nominal group.

Subject-Finite inversion (F, S) A structure where Finite precedes Subject, e.g., in interrogatives.

superordinate clause The clause in which a rankshifted clause is embedded.

syntagmatic relations The linguistic phenomenon of 'chaining'. In language, items are strung together 'horizontally' in structures, as in Subject + Finite + Predicator + Complement; or re+enter+ing. Contrasted with paradigmatic, the other major organizing principle of language.

system A set of lexicogrammatical choices, e.g., the POLARITY system: positive or negative; the VOICE system: active or passive.

textual metafunction One of the three metafunctions (the others being ideational, interpersonal). Concerns the organization of text: Theme and Rheme, conjunctive Adjuncts, cohesion.

textual Theme A Theme which is realized by a textual element such as a continuative (e.g., *now, well, so*) or a conjunctive Adjunct (e.g., *however, nevertheless*). Combines with topical Theme to make a multiple Theme. Subcategories include structural Theme.

textuality The quality of being coherent text, constructed by textual organization: Theme and Rheme; Given and New and cohesion.

Theme One of a pair of textual functions of the clause, the other being Rheme. Usually signalled by its position at the beginning of the clause. The Theme is the first experiential constituent plus preceding constituents, if any. Themes are topical, interpersonal or textual, corresponding to the three metafunctions: experiential, interpersonal, textual. Theme may be simple or multiple; topical Theme may be marked or unmarked. In a clause complex, the entire initial clause can be labelled Theme but it will contain its own Theme and Rheme.

Thing Experiential function at the rank of group. Key experiential item in a nominal group. Typically conflates with Head. Typically realized by a noun.

topical Theme An experiential constituent as Theme. The first experiential element in the clause. Conflates with S, P, C or A^{cir}.

unmarked Theme See marked Theme.

verb A word class realizing the elements of a verbal group. In traditional grammar or loosely, 'verb' sometimes also means what SFG calls a verbal group.

verbal group A group with verb as Head (and as Modifiers, if any). Usual congruent choice for a process. Realizes Finite and/or Predicator functions, which together conflate with Process. Its experiential functions are: Finite; Auxiliaries, Event.

vocative A nominal group in direct address: e.g., *Michael,* can you help? Be quiet, *you stupid idiot!*

VOICE A system offering the choices active and passive.

wh-word One of the closed set of words beginning with *wh-* (plus *how*), typically occurring thematically in interrogatives and relative clauses.

word Rank immediately below group and immediately above morpheme in the rank scale. Usually indicated in writing by a space on either side.

word class Category of lexical item, roughly equivalent to traditional 'part of speech'. Central word classes in SFG are: noun, adjective, numeral, determiner, verb, preposition, adverb, conjunction (though these can be grouped less delicately or subdivided into more delicate classes).

References

Adams, P., Heaton, B. and Howarth P. (eds) 1991: *Sociocultural issues in English for academic purposes*, Review of English Language Teaching 1.2, 1–13. London: Modern English Publications.

Andersen, R. 1988: *The power and the word*. London: Paladin Grafton Books.

Anderson, R.C. and Davison A. (eds) 1988: *Linguistic complexity and text comprehension*. New Jersey: Lawrence Erlbaum Associates.

Bach, E. and Harms, R.T. (eds) 1968: *Universals in linguistic theory*. New York: Holt, Rinehart and Winston.

Banks, D. 2003a: The evolution of grammatical metaphor in scientific writing. In Simon-Vandenbergen, A.M. *et al.*, *Grammatical metaphor*. London and Philadelphia: John Benjamins.

—— 2003b: Relativity as an antidote to incorrect linguistic analysis. In Delmas, C. (ed.), *Correct, incorrect en linguistique anglaise*. Saint Etienne: Université de Saint Etienne.

Beaugrande, R. de, 1991: *Linguistic theory: the discourse of fundamental works*. London and New York: Longman.

Bell, A. and Garrett, P. (eds) 1998: *Approaches to media discourse*. Oxford: Blackwell.

Berry, M. 1975: *Introduction to systemic linguistics: 1. Structures and systems*. London: Batsford.

—— 1977: *Introduction to systemic linguistics: 2. Levels and links*. London: Batsford.

—— 1989: Thematic options and success in writing. In Butler, C.S., Cardwell, R.A. and Channell, J. (eds), *Language and literature: theory and practice*. Nottingham Linguistic Circular Special Issue, University of Nottingham.

Biber, D., Johanson, S., Leech, G., Conrad, S. and Finegan, E. 1999: *The Longman grammar of spoken and written English*. London: Longman.

Birch, D. and O'Toole, L.M. (eds) 1988: *Functions of style*. London and New York: Pinter.

Bloomfield, L. 1934: *Language*. London: George Allen and Unwin.

Bloor, M. 1996: Academic writing in computer science: a comparison of genres. In Ventola, E. and Mauranen, A. (eds), *Academic writing: intercultural and textual issues.* Amsterdam and Philadelphia: John Benjamins.

—— 1998: Lexical and grammatical choices in innovative language use in computer science. In Sánchez-Macarro, A. and Carter, R. (eds), *Linguistic choice across genres.* Amsterdam and Philadelphia: John Benjamins.

—— 1999: Variation in the methods sections of research articles across disciplines: the case of fast and slow text. In Thompson, P. (ed.), *Issues in EAP: writing research and instruction.* Reading: Centre for Applied Language Studies, University of Reading.

—— (in press) 2004: Towards a systemic-functional model for comparing forms of discourse in academic writing. Florianapolis: *Ihla do Desterro: Special issue on systemic functional linguistics.*

Bloor, M. and Bloor, T. 1991: Cultural expectations and socio-pragmatic failure in academic writing. In Adams, P., Heaton, B. and Howarth, P. (eds), *Sociocultural issues in English for academic purposes*, Review of English Language Teaching 1.2, 1–13. London: Modern English Publications.

—— 1992: Given and new information in the thematic organization of text: an application to the teaching of academic writing. In Noel, D. (ed.) *Occasional papers in systemic linguistics* Nottingham: University of Nottingham, Vol. 6, 45–59.

—— 1993: How economists modify propositions. In Henderson, W., Dudley-Evans, T. and Backhouse, R. (eds), *Economics and language*. London and New York: Routledge.

—— 2001: There'll be some changes made: predicting future events in academic and business genres. In Hewings, M. (ed.), *Academic writing in context.* Birmingham: Birmingham University Press.

Bloor, T. 1996. Three hypothetical strategies in philosophical writing. In Ventola, E. and Mauranen, A. (eds), *Academic writing: intercultural and textual issues.* Amsterdam and Philadelphia: John Benjamins.

—— 1998: Conditional expressions: meaning and realizations in two genres. In Sánchez-Macarro, A. and Carter, R. (eds), *Linguistic choices across genres: variation in spoken and written English.* Amsterdam and Philadelphia: John Benjamins.

Bloor, T. and Norrish, J. (eds) 1987: *Written language.* London: Centre for Information on Language Teaching and Research and British Association for Applied Linguistics.

Boas, F. 1964 (originally written 1911): Linguistics and ethnology. Reprinted in Hymes, D. (ed.), *Language in culture and society.* New York: Harper and Row.

Brazil, D., Coulthard, M. and Johns, C. 1980: *Discourse intonation and language teaching.* Harlow: Longman.

Brieger, N. and Sweeney, S. 1994: *The language of business English: grammar and functions*. London: Prentice Hall.

Brown, G. and Yule, G. 1983: *Discourse analysis*. Cambridge: Cambridge University Press.

Brown, P. and Levinson, S.C. 1987: *Politeness: some universals in language use*. Cambridge: Cambridge University Press.

Butler, C.S. 1985: *Systemic linguistics: theory and applications*. London: Batsford Academic and Education.

—— 2003a: *Structure and Function. Part 1: Approaches to the simplex clause*. Amsterdam and Philadelphia: John Benjamins.

—— 2003b: *Structure and Function. Part 2: From clause to discourse and beyond*. Amsterdam and Philadelphia: John Benjamins.

Butler, C.S., Cardwell, R.A. and Channell, J. (eds) 1989: *Language and literature: theory and practice*. Nottingham Linguistic Circular Special Issue, University of Nottingham.

Butt, D., Fahey, R., Feez, S., Spinks, S. and Yallop, C. 2000: *Using functional grammar: an explorer's guide* (second edition). Sydney: Macquarie University. (First edition: 1994.)

Caldas-Coulthard, C.R. and Coulthard, M. (eds) 1996: *Texts and practices: Readings in critical discourse analysis*. London and New York: Routledge.

Carter, R.A. 1997: *Investigating English discourse*. London and New York: Routledge.

Carter, R.A. and McRae, J. (eds) 1996: *Language, literature and the learner: creative classroom practice*. London: Longman.

Castello, E. 2002: *Tourist information texts: a corpus-based study of four related genres*. Padua: Unipress.

Channell, J. 1994: *Vague language*. Oxford: Oxford University Press.

Chomsky, N. 1993: Linguistics and adjacent fields: a personal view. In Kasher, A. (ed.) *The Chomskyan turn*. Oxford U.K. and Cambridge U.S.A.: Blackwell.

Christie, F. (ed.) 1999: *Pedagogy and the shaping of consciousness: linguistic and social processes*. London and New York: Cassell.

—— 2002: *Classroom discourse analysis: a functional perspective*. London and New York: Continuum.

Christie, F. and Martin, J.R. (eds) 1997: *Genre and institutions: Social processes in the workplace and school*. London: Cassell.

Christie, F. and Mission, R. (eds) 1998: *Literacy and schooling*. London: Routledge.

Clark, R. and Fairclough, N. (eds) 1990: *Language and power*. British studies in applied linguistics 5. London: Centre for Information on Language Teaching and Research for the British Association for Applied Linguistics.

Cmerjrková, S., Daneš, F. and Havlová, E. (eds) 1994: *Writing versus speaking*. Tübingen: Gunter Narr Verlag.

Coffin, C., Hewings, A. and O'Halloran, K. 2004. *Applying English grammar: functional and corpus approaches.* London: Open University and Arnold.

Collins Cobuild English grammar, 1990. London: Collins.

Cotterill, J., 2003: *Language and power in court: a linguistic analysis of the O.J. Simpson trial.* Basingstoke: Palgrave Macmillan.

Cotterill, J. (ed.), 2004: *Language in the legal process.* Basingstoke: Palgrave Macmillan.

Coulthard, R.M. 1985: *An introduction to discourse analysis.* London: Longman.

—— (ed.) 1992: *Advances in spoken discourse analysis.* London and New York: Routledge.

—— (ed.) 1994: *Advances in written text analysis.* London and New York: Routledge.

Cummings, M., 1995: A systemic functional approach to the thematic structure of the Old English clause. In Hasan, R. and Fries, P.H. (eds) *On subject and theme: a discourse functional perspective.* Amsterdam and Philadelphia: John Benjamins.

Cummings, M. and Simons, R. 1983. *The language of literature.* Oxford: Pergamon Press.

Daneš, F. 1970: An instance of Prague School methodology: functional analysis of utterance and text. In Garvin, P.L. (ed.), *Method and theory in linguistics,* The Hague: Mouton.

—— (ed.) 1974: *Papers on functional sentence perspective.* The Hague: Mouton; Prague: Academia.

Davidse, K. 1987: M.A.K. Halliday's functional grammar and the Prague School. In Dirven, R. and Fried, V. (eds) *Functionalism in linguistics.* Amsterdam/Philadelphia: John Benjamins.

Davies, M. 1994: Intonation is visible in written English. In Cmerjrková, S., Daneš, F. and Havlová, E. (eds), *Writing vs speaking,* Tübingen: Gunter Narr Verlag.

Delmas, C. (ed.) 2003: *Correct, incorrect en linguistique anglaise.* Saint Etienne: Université de Saint Etienne.

Dennett, D.C. 1991: *Consciousness explained.* Harmondsworth: Penguin.

—— (translated W. Baskin) 1959: *Course in general linguistics.* London: Peter Owen.

Dik, S. 1978: *Functional grammar.* London: Academic Press.

Dirven, R. and Fried V. (eds) 1987: *Functionalism in linguistics.* Amsterdam: John Benjamins.

Downing, A. and Locke, P. 2002: *A university course in English grammar* (second edition). London: Routledge. (First edition 1992: Prentice Hall International.)

Drury, H. 1991: The use of systemic linguistics to describe student summaries at university level. In Ventola, E. (ed.), *Functional and systemic linguistics:*

approaches and uses. Trends in Linguistics Studies and Monographs 55. Berlin: Mouton de Gruyter, 431–56.

Drury, H. and Webb, C. 1994: Teaching academic writing at the tertiary level. *Prospect* 7, 2–17.

Dudley-Evans, T. 1993: The debate over Milton Friedman's theoretical framework: an applied linguist's view. In Henderson, W., Dudley-Evans, T. and Backhouse, R. (eds), *Economics and language.* London and New York: Routledge.

Dudley-Evans, T. and St John, M.J. 1998: *Developments in English for specific purposes.* Cambridge: Cambridge University Press.

Duskova, L. (ed.) 2003: *Dictionary of the Prague school of linguistics.* Amsterdam and Philadelphia: John Benjamins.

Eggins, S. 1994: *An introduction to systemic functional linguistics.* London: Pinter.

Eggins, S. and Slade, D. 1997: *Analyzing casual conversation.* London: Cassell.

Fairclough, N. 1989: *Language and power.* London and New York: Longman.

—— 1999: Linguistic and intertextual analysis within discourse analysis. In Jaworksi, A. and Coupland N. (eds), *The discourse reader.* London and New York: Routledge.

Fawcett, R.P. 1974: Some proposals for systemic syntax. Parts 1, 2 and 3. Midlands Association for Linguistic Studies: *MALS Journal No. 1.* Vol. 1.2: 1–15; Vol. 2.1: 43–68; Vol. 2.2: 36–68.

—— 1984: System networks, codes and knowledge of the universe. In Fawcett, R.P., Halliday, M.A.K., Lamb, S.M. and Makkai, A. (eds), *The semiotics of culture and language.* London: Francis Pinter.

—— 1987: The semantics of clause and verb for relational processes in English. In Halliday, M.A.K. and Fawcett, R.P. (eds), *New development in systemic linguistics: Volume I: Theory and description.* London: Pinter.

—— 1999: On the subject of the Subject in English. *Functions of language,* 6.2: 243–73.

—— 2000a: *A theory of syntax for systemic functional linguistics.* Amsterdam and Philadelphia: John Benjamins.

—— 2000b: In place of Halliday's 'verbal group', Part 1. *Word* 51.2: 157–203.

—— 2000c: In place of Halliday's 'verbal group', Part 2. *Word* 51.3: 327–75.

—— in press: *The functional syntax handbook: analyzing English at the level of form.* London: Equinox.

—— forthcoming: *The functional semantics handbook: analyzing English at the level of meaning.* London: Equinox.

Fawcett, R., Halliday, M.A.K., Lamb, S.M. and Makkai, A. (eds) 1984: *The semiotics of culture and language*. London: Francis Pinter.

Fawcett, R., Tucker, G.H. and Lin, Y.Q. 1993: How a systemic functional grammar works: the role of realization in realization. In Horacek, H. and Zock, M. (eds) *New prospects in natural language generation: realization and systems*. London: Pinter.

Fillmore, C. 1968: The case for case. In Bach, E. and Harms, R.T. (eds), *Universals in linguistic theory*. New York: Holt, Rinehart and Winston.

Firbas, J. 1972: On the interplay of prosodic and non-prosodic means of functional sentence perspective. In Fried, V. (ed.), *The Prague School of linguistics and language teaching*. Oxford: Oxford University Press.

Firth, J.R. 1957: *Papers in linguistics 1934–1951*. London: Oxford University Press.

—— 1964: *The tongues of men and speech*. Oxford: Oxford University Press.

Francis, G., Hunston, S. and Manning, E. 1996: *Collins Cobuild Grammar Patterns 1: Verbs*. London: HarperCollins.

Francis, G. 1986: *Anaphoric nouns*. Discourse Analysis Monograph 11. English Language Research. University of Birmingham.

—— 1990: Theme workshop. *Network* 13/14, 8–9.

Francis, G. and Kramer-Dahl, A. 1991: From clinical report to clinical story: two ways of writing about a medical case. In Ventola, E. (ed.), *Functional and systemic linguistics: approaches and uses*. Trends in Linguistics, Studies and Monographs 55. Berlin: Mouton de Gruyter, 339–68.

Fried, V. (ed.) 1972: *The Prague School of linguistics and language teaching*. Oxford: Oxford University Press.

Fries, C.C. 1952: *The structure of English*. London: Longman.

Fries, P.H. and Francis, G. 1992: Exploring theme: problems for research. *Occasional papers in systemic linguistics* 6, 45–59.

Fries, P.H. and Gregory, M. (eds) 1995: *Discourse in society: systemic functional perspectives*. Advances in discourse processes. Vol. 50. Norwood, NJ: Ablex Publishing Corporation.

Garvin, P.L. (ed.) 1970: *Method and theory in linguistics*. The Hague: Mouton.

Ghadessy, M. (ed.) 1995: *Thematic development in English texts*. London and New York: Pinter.

—— (ed.) 1999: *Text and context in functional linguistics*. Amsterdam and Philadelphia: John Benjamins.

Ghadessy, M., Henry, A. and Roseberry R.L. (eds) 2001: *Small corpus studies and ELT*. Amsterdam and Philadelphia: John Benjamins.

Givón, T. 1995: *Functionalism and grammar*. Amsterdam and Philadelphia: John Benjamins.

Gledhill, C. 2000: *Collocations in science writing*. Tübingen: Gunter Narr Verlag.

Gouveia, C. 2002: Critical discourse analysis and the development of the new science. In Weiss, G. and Wodak, R. *Critical discourse analysis: theory and interdisciplinarity.* Basingstoke: Palgrave Macmillan.

Gregory, M.J. 1974: A theory for stylistics – exemplified: Donnes's Holy Sonnet XIV. *Language and Style* 7.2, 177–98.

—— 1978: Marvell's 'To his coy mistress': the poem as a linguistic and social event. *Poetics 7.4*, 351–62.

—— 1995: Generic expectancies and discoursal surprises: John Donne's 'The good morrow.' In Fries, P.H. and Gregory, M. (eds), *Discourse in society: systemic functional perspectives.* Advances in discourse processes. Vol. 50. Norwood, NJ: Ablex Publishing Corporation.

Halliday, M.A.K. 1967, 1968: Notes on transitivity and theme in English, 1–3. *Journal of Linguistics*, 3, 37–87 and 199–244; 4, 179–215.

—— 1971: Linguistic function and literary style: an enquiry into the language of William Golding's *The inheritors.* In Halliday, M.A.K. *Explorations in the functions of language.* London: Edward Arnold.

—— 1972: Options and functions in the English clause. In Householder, F.W. (ed.), *Syntactic theory I: structuralist.* Harmondsworth: Penguin.

—— 1973: *Explorations in the functions of language.* London: Edward Arnold.

—— 1974: The place of functional sentence perspective in the system of linguistic description. In Daneš, F. (ed.), *Papers on functional sentence perspective.* The Hague: Mouton; Prague: Academia.

—— 1975: *Learning how to mean.* London: Edward Arnold.

—— 1978: *Language as social semiotic.* London: Edward Arnold.

—— 1989: *Spoken and written language.* Oxford: Oxford University Press.

—— 1990: *New ways of meaning: a challenge to applied linguistics.* Paper presented to the Ninth World Congress of Applied Linguistics, Thessaloniki-Halkidiki, Greece.

—— 1993: *Language in a changing world.* Sydney: Applied Linguistics Association of Australia Occasional Paper 13.

—— 1994 (first edition 1985): *Introduction to functional grammar* (second edition). London: Edward Arnold.

—— 2002a: *On grammar.* Collected works of Michael Halliday, Vol. 1: London and New York: Continuum.

—— 2002b: *Linguistic studies of text and discourse.* Collected works of Michael Halliday, Vol. 2: London and New York: Continuum.

—— 2003a: *On language and linguistics.* Collected works of Michael Halliday, Vol. 3. London and New York: Continuum.

—— 2003b: *The language of early childhood.* Collected works of Michael Halliday, Vol. 4. London and New York: Continuum.

—— 2004a: *The language of science.* Collected works of Michael Halliday, Vol. 5. London and New York: Continuum.

—— 2004b: *Computational and quantitative studies.* Collected works of Michael Halliday, Vol. 6: London and New York: Continuum.

Halliday, M.A.K. and Fawcett, R.P. (eds) 1987: *Developments in systemic linguistics: Volume I: Theory and description.* London: Pinter.

Halliday, M.A.K. and Hasan, R. 1976: *Cohesion in English.* London: Longman.

—— 1989: *Language, context and text: aspects of language in a social-semiotic perspective.* Oxford: Oxford University Press. (orig. edition 1985: Geelong, Vic: Deakin University Press).

Halliday, M.A.K. and James, Z.L. 1993: A quantitative study of polarity and primary tense in the English finite clause. In Sinclair, J. *et al.* (eds) *Techniques of description.* London: Routledge.

Halliday, M.A.K. and Martin, J.R. 1993: *Writing science: literacy and discursive power.* London: The Falmer Press.

Halliday, M.A.K. and Matthiessen, C.M.I.M. 1999: *Construing experience through meaning: a language-based approach to cognition.* London and New York: Continuum.

Halliday, M.A.K. and Matthiessen, C.M.I.M. 2004: *An introduction to functional grammar* third edition. London: Arnold.

Halliday, M.A.K., McIntosh, A. and Strevens, P. 1964: *The linguistic sciences and language teaching.* London: Longman.

Harris, J. 1824: *The infant's grammar or a picnic party of the parts of speech.* London: Harris and Son. Republished 1977 by The Scolar Press Ltd., London.

Hasan, R. 1996: *Ways of saying: ways of meaning.* (Edited by Cloran, C., Butt, D.G. and Williams, G.) London and New York: Cassell.

Hasan, R. and Fries, P.H. 1995: *On subject and theme.* Amsterdam and Philadelphia: John Benjamins.

Henderson, W., Dudley-Evans, T. and Backhouse, R. (eds) 1993: *Economics and language.* London and New York: Routledge.

Hewings, A. 1999: Disciplinary engagement in undergraduate writing: an investigation of clause-initial elements in geography essays. Unpublished PhD thesis, University of Birmingham.

—— 2001: Undergraduate writing: linguistic indicators of success in undergraduate writing. In Hewings, M. (ed.) *Academic writing in context.* Birmingham: Birmingham University Press.

Hewings, A. and Coffin, C. 2004: Grammar in the construction of online messages. In Coffin, C., Hewings, A. and O'Halloran, K.A. (eds), *Applying English grammar: Functional and corpus approaches.* London: Open University and Arnold.

Hewings, M. 2001: *Academic writing in context.* Birmingham: Birmingham University Press.

Hillier, H. 2004: *Analysing real texts.* Basingstoke: Palgrave Macmillan.

Hoey, M. 1983: *On the surface of discourse*. London: George Allen and Unwin.
—— 1991: *Patterns of lexis in text*. Oxford: Oxford University Press.
—— (in press) *Lexical priming*. London: Routledge.
Householder, F.W. (ed.) 1972: *Syntactic theory I: structuralist*. Harmondsworth: Penguin.
Hudson, R. 1992: A spectator's guide to syntactic theories. *Links and Letters* 1, 25–50. Universitat Autonoma de Barcelona.
Hunston, S. (ed.) 1998. *Language at work*. Clevedon: Multilingual Matters.
Hunston, S. and Francis, G. 2000: *Pattern grammar: a corpus-driven approach to the lexical grammar of English*. Amsterdam: John Benjamins.
Hunston, S. and Thompson, G. (eds) 2000: *Evaluation in text: authorial stance and the construction of discourse*. Oxford: Oxford University Press.
Hyland, K. 1994: Hedging in academic writing and EAP textbooks. *English for Specific Purposes* 13, 239–56.
—— 1998: *Hedging in scientific research articles*. Amsterdam: John Benjamins.
—— 2000. *Disciplinary discourses: social interactions in academic writing*. Harlow: Longman.
Iedema, R. 2003: *Discourses of post-bureaucratic organization*. Document Design Companion. Series 5. Amsterdam and Philadelphia: John Benjamins.
Innis, R.E. 1987: Entry for 'Bühler, Karl'. In Turner R. (ed.), *Thinkers of the twentieth century*, London: St James Press.
Jaworski, A. and Coupland, N. (eds) 1999: *The discourse reader.* London and New York: Routledge.
Jespersen, O. 1909–49: *A modern English grammar on historical principles*. London: Allen and Unwin.
Johnston, S. and Meinhof, U.H. 1997: *Language and masculinity*. Oxford: Blackwell.
Jordan, R.R. 1997: *English for academic purposes*. Cambridge: Cambridge University Press.
Koller, V. and Mauntner, G. 2004: Computer applications in critical discourse analysis. In Coffin, C., Hewings, A. and O'Halloran, K.A. (eds), *Applying English grammar: Functional and corpus approaches*. London: Open University and Arnold.
Kress, G.R. (ed.) 1976: *Halliday: system and function in language*. London: Oxford University Press.
—— 1989: *Linguistic processes in sociocultural practice*. Oxford: Oxford University Press.
—— 1998: Meaning as work: individuals, society and the production of representational resources. In Sánchez-Macarro, A. and Carter, R. (eds),

Linguistic choice across genres: variation in spoken and written English. Amsterdam and Philadelphia: John Benjamins.

Kress, G.R. and Hodge, R.I.V. 1979: *Language as ideology.* London: Routledge and Kegan Paul.

Kress, G. and van Leeuwen, T. 1996: *Reading images: the grammar of visual design.* London and New York: Routledge.

—— 1998: Front pages: the critical analysis of newspaper layout. In Bell, A. and Garrett, P. (eds) *Approaches to media discourse.* Oxford: Blackwell.

Lakoff, G. 1987: *Women, fire and dangerous things: what categories reveal about the mind.* Chicago: University of Chicago Press.

—— 1992: Metaphor and war: the metaphor system used to justify war in the Gulf. In Pütz, M. (ed.) *Thirty years of linguistic evolution.* Amsterdam: Benjamins.

Lakoff, G. and Johnson, M. 1980: *Metaphors we live by.* Chicago: Chicago University Press.

Lassen, I. 2003: *Accessibility and acceptability in technical manuals.* Amsterdam and Philadelphia: John Benjamins.

Leech, G.N. 1969: *A linguistic guide to English poetry.* London: Longman.

Leech, G.N. and Short, M. 1981: *Style in fiction.* London: Longman.

Lock, G. 1996: *Functional English grammar: an introduction for second language teachers.* Cambridge: Cambridge University Press.

McCabe, A.M. 1999: Theme and thematic patterns in Spanish and English history texts. Unpublished PhD thesis, Aston University, UK.

McCarthy, M. 1991: *Discourse analysis for language teachers.* Cambridge: Cambridge University Press.

McCarthy, M. and Carter, R. 1994: *Language as discourse: perspectives for language teaching.* London: Longman.

Mann, W.C. and Thompson, S.A. (eds) 1992: *Discourse description: diverse linguistic analyses of a fund-raising text.* Amsterdam: John Benjamins.

Martin, J.R. 1989: *Factual writing: exploring and challenging social reality.* Oxford: Oxford University Press.

—— 1993: Literacy in science: learning to handle text as technology. In Halliday, M.A.K. and Martin J. (eds), *Writing science: literacy and discursive power.* London: The Falmer Press.

Martin, J.R. 1992: *English text: system and structure.* Amsterdam: John Benjamins.

—— 1998: Practice into theory: catalysing change. In Hunston, S. (ed.) *Language at work.* Clevedon: Multilingual Matters.

Martin, J.R., Matthiessen, M.I.M. and Painter, C. 1997: *Working with functional grammar.* London and Sydney: Arnold.

Martin, J.R. and Veel, R. (eds) 1998: *Reading science: critical and functional perspectives on discourses of science.* London and New York: Routledge.

Matthews, P.H. 1966: The concept of rank in 'neo-Firthian' linguistics. *Journal of Linguistics* 2.1: 101–18.

Matthiessen, C.M.I.M. and Bateman, J.A. 1991: *Text generation and systemic-functional linguistics: experiences from English and Japanese.* London: Pinter.

Mauranen, A. 2001: Descriptions or explanations? In Hewings, M. (ed.) *Academic writing in context.* Birmingham: Birmingham University Press.

Mey, J.L. 1993: *Pragmatics.* Oxford: Blackwell.

Moore, J. 1979: *Reading and thinking in English.* Oxford: Oxford University Press.

Moore, T. and Carling, C. 1982: *Understanding language: towards a post-Chomskyan linguistics.* London: Macmillan.

Morley, G. 2000: *Syntax in functional grammar.* London and New York: Continuum.

Munby, J. 1978: *Communicative syllabus design.* Cambridge: Cambridge University Press.

Myers, G. 1989: The pragmatics of politeness in scientific articles. *Applied linguistics* 10, 1–35.

—— 1990: *Writing biology: texts in the social construction of scientific knowledge.* Madison, WI: University of Wisconsin.

Noel, D. (ed.) 1992: *Occasional papers in systemic linguistics.* Vol. 6. Nottingham: English Studies Dept., University of Nottingham.

Nuttall, C. 1985: *Teaching reading skills in a foreign language.* London: Heinemann Educational Books.

Nwogu, K. and Bloor, T. 1991: Thematic progression in professional and popular medical texts. In Ventola, E. (ed.), *Functional and systemic linguistics: approaches and uses.* Trends in linguistics studies and monographs 55, 369–84. Berlin: Mouton de Gruyter.

O'Halloran, K.A. and Coffin, C. 2004: Checking overinterpretation and underinterpretation: help from corpora in critical linguistics. In Coffin, C., Hewings, A. and O'Halloran, K.A. (eds), *Applying English grammar: functional and corpus approaches.* London: Open University and Arnold.

Ouhalla, J. 1999: *Introducing transformational grammar.* (Second edition.) London: Edward Arnold.

Painter, C. 1984: *Into the mother tongue.* London: Pinter.

—— 1989: *Learning the mother tongue.* Oxford: Oxford University Press.

—— 1999: *Learning through language in early childhood.* London and New York: Cassell.

Palmer, F.R. 1974: *The English verb.* Harlow: Longman.

—— 1979: *Modality and the English modals.* London: Longman.

—— 1986: *Mood and modality.* Cambridge: Cambridge University Press.

Pindi, M. and Bloor, T. 1987: Playing safe with predictions: hedging, attribution and conditions in economics forecasting. In Bloor, T. and Norrish, J.

(eds), *Written language*. London: Centre for Information on Language Teaching Research for the British Association for Applied Linguistics.

Pütz, M. (ed.) 1992: *Thirty years of linguistic evolution*. Amsterdam: John Benjamins.

Quirk, R., Greenbaum, S., Leech, G. and Svartvik, J. 1972: *A grammar of contemporary English*. London: Longman.

—— 1985: *A comprehensive grammar of the English language*. London: Longman.

Radford, A. 1997: *Syntax: a minimalist introduction*. Cambridge: Cambridge University Press.

Reynolds, M. 1990: Classroom power: some dynamics of classroom talk. In Clark, R. and Fairclough, N. (eds), *Language and power*. British Studies in Applied Linguistics 5. London: Centre for Information on Language Teaching Research for the British Association for Applied Linguistics.

Richards, I.A. 1929: *Practical criticism*. London: Routledge and Kegan Paul.

Robins, R.H. 1967: *A short history of linguistics*. London: Longman.

Sampson, R.E. 1987: Entry for 'Malinowski, Bronislaw (Kaspar)'. In Turner, R. (ed.) *Thinkers of the twentieth century*, London: St James Press.

Sánchez-Macarro, A. and Carter, R. 1998 (eds): *Linguistic choice across genres: variation in spoken and written English*. Amsterdam and Philadelphia: John Benjamins.

Sapir, E. 1921: *Language: an introduction to the study of speech*. New York: Harcourt, Brace and World.

Saussure, F. de. 1916: *Cours de linguistique générale*. Paris: Payot.

Scott, F., Bowley, C., Brockett, C., Brown, J. and Goddard, P. 1968: *English grammar*. London: Heinemann Educational.

Short, M. (ed.) 1988: *Reading, analysing and teaching literature*. London and New York: Longman.

Siewierska, A. 1991: *Functional grammar*. London: Routledge.

Simon-Vandenbergen, A.M., Taverniers, M. and Ravelli, L.J. (eds) 2003: *Grammatical metaphor: views from systemic functional linguistics*. Amsterdam and Philadelphia: John Benjamins.

Sinclair, J. 1972: *A course in spoken English: grammar*. London: Oxford University Press.

—— 1991: *Corpus, concordance, collocation*. Oxford: Oxford University Press.

Sinclair, J. and Coulthard, R.M. 1975: *Towards an analysis of discourse: the English used by teachers and pupils*. Oxford: Oxford University Press.

Sinclair, J., Fox, G. and Hoey, M. (eds) 1993: *Techniques of description*. London: Routledge.

Stubbs, M. 1986: A matter of prolonged fieldwork: notes towards a modal grammar of English. *Applied Linguistics* 7, 1–25.

—— 1996: *Text and corpus analysis: computer-assisted studies of language and culture*. Oxford: Blackwell.

Swales, J.M. 1984: Research into the structure of introductions to journal articles and its application to the teaching of academic writing. In Williams, R., Swales, J. and Kirkman, J. (eds), *Common ground: shared interests in EAP and communication studies*. Oxford: Pergamon.

—— 1990: *Genre analysis*. Cambridge: Cambridge University Press.

Tadros, A. 1981: *Prediction in text*. Discourse Analysis Monograph 10. Birmingham: English Language Research, University of Birmingham.

Tench, P. 1996. *The intonation systems of English*. London: Cassell Academic.

Terauchi, H. 2001: *English for academic legal purposes in Japan*. Tokyo: Liber Press.

Thomas, S. and Hawes, T.P. 1994: Reporting verbs in medical journal articles. *English for specific purposes* 13, 171–86.

Thompson, G. 1994: *Reporting: Collins Cobuild English guides*. London: HarperCollins.

—— 2004: *Introducing functional grammar* (second edition). London: Arnold. (First edition: 1996.)

Thompson, G. and Yiyun, Ye 1991: Evaluation in the reporting verbs used in academic papers. *Applied Linguistics* 12, 365–82.

Toolan, M. 1992: *Language, text and context: essays in stylistics*. London and New York: Routledge.

—— 1998. *Language in literature*. London: Arnold.

Tucker, G. 1998: *The lexicogrammar of adjectives: a systemic functional approach to lexis*. London: Cassell Academic.

Tyler, A. 1994: The role of syntactic structure in discourse structure: signaling logical and prominence relations. *Applied Linguistics* 15, 243–62.

Ventola, E. 1983: Contrasting schematic structures in service encounters. *Applied Linguistics* 5, 275–86.

—— 1987: *The structure of social interaction: a systemic approach to the structure of service encounters*. London: Francis Pinter.

—— (ed.) 1991: *Functional and systemic linguistics: approaches and uses*. Trends in Linguistics Studies and Monographs 55. Berlin: Mouton de Gruyter.

Ventola, E. and Mauranen, A. 1991: Non-native writing and native revising of scientific articles. In Ventola, E. (ed.), *Functional and systemic linguistics: approaches and uses*. Trends in Linguistics Studies and Monographs 55. Berlin: Mouton de Gruyter.

—— (eds) 1996: *Academic writing: intercultural and textual issues*. Amsterdam and Philadelphia: John Benjamins.

Weiss, G. and Wodak, R. (eds) 2002: *Critical discourse analysis; theory and interdisciplinarity*. Basingstoke: Palgrave Macmillan.

White, P.R. 2003: Appraisal – the language of evaluation and stance. In Verschueren, J., Östman, J.J., Bommaert, J. and Bulcaen, C. (eds), *The handbook of pragmatics*. Amsterdam: John Benjamins.

White, P.R. 2004: Subjectivity, evaluation and point of view in media discourse. In Coffin, C., Hewings, A. and O'Halloran, K.A. (eds), *Applying English grammar: functional and corpus approaches.* London: Open University and Arnold.

Whorf, B.L. (edited and with an introduction by J.B. Carroll) 1956: *Language, thought and reality: selected writings of Benjamin Lee Whorf.* Cambridge, MA: MIT Press.

Williams, R., Swales, J. and Kirkman, J. (eds) 1984: *Common ground: shared interests in EAP and communication studies.* Oxford: Pergamon.

Willis, D. 1991. *Collins Cobuild student's grammar.* London: HarperCollins.

Young, D.J. 1980: *The structure of English clauses.* London: Hutchinson.

Index of authors

Note: As this book largely concerns Halliday's model of grammar, his name and work appears too frequently in the text to be referred to in this index of authors.

Subject index